Parenting After the Death of a Child

☐ The Series in Death, Dying, and Bereavement

Robert Neimeyer, Consulting Editor

Beder—Voices of Bereavement: A Casebook for Grief Counselors
Berger – Music of the Soul: Composing Life Out of Loss
Buckle & Fleming—Parenting After the Death of a Child: A Practitioner's Guide
Davies—Shadows in the Sun: The Experiences of Sibling Bereavement in Childhood
Doka & Martin—Grieving Beyond Gender: Understanding the Ways Men and Women Mourn, Revised Edition
Harvey—Perspectives on Loss: A Sourcebook
Katz & Johnson —When Professionals Weep: Emotional and Countertransference Responses in End-of-Life Care
Klass—The Spiritual Lives of Bereaved Parents
Jeffreys—Helping Grieving People – When Tears Are Not Enough: A Handbook for Care Providers
Jordan & McInotsh—Grief After Suicide: Understanding the Consequences and Caring for the Survivors
Leenaars—Lives and Deaths: Selections from the Works of Edwin S. Shneidman
Leong & Leach—Suicide among Racial and Ethnic Minority Groups: Theory, Research, and Practice
Lester—Katie's Diary: Unlocking the Mystery of a Suicide
Martin, Doka—Men Don't Cry...Women Do: Transcending Gender Stereotypes of Grief
Nord—Multiple AIDS-Related Loss: A Handbook for Understanding and Surviving a Perpetual Fall
Roos—Chronic Sorrow: A Living Loss
Rogers – The Art of Grief: The Use of Expressive Arts in a Grief Support Group
Rosenblatt—Parent Grief: Narratives of Loss and Relationship
Rosenblatt & Wallace—African-American Grief
Tedeschi & Calhoun—Helping Bereaved Parents: A Clinician's Guide
Silverman—Widow to Widow, Second Edition
Werth—Contemporary Perspectives on Rational Suicide
Werth & Blevins—Decision Making near the End of Life: Issues, Developments, and Future Directions

☐ Formerly the Series in Death Education, Aging, and Health Care

Hannelore Wass, Consulting Editor

Bard—Medical Ethics in Practice
Benoliel—Death Education for the Health Professional
Bertman—Facing Death: Images, Insights, and Interventions

Brammer—How to Cope with Life Transitions: The Challenge of Personal Change
Cleiren—Bereavement and Adaptation: A Comparative Study of the Aftermath of Death
Corless, Pittman-Lindeman—AIDS: Principles, Practices, and Politics, Abridged Edition
Corless, Pittman-Lindeman—AIDS: Principles, Practices, and Politics, Reference Edition
Curran—Adolescent Suicidal Behavior
Davidson—The Hospice: Development and Administration, Second Edition
Davidson, Linnolla—Risk Factors in Youth Suicide
Degner, Beaton—Life-Death Decisions in Health Care
Doka—AIDS, Fear, and Society: Challenging the Dreaded Disease
Doty—Communication and Assertion Skills for Older Persons
Epting, Neimeyer—Personal Meanings of Death: Applications for Personal Construct Theory to Clinical Practice
Haber—Health Care for an Aging Society: Cost-Conscious Community Care and Self-Care Approaches
Hughes—Bereavement and Support: Healing in a Group Environment
Irish, Lundquist, Nelsen—Ethnic Variations in Dying, Death, and Grief: Diversity in Universality
Klass, Silverman, Nickman—Continuing Bonds: New Understanding of Grief
Lair—Counseling the Terminally Ill: Sharing the Journey
Leenaars, Maltsberger, Neimeyer—Treatment of Suicidal People
Leenaars, Wenckstern—Suicide Prevention in Schools
Leng—Psychological Care in Old Age
Leviton—Horrendous Death, Health, and Well-Being
Leviton—Horrendous Death and Health: Toward Action
Lindeman, Corby, Downing, Sanborn—Alzheimer's Day Care: A Basic Guide
Lund—Older Bereaved Spouses: Research with Practical Applications
Neimeyer—Death Anxiety Handbook: Research, Instrumentation, and Application
Papadatou, Papadatos—Children and Death
Prunkl, Berry—Death Week: Exploring the Dying Process
Ricker, Myers—Retirement Counseling: A Practical Guide for Action
Samarel—Caring for Life and Death
Sherron, Lumsden—Introduction to Educational Gerontology, Third Edition
Stillion—Death and Sexes: An Examination of Differential Longevity Attitudes, Behaviors, and Coping Skills
Stillion, McDowell, May—Suicide Across the Life Span—Premature Exits
Vachon—Occupational Stress in the Care of the Critically Ill, the Dying, and the Bereaved
Wass, Corr—Childhood and Death
Wass, Corr—Helping Children Cope with Death: Guidelines and Resource, Second Edition
Wass, Corr, Pacholski, Forfar—Death Education II: An Annotated Resource Guide
Wass, Neimeyer—Dying: Facing the Facts, Third Edition
Weenolsen—Transcendence of Loss over the Life Span
Werth—Rational Suicide? Implications for Mental Health Professionals

Parenting After the Death of a Child

A Practitioner's Guide

Jennifer L. Buckle and Stephen J. Fleming

Routledge
Taylor & Francis Group
711 Third Avenue,
New York, NY 10017

Routledge
Taylor & Francis Group
27 Church Road,
Hove, East Sussex BN3 2FA, UK

First issued in paperback 2014

Routledge is an imprint of the Taylor and Francis Group, an informa business

© 2011 by Taylor and Francis Group, LLC

ISBN 978-0-415-99573-3 (hbk)
ISBN 978-1-138-88441-0 (pbk)

For permission to photocopy or use material electronically from this work, please access www.copyright.com (http://www.copyright.com/) or contact the Copyright Clearance Center, Inc. (CCC), 222 Rosewood Drive, Danvers, MA 01923, 978-750-8400. CCC is a not-for-profit organization that provides licenses and registration for a variety of users. For organizations that have been granted a photocopy license by the CCC, a separate system of payment has been arranged.

Trademark Notice: Product or corporate names may be trademarks or registered trademarks, and are used only for identification and explanation without intent to infringe.

Library of Congress Cataloging-in-Publication Data

Buckle, Jennifer L.
  Parenting after the death of a child : a practitioner's guide / Jennifer L. Buckle and Stephen J. Fleming.
    p. cm.
  Includes bibliographical references and index.
  ISBN 978-0-415-99573-3 (hardcover : alk. paper)
  1. Bereavement--Psychological aspects. 2. Children--Death--Psychological aspects. 3. Brothers and sisters--Death--Psychological aspects. 4. Parents--Psychology. 5. Parent and child. I. Fleming, Stephen J. II. Title.

BF575.G7.B767 2010
155.9'37--dc22   2010004638

Visit the Taylor & Francis Web site at
http://www.taylorandfrancis.com

and the Routledge Web site at
http://www.routledgementalhealth.com

To the bereaved parents who so generously shared their anguish and their children's legacies.

With love and gratitude to

Ken and Kate,

and my parents,

Norma and Dave

(JB)

To the bereaved parents whose courage and eloquence made the book possible

And to Sean, Jennifer, Erin, Maggie, and Leslie ... thank you for your sustaining presence in my life.

(SF)

CONTENTS

Series Editor's Foreword	xi
Preface	xv
About the Authors	xix

1	Setting the Stage	1
2	Discovering the Theory of Bereaved Parenting: Method, Participants, and Overview of Results	21
3	The Devastation of Parental Bereavement	41
4	Picking Up the Pieces: Regeneration of Self	73
5	Picking Up the Pieces: Regeneration of Family	91
6	Dual Tasks of Parenting and Grieving	113
7	Parenting, Protecting, and Priorities	129
8	Parenting Bereaved Children: The Challenges	145

9 **Afterword** **169**

Appendix A **177**

Appendix B **187**

References **189**

Index **203**

SERIES EDITOR'S FOREWORD

Some years ago, Carol and Ken consulted me in the aftermath of the death of their 18-year-old son, Mark, in a vehicular accident. They felt that they had been catapulted into a hostile and alien landscape, one that overturned every assumption that once supported their sense of security in a previously familiar world. Confronted with anguishing existential questions, corrosive yearning for Mark, and an unsettling sense of vulnerability to further loss, they faced the challenge of not only rebuilding their own lives as individuals and as a couple, but also continuing to parent Mark's younger brother, Keith, whose own grief and disorientation in the wake of his sibling's death was palpable. Aching and uncertain, they turned to me for guidance, and I, as a clinician who at that time had limited experience in working with loss, turned to the professional literature.

What I found there told me more than little, but less than much, about what Ken and Carol might confront in their attempt to rebuild a livable world from the ruins of the one they once inhabited. Ample evidence indicated that parental grief over the lost of a child was perhaps the most intense and sustained of that following any form of bereavement. Further, simple, stage-like patterns of adaptation to such loss did little to capture the variations in individual pathways through the experience. A handful of research studies had documented the despair of parents, their tendency to memorialize the child, and their susceptibility to depression, anxiety states, and a variety of worrisome medical outcomes. More was being learned about the distinctive complications that could arise in the wake of traumatic loss, which accounted for a large percentage of the deaths of children and adolescents. But comparatively little was known about the implications of loss of a child for the family system, as such, with "clinical wisdom"—now disputed by recent research—trumpeting the heightened likelihood of subsequent parental divorce and the critical importance of expression of feelings between spouses in promoting healthy "grief work." When it came to the critical question of how mothers and fathers continue to parent surviving children while simultaneously grieving those who are lost, the research literature said almost nothing beyond cautioning against seeking a "replacement child"—another truism called into question by recent studies. As a result, clinicians who worked with bereaved families could find little reliable guidance in the research literature, especially when they shifted their attention from the private agony of individual parents to their complex immersion in a family system, one that included surviving children with their own unique needs.

It is in this context that Buckle and Fleming's sensitive book, Parenting after the Death of a Child, makes a distinctive contribution. Like a sturdy stool, it stands on three strong legs: first, a solid summary of the contemporary bereavement literature; second, a revealing qualitative study of bereaved parents; and third, a wealth of clinical case illustrations that weave together the insights garnered from the previous two sources in a way that elucidates their implications for the helping relationship. A few words about each of these legs should suffice to convey the contributions the book can make to understanding the challenges faced by bereaved parents, whether for bereavement theorists and researchers, grief therapists, or even the parents themselves.

To begin with, Buckle and Fleming provide a thoughtful review of cutting-edge developments in bereavement theory, including critical distinctions between normal sadness, grief, depression and posttraumatic stress disorder; cognitive dimensions of grieving; disruptions in the survivor's world of meaning; and the collapse of the traumatically bereaved person's assumptive world. They further offer the reader summaries of conceptually useful models for understanding adjustment to loss, ranging from foundational work in attachment theory to contemporary models explicating the dual processes of coping with loss and restoration, or managing biopsychosocial stressors while also realigning one's multifaceted relationship to the deceased. In each case, the authors bring to bear existing qualitative and quantitative research in a readable style, producing an evidence-informed discussion that situates the reader securely in the contemporary literature.

And yet, despite the impressive growth in sophistication in bereavement studies that Buckle and Fleming review, it is clear that much remains to be done by way of constructing a clear and practical model of parent grief, particularly as it bears on the seemingly impossible task of mourning and moving forward with parenting another child at the same time. To provide this more cohesive framework, the authors detail their qualitative research into the experience of 10 bereaved parents, 5 mothers and 5 fathers who together participated in interviews that yield more than 800 pages of text plumbing the depths of their despair, disorientation, struggle, teamwork, and, in most cases, resilience. Combing through this very personal archive of concerns, observations, and insights about one of life's greatest traumas, Buckle and Fleming bring to light the central themes encountered by parents as they deal with the daily duality of devastation and regeneration. The result is a compelling portrait of parental bereavement, one studded with memorable metaphors (e.g., the "house of refracting glass" reflecting the fragile illusion of security that preceded the death) and counterintuitive conclusions (e.g., bearing on the differences in mothers and fathers in their styles of both grieving and parenting after loss).

And finally, the book benefits from the long and deep engagement in psychotherapy with bereaved parents on the part of the second author. Time and again, fragments of evocative text from the qualitative interviews conducted by Buckle are given context and continuity by being juxtaposed with case vignettes offered by Fleming, allowing readers a rare glimpse into the consulting room where traumatic imagery is assimilated, anguishing self-accusations softened, and opposing needs for honest expression of grief and protection of vulnerable family members are negotiated. As a result, the practicing clinician is better able to bridge the learning packed into these pages with the exigencies of grief therapy and counseling "in the trenches."

In summary, Buckle and Fleming have offered a comprehensive and multifaceted examination of the world of bereaved parents, drawing on the best of the current literature, the insights of a master clinician, and, perhaps most impressively, the stories of the mothers and fathers themselves. The result is a unique contribution to our understanding, and one I will not hesitate to recommend to the current generation of clinicians seeking orientation in the anguishing terrain accompanying the loss of a child.

Robert A. Neimeyer, PhD
Series Editor

PREFACE

The death of a child has an overwhelming impact on a parent because a tragedy of this magnitude assaults one's identity, challenges one's worldview, stresses the marital bond, immutably alters the psychosocial landscape of the family, and leaves its irrevocable imprint on the surviving children. Whereas there is a substantial body of research exploring the unspeakable catastrophe of parental bereavement, relatively little systematic attention has been paid to the unique challenges and daunting responsibilities mothers and fathers face in having to parent their surviving, bereaved children. This book addresses the complex and delicate dilemma facing bereaved parents; namely, in the midst of grief, how do you cease parenting the deceased child while simultaneously continuing in this role with surviving children?

In order to comprehensively and sensitively understand the myriad nuances of such an intimidating and overwhelming predicament, the authors opted for a qualitative approach. The methodology used in this study is based on modifications to the grounded theory approach (Glaser & Strauss, 1967) suggested by Rennie, Phillips, and Quartaro (1988). A total of 10 bereaved parents (five mothers and five fathers) were interviewed at length; audiotapes of each interview were transcribed and analyzed. The use of established grounded theory procedures (theoretical sampling, constant comparative analysis, and theoretical memoing) in the painstaking analysis of more than 800 pages of transcripts gradually exposed levels of categories and culminated in the recognition of a core category under which all other categories were subsumed. In addition to this detailed empirical exploration, vignettes and case studies from clinical practice are included throughout the book to supplement the core themes and provide practical guidance to professionals working with bereaved parents.

The core category that ultimately surfaced was elusive and, much like an archeological dig, was not readily discernible. We were puzzled by the juxtaposition of life and death in the lives of bereaved parents; by the co-existence of suffocating loss and the constant, daily demands of parenting surviving children; and by the chaos and confusion inherent in grief and the need for meticulous planning and structure in family life. Gradually, the data yielded the core category that reflected the lived duality of a bereaved parent's experience; we termed this central concept "bereaved parenting." Bereaved parenting is not a discrete reality in which one engages the pain of one's loss, or is solely grieving, and then moves to rebuilding one's life and meeting family responsibilities, what Stroebe and Schut (1999) would term a restoration-orientation. Rather, bereaved parenting is living this continuous duality, where one informs the other and one can take precedence over the other at any time; it represents an ongoing fluctuation between the two extremes of loss and life. Consequently, the core category reflecting the totality of this experience is titled "Bereaved Parenting: Living the Duality of Devastation and Regeneration."

Parental devastation caused by the death of a child is well documented and the term accurately describes the sense of personal annihilation in the face of such an overpowering tragedy. In this study, a salient feature of the parents' responses was that they could not remain emotionally enveloped in this devastated state for long. Virtually from the moment of their child's death the parents were confronted by numerous, emergent demands to parent remaining children. A poignant illustration of this duality is the parent, at the accident scene where one of her children had just died, giving consent for emergency surgery to save the life of her son who sustained life-threatening injuries in the same motor vehicle accident. Even if they preferred to stay in the pain of their grief and, paradoxically, remain connected to their deceased child, parents had little choice as they were pulled into the process of regeneration, of rebuilding shattered assumptions of the world and self, by the demands of parenting their remaining children.

We have chosen the term "regeneration" with considerable forethought because it does not simply represent the opposite of devastation, nor does it imply a "recovery" to a pre-loss state—that state of existence has been irrevocably shattered. To regenerate is to "bring or come into renewed existence; to generate again; to impart new and more vigorous life; to regrow lost or injured tissue; to invest with a new and higher nature" (*Oxford English Reference Dictionary*, 1996). With clarity and courage, these parents spoke of painfully regenerating a sense of self and a sense of family; and in a forthright, honest fashion acknowledged their often halfhearted attempts to reengage their parental responsibilities. They were not always successful; at times they actually failed, but they persevered in "picking up the pieces" and, ultimately, they succeeded in reclaiming their lives. They were able to regenerate some of the lost and injured pieces, but not all. Like a starfish barely surviving a fatal blow, they restored lost aspects of their shattered lives, but never to their full strength and beauty. They survived and they functioned and, in some ways, they thrived, but there is forever the missing piece, the unfillable hole, the unfathomable depth. Bereaved parenting, then, is an act of engaging in regeneration, but it is not an act of "acceptance," "resolution," "moving on," or "getting over" the death of a beloved child. It is an act of "picking up the pieces" in the face of the devastation, forever respectful and informed by the weight of their child's absence.

☐ Who Should Read This Book?

This book is intended for a broad audience; anyone interested in appreciating the oppressive impact of the death of a child on parents, surviving siblings, and the family as a whole will find useful, practical information in this text. It represents a rich and informative reference for clinicians and other health professionals working with bereaved parents, especially regarding issues of ongoing parenting. The rigorous, detailed, grounded theory approach to the complex, relatively unknown, and often-misunderstood phenomenon of bereaved parenting makes this a valuable resource for educators, researchers, and students interested in qualitative methodology. Finally, we have liberally included excerpts taken directly from the interviews with bereaved parents to illustrate the themes and ground the theory. It is hoped that bereaved parents who read this book will resonate with the horrific eloquence of the participants' grief and have their experiences affirmed and validated.

We would like to thank those who assisted in the editorial process and were instrumental in bringing this book to fruition. The foundation of this book is the first author's doctoral dissertation, supervised by the second author. We would like to thank the Bereaved Families of Ontario for facilitating the study. We would like to recognize the dissertation committee members who, each in his own way, contributed to the development of this work: Drs. David Rennie, Shaké Toukmanian, David Reid, John Unrau, and Jack Morgan. We would like to thank Mr. Dana Bliss, editor at Routledge, for his support and patience throughout the preparation of this book. Our gratitude is also extended to those who reviewed the manuscript and offered suggestions that strengthened the final version. None of this would have been realized without the bereaved parents who gave so graciously and selflessly of their lives. This book is a testament to their courage as they revisited and exposed their anguish and vulnerability; it is a testament to their resiliency as they moved from devastation to regeneration and embraced life in a new and meaningful way; and it is a testament to the trust they placed in us to tell the story of their survival. We hope we have met that trust.

ABOUT THE AUTHORS

☐ Jennifer L. Buckle, Ph.D., R. Psych.

Dr. Buckle is a registered psychologist and assistant professor of psychology at Sir Wilfred Grenfell College, Memorial University of Newfoundland, Newfoundland and Labrador, Canada. She received her Ph.D. in clinical psychology at York University in Toronto, Ontario, Canada. She was awarded the Ivana Guglietti-Kelly Award for excellence in qualitative research from York University and the Doctoral Thesis Certificate of Academic Excellence from the Canadian Psychological Association. Dr. Buckle has authored publications and presentations on the grief experiences of bereaved parents and the application of qualitative research methods in the study of bereavement. In addition, she teaches a variety of psychology courses including the Psychology of Death and Dying.

☐ Stephen J. Fleming, Ph.D., C. Psych.

Dr. Fleming is a professor in the Department of Psychology, Faculty of Health, at York University in Toronto, Ontario, Canada. The author of numerous book chapters, articles, and presentations on the grief experiences of children, adolescents, and adults, he has lectured in Canada, the United States, South America, Asia, and Europe. In addition to teaching graduate and undergraduate courses on the psychology of death, Dr. Fleming has qualified as an expert witness in litigation involving trauma, and he has served on the editorial boards of the *Journal of Palliative Care* and *Death Studies*. He has been the recipient of numerous awards and honors including the Noah Thorek Award for outstanding volunteer contribution to the Bereaved Families of Ontario; the Clinical Practice Award for outstanding contribution to clinical thanatology from the Association for Death Education and Counselling; the Dr. Beatrice Wickett Award for outstanding contribution to mental health education in Ontario; and the Citizen of Distinction Award from MADD Canada. A member of the Canadian Academy of Psychologists in Disability Assessment, he currently is Secretary-Treasurer of the International Work Group on Death, Dying, and Bereavement.

Setting the Stage

The death of a child, a parent's worst nightmare and the most excruciating of losses, results in devastating, ever-present grief. Parental bereavement is generally considered a permanent state of attempting to adjust to a diminished world empty of the beloved child (Klass, 1988). For a parent, the death of a child changes everything, forever.

The death of a child also brings multiple levels of loss. It begins with the physical loss of the child and quickly penetrates every aspect of a parent's functioning, affecting the view and experience of self, family, and the world. Even when surviving children remain, losing a child assaults basic aspects of a parent's identity (Edelstein, 1984). The more of ourselves we invest in another human being, the greater the loss to self when that person dies (Rosof, 1994). Clearly there are significant losses to the self with the death of a child due to the intimate and interconnected nature of the parent-child relationship with its substantial self-investment. The dynamics of the relationship intensify the losses, since parental attachment consists of both love for the child and love for oneself (Rando, 1986a). Furthermore, the pain of separation from their deceased children is especially intense for parents due to this unique physical and psychological closeness in the parent-child relationship (Rando, 1991).

A second level of loss involves the family. When a child dies, the family that was cannot be reclaimed and, although it will continue to exist, it will be forever transformed and diminished by the absence of a significant member (Rando, 1986a; Walsh & McGoldrick, 2004). The loss of the roles assumed by the deceased child, the changes in siblings who are now bereaved and, in some cases, now an only child, in addition to the loss of parts of each parent's self-identity, combine to create a new family system (Rando, 1993).

A third level of loss is the loss of future hopes and expectations (Edelstein, 1984; Rando, 1986a; Roach & Nieto, 1997; Rosof, 1994; Rubin & Malkinson, 2001). With the death of a child, a parent must grieve all the things that the child will never do: the graduation that will not occur, the wedding that will never happen, the grandchildren that will never be. Parents feel cheated. They experience a gaping sense of incompletion as they are forced to abandon all of the hopes, dreams, and expectations they held for their child (Rando, 1986a; Rosof, 1994). Even when there are surviving children, there is an ongoing longing for completion that will never occur with the deceased child (Edelstein, 1984). The child who died remains static, unchanging, in the hearts and minds of bereaved parents, while all else changes, develops, and grows.

A fourth level of loss involves the forced surrendering of comforting illusions and assumptions that are violated by the death. Parental beliefs in the benevolence of the world, the order of the universe in which the young replace the old, and the belief in one's self are significantly destabilized (Janoff-Bulman & Berg, 1998; Parkes, 1971; Rando, 1993). A bereaved parent's assumptive world—that set of assumptions or beliefs that secure and ground individuals and provide a sense of reality, purpose, and meaning (Kauffman, 2002)—is sorely challenged, if not destroyed. The fracturing of one's assumptive world results in substantial psychological upheaval, and the reluctant recognition that the world is no longer safe, orderly, and fair leaves bereaved parents feeling fearful and vulnerable. The illusions of security and protection from tragedy have been replaced by perceptions of the world as random, chaotic, unnatural, and cruel. Gone is the belief that there are answers to fundamental questions. The death of a child is simply incomprehensible.

When a child dies, parents lose so much on so many levels. Mothers and fathers lose the special relationship that exists between a parent and child, a relationship that is unique with each child. They lose aspects of self that were invested in and contingent on the life of their child, including their self-efficacy and self-worth. They lose their family as they knew it. They lose their sense of the future that was embodied in the child, the expectations, the hopes, the dreams. Finally, they lose the illusions and assumptions that provided support, security, and meaning. The insidious, obliterating nature of the loss of a child is not to be underestimated.

In a landmark study, Sanders (1980) administered the Grief Experience Inventory and the Minnesota Multiphasic Personality Inventory to individuals who had experienced the death of a child, a parent, or a spouse, and a non-bereaved control group. In contrast to those who had lost a parent or spouse, she found bereaved parents reported more intense grief reactions over a wide range of symptoms including greater somatization, depression, anger, guilt, and despair. This finding has since been replicated in numerous studies (e.g., Cleiren, Diekstra, Kerkhof, & van der Wal, 1994; Leahy, 1992–1993; Middleton, Raphael, Burnett, & Martinek, 1998; Rubin, 1993). Moreover, research has demonstrated that bereaved parents are at increased risk for affective disorders requiring hospitalization (Li, Laursen, Precht, Olsen, & Mortensen, 2005), physical illness (e.g., cancer, multiple sclerosis, myocardial infarction) (Li, Hansen, Mortensen, & Olsen, 2002; Li, Johansen, Bronnum-Hansen, Stenager, Koch-Henriksen, & Olsen, 2004; Li, Johansen, Hansen, & Olsen, 2002), and higher mortality rates than non-bereaved parents (Li, Precht, Mortensen, & Olsen, 2003).

Interestingly, Sanders (1980) failed to find significant differences between the grief of parents whose children died after a lengthy illness versus a sudden and unexpected death. Further to this finding, Buckle (1998), in a study of the efficacy of mutual-help groups for bereaved mothers, found they overwhelmingly experienced their children's deaths as sudden and unexpected regardless of the cause (a protracted dying period or sudden death). Although there may be challenges or issues unique to different types of death, the grief experienced by bereaved parents tends to have much in common irrespective of the cause of death (Sprang & McNeil, 1995; Tedeschi & Calhoun, 2004a). These findings further highlight the devastating impact of a child's death and illustrate that forewarning of the impending loss does little to this stark violation of the natural order of things—it is virtually always considered a shock.

☐ Definition of Terms: Bereavement, Mourning, and Grief

There seems to be a consensus in the literature on the definition of "bereavement." The term has been variously defined as "the state of having suffered a loss" (Rando, 1986b, p. 343), "the objective situation of having lost someone significant through death" (Stroebe, Hansson, Schut, & Stroebe, 2008, p. 4), and "... the loss to which the person is trying to adapt" (Worden, 2009, p. 17). What is common to all of these definitions is the objective state of having experienced a loss. Certainly there are many types of losses (e.g., the loss of a limb, termination of one's employment, or the loss of reputation); however, in this book "bereavement" will refer to the rupture of a loving relationship through death.

In contrast, although the terms "mourning" and "grief" have been used interchangeably, there is an emerging consensus that they are conceptually distinct. "Grief" is understood to be one's (personal) reaction to the death of a loved one; in the context of this book, it principally refers to the affective, cognitive, behavioral, physiological, social, and spiritual reactions of a parent subsequent to the death of their child. Grief is simply the price we pay for loving. It is an expected, human response to the death of someone significant or meaningful in our lives—and it does not necessarily require professional intervention.

With respect to "mourning," Rando (1986b) points out that, historically, the term has had two meanings. First, mourning was associated with the psychoanalytic process of decathecting or relinquishing the psychological bonds to the deceased and reinvesting this energy in other relationships. The second meaning is associated with the cultural, social, and religious rites and rituals that shape, and give expression to, an individual's and community's response to bereavement. From this perspective, mourning, or the response to bereavement (including cognitions, affect, and physiological responses), will vary considerably from one society, or religious or cultural group to the next. Whether one implements mourning rites prior to a death or after it, and for how long (days, weeks, months, or even years); whether communication with the deceased is promoted or discouraged; whether feelings must be suppressed or publicly displayed, or camouflaged behind a more socially palatable emotion (e.g., humor) will reflect the complex matrix of cultural, religious, and social prescriptions. As Rosenblatt (2008) observed, "everything written and everything known about grief through study and personal experience is saturated with cultural perspectives, concepts, and beliefs. No knowledge about grief is culture free" (p. 207).

Although not psychoanalytically trained, both Worden (2009) and Rando (1993) refer to mourning as a "process." For Worden, "mourning is the term applied to the '*process*' that one goes through in adapting to the death of the person" (p. 17). Rando is quite specific in referring to mourning as the process of accommodating the loss of a loved one through three reorientation operations related to the deceased (i.e., the transformation and reestablishing of new attachments while acknowledging physical absence), the mourner (i.e., revisiting one's assumptive world and identity and adjusting to the new reality), and the external world (i.e., adopting new, healthier ways of being in the world that acknowledge the absence of the deceased).

Other authors, when referring to mourning, tend to stress the interplay of social, cultural, and religious influences on how one interprets and reacts to the objective state of loss (bereavement). For example, Stroebe et al. (2008) interpret mourning to represent "... the public display of grief, the social expressions or acts expressive of grief that are shaped by the (often religious) beliefs and practices of a given society or cultural group" (p. 5), while Malkinson (2007) uses the term to refer "... to a set of practices and acts that are defined in cultural, social, and religious terms" (p. 3). In this book, we will restrict the term "mourning" to the external, more public expressions of loss that are shaped by cultural influences, religious beliefs, and social prescriptions. It represents how grief is expressed more so than how it is felt or experienced.

☐ Grief and Depression

In the *Diagnostic and Statistical Manual of Mental Disorders* (DSM-IV-TR; American Psychiatric Association (APA), 2000) "bereavement" is considered in the category "other conditions that may be the focus of clinical attention." Acknowledging that the duration and expression of "normal bereavement" are culturally determined, and that symptoms of acute grief and depression may be virtually indistinguishable, DSM-IV-TR excludes conditions due to bereavement within the two-month post-loss period (referred to as the bereavement exclusion). If the symptoms persist and meet the symptomatic criteria for depression, then the individual is diagnosable. To meet the threshold for major depressive disorder, an individual must report at least five of the following nine symptoms during a two-week period (the five must include either depressed mood or diminished interest or pleasure): depressed mood, diminished interest or pleasure, significant weight loss or weight gain, insomnia or hypersomnia, psychomotor agitation or retardation, fatigue or loss of energy, feelings of worthlessness or inappropriate guilt, diminished concentration or indecision, and recurrent thoughts of death or recurrent suicidal ideation with a plan (DSM-IV-TR; APA, 2000).

Without the bereavement exclusion, there are data to suggest that between 20% and 40% of bereaved spouses acknowledge symptoms consistent with a major depressive disorder within the first few months of bereavement (Clayton & Darvish, 1979; Zisook & Shuchter, 1991). Although there are many symptoms of a "normal" or uncomplicated grief reaction that are similar to depression, evidence suggests there may be important differences between grief and depression particularly in the nature and type of cognitive schemas and thoughts that underlie depressive symptoms.

According to Beck's cognitive theory of depression (1967, 1976), depressed individuals are prone to commit cognitive errors (e.g., overgeneralization, arbitrary inference) and, on the basis of childhood experiences, to think negatively about themselves, their world, and their future, what Beck referred to as the (depressive) cognitive triad. After a series of detrimental life events (usually in childhood), an individual formulates a number of "core assumptions" or interpretations that ultimately develop into an enduring negative cognitive belief system or "schema." Beck (1967) defined a schema as "elements constructed of past experience that form a relatively cohesive and persistent body of knowledge capable of guiding subsequent perceptions and appraisals" (p. 147). For example, an individual with a negative self-evaluation schema has the entrenched belief they can "never do anything right," while someone with a self-blame schema will feel personally responsible for anything untoward that occurs. In each dimension of the cognitive triad (self, world, and the future) there are data to show that the cognitions of depressed individuals are consistently more negative and self-critical than the cognitions of non-depressed individuals (Dobson & Shaw, 1987; Zuroff, Blatt, Sanislow, Bondi, & Pilkonis, 1999), that depressive cognitions are the product of distorted information processing, and that they happen rapidly, outside of awareness—in other words, they are automatic. We may not even be aware how cognitive errors and schemas shape our understanding of, and reaction to, life events.

Given the symptom overlap and co-morbidity of grief and depression begs the question, could cognitive theory assist in distinguishing these two phenomena? Are the cognitive profiles of depression and grief distinctive? Fortunately, there are data to show that certain depressogenic cognitions are unique to clinically depressed individuals but not to the bereaved, whether depressed or not. Leahy (1992-1993) found that grieving, depressed participants did not endorse as many negative subjective items on the Beck Depression Inventory as a clinically depressed sample. Further, in a study of nondepressed/bereaved, depressed/bereaved, depressed/non-bereaved, and control participants, Robinson and Fleming (1992) reported that bereaved individuals (nondepressed or depressed) were characterized by a different cognitive style than the clinically depressed subjects—they reported less intense depressed affect, and a less dysfunctional pattern of depressotypic thinking than their non-bereaved depressed counterparts. It would appear that the depressive mood, negative automatic thoughts, cognitive errors, and dysfunctional attitudes endorsed by the bereaved and the depressed bereaved are less intense than those who have a major depressive episode without bereavement.

It is our opinion that neurovegetative symptoms, e.g., sadness, apathy, difficulty eating, non-restorative sleep, problems concentrating, fatigue, anhedonia, and loss of libido, often blur the distinction between grief and depression. Although more research is needed, one of the keys to differentiating the two phenomena may be in the assessment of problematic cognitions, more specifically, the nature and intensity of negative thoughts of self, world, and future (Fleming & Robinson, 1991). In therapy, one of the authors (SF) has consistently noted the internalization of self-condemning cognitions ("I am worthless," "I'm a failure"), and not the aforementioned neurovegetative symptoms, in distinguishing an acute grief response complicated by clinically significant depressed affect. (Perhaps Freud [1917/1957] had it right in his seminal paper "Mourning and Melancholia" when he observed that bereaved individuals feel the *world* is impoverished and barren while the depressed are convinced they, *personally*, are unworthy, unloved, and disconsolate).

In their timely book *The Loss of Sadness*, Horwitz and Wakefield (2007) argue that contemporary psychiatry fails to distinguish sadness (the "normal response to misfortune," p. xi) from major depressive disorder by relying exclusively on the symptom profile while ignoring the context within which the symptoms occur. While they recognize and support the legitimacy of the bereavement exclusion, Horwitz and Wakefield are concerned that bereavement reactions (along with other negative experiences such as the ending of a romantic relationship, the loss of one's professional career, or a threatening medical diagnosis) that extend beyond the two-month post-loss period may be manifestations of "intense sadness" and not a psychiatric disorder. For example, Zisook, Paulus, Shuchter, and Judd (1997) found that 12% of a sample of 328 bereaved spouses had major depression at 13 months, and 6% were depressed at 25 months (compared to 1% of an age-matched comparison group diagnosed with depression).

The misdiagnosis of an uncomplicated grief reaction (Horwitz and Wakefield's [2007] "normal sadness") as major depressive disorder creates a number of unfortunate and destructive consequences: treating normal responses to loss as a disorder may eventuate in a self-fulfilling prophecy and lead to further difficulties in adjusting to the loss by exacerbating and prolonging symptoms; it wreaks havoc with prognostic accuracy; and it may thwart research efforts to identify treatment interventions for conditions that are distinct but present as symptomatically similar (Horwitz & Wakefield, 2007). This book bears witness to the agony of bereaved parents and we do not intend to minimize their suffering by referring to "normal" grief or sadness; we are simply arguing for conceptual clarity and diagnostic accuracy. The informed clinician will thoroughly assess for a variety of symptoms that may have preceded the loss, or developed subsequently. When a bereaved parent presents with the aforementioned symptoms of major depressive disorder, particularly with self-loathing, guilt, and self-destructive urges, psychotherapy is indicated and, in extreme cases, a psychiatric referral for medication may be indicated to supplement therapy.

☐ Grief and Posttraumatic Stress Disorder

In addition to major depressive disorder, another ticklish diagnostic and treatment issue for clinicians is the distinction between grief symptoms (affective, cognitive, physical, social, and spiritual) and subsyndromal or syndromal symptoms of posttraumatic stress disorder (PTSD). The core symptoms of PTSD are re-experiencing, avoidance, and increased arousal following exposure to a traumatic event during which one's peritraumatic response involves fear, helplessness, or horror (DSM-IV-TR; APA, 2000). The reexperiencing is often in the form of nightmares, memories and, when there is a profound and frightening sense of reliving the traumatic event, flashbacks. Because the memories and emotions associated with the trauma are so painful and debilitating, there is a tendency to avoid reminders of the trauma; this may involve actually quashing the experience of emotion, for this triggers traumatic memories. Finally, with the destruction of one's assumptive world, survivors are hypervigilant as the world is now a dangerous place and one must pay constant and close attention to ensure safety.

In a detailed analysis, Simpson (1997) commented on the striking similarity between the symptom presentation of grief and PTSD. PTSD symptoms of reexperiencing (e.g., dreams, nightmares, intense distress when exposed to reminders of the trauma accompanied by physiological reactivity) are not uncommon in bereaved individuals. Similarly, in PTSD, avoidance and emotional numbing (e.g., distancing from painful reminders of the deceased, loss of interest in previously enjoyed activities, feelings of detachment or not belonging, restricted range of affect, and thoughts of a foreshortened future) are prevalent among bereaved parents. And PTSD symptoms of hyperarousal (constant vigilance, difficulty falling and/or staying asleep, irritability and anger, concentration difficulties, and an exaggerated startle response) are frequently reported by those suffering the death of a child.

Although there is considerable overlap between the phenomena of grief and trauma, Nader's (1997) analysis of their differences and similarities is instructive. Although referring principally to traumatized children, she notes distinctive features of PTSD reexperiencing compared to grief reexperiencing; in the latter, particularly during the acute phase of grief, one pines or yearns for the deceased and wishes mightily for their return. In contrast, the reexperiencing typically found in PTSD takes the form of unbidden, intrusive, and often destabilizing images, memories, and dreams of the horror of experience. Similarly, there are distinctive features of the avoidance/numbing response; this response is common during the early weeks/months of grieving and tends to reduce in intensity with resignation to the loss. With PTSD, in contrast, this reaction tends to persist and actually hamper the emergence of a grief response. Nader noted, "Avoidance of reminders of the event and its traumatic circumstances (e.g., of thoughts, conversations, feelings, activities, people, locations, or other items that arouse recollection of the trauma) may interfere with expressing sadness, reminiscing … in order to work through the loss" (p. 25). With respect to arousal, shared symptoms include nonrestorative sleep, impaired focus and concentration, and anger/irritability (not unlike depression), but grief and PTSD differ as symptoms of hypervigilance and an exaggerated startle response are unique to the latter.

The death of a loved one will not unequivocally result in trauma symptoms or the formal diagnosis of PTSD and, of course, one can develop PTSD symptoms after exposure to a traumatic event that does not involve death (e.g., a serious motor vehicle accident, sexual assault). According to Rando (1994), grief with an overlay of trauma is more likely to follow a "traumatic death," i.e., death characterized by such features as suddenness, violence and mutilation, preventability and/or randomness, multiple deaths, and the loss of a child.

☐ What Constitutes "Complicated Grief"?

There are occasions when the risk for complications in the grief response is heightened, e.g., when the death is sudden and/or violent, when the pre-morbid relationship with the deceased is characterized by dependency or ambivalence, when the survivor's preexisting mental health has been precarious, or when the perceived quality of social support is reduced or nonexistent. Although it has long been recognized that a subset of individuals experience unremitting distress and significant functional impairment following the death of a loved one, the systematic investigation of bereavement-related physical and psychological morbidity is relatively recent (Prigerson, Maciejewski, et al., 1995). There have been several attempts at defining a type of grief response that involves intense inner perturbation and debilitating dysfunction, a response that severe, prolonged, and maladaptive, and that is not bet[ter accounted] for by major depressive disorder or PTSD (Horowitz et [al.,] & Jacobs, 1991; Prigerson, Bridge, et al., 1999). Several [terms have be]en used to refer to such enervating symptoms including morbid, atypical, pathological, unresolved, and complicated grief; consequently, attempts at operationalizing and classifying this syndrome have proven to be elusive. Prigerson and her colleagues originally referred to grief accompanied by intense distress and disability as *complicated*, as the symptoms were thought to be unresolved and associated with, or predictive of, significant impairment in daily functioning (Frank, et al., 1995; Prigerson, Maciejewski, et al., 1995; Prigerson).

When complicated grief was confused with complicated bereavement (i.e., symptoms of depressed affect secondary to bereavement), and when research revealed separation distress and traumatic distress as the underlying dimensions of the syndrome, Prigerson abandoned the term "complicated" in favor of "traumatic grief" (Prigerson, Shear, et al., 1997). Although she emphasized that the use of "traumatic" referred to the subjective experience of the event and not to its etiology, Prigerson, Vanderwerker, and Maciejewski (2008) acknowledged that the term had been frequently confused with posttraumatic stress disorder. As a result, "prolonged grief disorder" (PGD) is the current nomenclature for the constellation of symptoms marked by chronically high levels of yearning and pining for the deceased, chronic sorrow and rumination, lack of meaning in life, an inability to find potentially rewarding activities, the sense that "part of me" has died with the deceased, and the conviction that one's life will remain empty and unfulfilled without the deceased. For a diagnosis of PGD, symptoms must cause significant impairment in social, occupational, or other important areas of functioning, and they must persist for at least six consecutive months. This six-month time specification was implemented to minimize the number of false positives (i.e., individuals experiencing "normal sadness" immediately following the death of a loved one) and pathologizing a relatively normal acute bereavement response. However, as we will demonstrate in the chapters to follow, it is not atypical for bereaved parents to exhibit many of the above symptoms (and more) well beyond the six-month period.

PGD symptoms are chronic and etiologically distinct, and they're associated with significant functional impairments, as well as physical morbidity including cancer, cardiac disease, suicidal ideation, and increased alcohol and tobacco use (Ott, 2003; Prigerson, Bierhals, et al., 1997; Prigerson, Bridge, et al., 1999; Prigerson, Frank, et al., 1995; Silverman et al., 2000). Although symptoms of bereavement-related depression and PGD may not be completely independent, there are data to show that PGD symptoms form a distinct and coherent cluster that (a) has distinct etiological underpinnings (Silverman, Johnson, & Prigerson, 2001) and (b) differentiates this syndrome from bereavement-related depression and anxiety, including PTSD (Boelen, van den Bout, & de Keijser, 2003; Prigerson, Frank, et al., 1995; Prigerson et al., 2008).

It has been argued that current diagnostic categories used to account for "complicated" grief reactions (e.g., major depressive disorder, PTSD, adjustment disorder) often fail to identify individuals suffering from debilitating and intense grief symptoms (Horowitz et al., 1997; Silverman et al., 2000) and, as a result, there may well be an underestimation of the prevalence of increased psychiatric symptoms following the death of a significant other (Horowitz et al., 1997; Prigerson et al., 2008). To rectify this situation, Prigerson has consistently advocated that PGD meets the criteria for a mental disorder as defined in the DSM-IV and, consequently, it ought to be included as an Axis I disorder in the DSM-V (Prigerson et al., 2008).

In anticipation of the DSM-V in 2010, controversy continues over how to operationally define and classify complications in the grieving process and as to whether such reactions should be considered a separate diagnostic category (Bonanno & Kaltman, 1999; Ogrodniczuk & Piper, 2003). Those opposed to Prigerson's position maintain that complicated grief reactions can be subsumed under, or accounted for, by existing diagnostic categories (Stroebe & Schut, 2005–2006), and, as we've previously mentioned, others emphasize the importance of including complicated grief reactions under the rubric of their own clinical entity.

Bypassing the DSM controversy, Worden (2009) has proposed four distinct types of "complicated mourning" reactions—chronic (prolonged in duration and without a satisfactory conclusion), delayed (emotional responses to loss appear at a much later date, often in response to another loss), exaggerated (intense grief responses leave one feeling overwhelmed), and masked (grief symptoms are not recognized as such and emerge in physical responses or maladaptive behavior). Whether one conceptualizes grief as a distinct nosological entity worthy of a separate diagnostic category, or subsumed under one of the current diagnostic categories, or as one of Worden's complicated mourning reactions, it is imperative that a thorough assessment of the presenting problems be undertaken and treatment be directed at the appropriate symptoms. (A comprehensive discussion of the assessment and treatment of complications in grieving is beyond the scope of this book. The reader is referred to Malkinson [2007], Rando [1993], and Worden [2009] for a more in-depth discourse on these topics.)

☐ Theoretical Perspectives on Grief

Because the death of a child so devastates the parental landscape, numerous authors have argued that a different model of grief is required to account for the unique experiences of bereaved parents and to guide assessment and treatment (Davies, 2004; Kagan, 1998; Rando, 1993; Sprang & McNeil, 1995). What is considered abnormal in other losses is quite typical after the death of a child; therefore, the need for an appropriate model to adequately depict parental grief and to avoid propagating unrealistic expectations of bereaved parents is of the utmost importance (Kamm & Vandenberg, 2001; Rando, 1993). Not only has there been a reconsideration of parental grief, but there has also been a significant shift in the conceptualization of grief over the past two decades. Traditional theories of grief have been evaluated, their limitations unearthed, and new theories have emerged.

The classical *psychoanalytic* approach to loss (Freud, 1917/1957) proposed that "grief work" involved decathecting or detaching the emotional energy invested in the relationship with the deceased and reinvesting in other relationships (re-cathexis). According to Freud, grief was resolved and adaptive functioning was restored when the bereaved accepted the finality of the loss and severed the bonds of attachment to the deceased. Hagman (1995), in a critical review of this model, deemed "the cornerstone of the contemporary western understanding of bereavement" (p. 909), concluded that it lacked reliability and validity. Rather than reflecting on the painful process of decathexis and re-cathexis, Hagman posited that disengagement did not typically signal the resolution of grief; rather, "there is a revitalised engagement with the object internally ... to such an extent that one can observe not decathexis but a heightened reengagement with the dead person and eventually a transformation of memory into a permanent part of the patient's internal world" (p. 91).

Hagman's (1995) reformulation of psychoanalytic theory is more consistent with the experiences of bereaved parents in our study as it suggests an ongoing attachment or continuing bond with the deceased. Klass (1995) noted that bereaved parents felt consoled and comforted by the enduring ongoing attachment to their deceased children. Attachments were maintained and nurtured through linking objects (objects connecting parent and child, e.g., a toy, a piece of jewelry), religious devotion or one's "sense of connectedness to that which transcends death" (Klass, 1995, p. 253), and memories. Attachments may also take the form of feeling the presence of one's deceased child, assuming personality qualities or interests of the child, or developing an inner representation of the deceased. We will return to the notion of ongoing attachment as it applies to the sense of connection bereaved parents feel toward their deceased child in Chapter 5.

In addition to the grief work theory, numerous alternatives focusing on "stages," "phases," or "tasks" have been proposed. The most prominent of the *stage* theorists is Kübler-Ross (1969), whose work with dying patients has been applied to the grieving process. For Kübler-Ross, the successful resolution of grief is marked by movement from denial of the painful reality through anger, bargaining, depression, and, ultimately, acceptance. Although stage theory may have documented useful observations of many common emotional responses to loss, it has been criticized for being too rigid, too linear, and too prescriptive, and for failing to consider the influence of individual and cultural influences on mourning (Kastenbaum, 2007; Wortman & Silver, 2001).

Rando (1993) has proposed a theory of mourning that divides the grief process into three distinct time periods or *phases;* namely, avoidance, confrontation, and accommodation. The avoidance phase includes learning of the death and the time period shortly thereafter; it is marked by feelings of denial, shock, numbness, confusion, and incomprehension. As the emotional anesthesia of this period recedes and the painful recognition of the loss surfaces, the full intensity of the grief response is experienced (the confrontation phase). Finally, with the gradual reduction of symptom intensity, the mourner experiences the third phase, accommodation. Accommodation, or reconciling oneself with the death of a loved one, is an active process, the goal of which is "… to learn to live with the loss and readjust one's new life accordingly. Adjustments must occur in the relationship with the deceased (developing a new relationship), in oneself (revising the assumptive world and forming a new identity), and the external world (readjusting roles, skills, and behaviors and, at the appropriate time, reinvesting emotional energy in new people, objects, roles, hopes, beliefs, causes, ideals, goals, and other pursuits)" (Rando, 1993, p. 41). Rando rejected the use of such terms as "resolve" and "recovery"—and we would add "closure"—as they inaccurately imply an end point to the mourning process, a time when grieving is finished. In reality, one does not "get over" the death of a child; as we will illustrate, although the intensity may diminish, one grieves this loss for the remainder of one's life and the pain may never recede. For example, in comparison with a non-bereaved control group, Rubin (1996) found that Israeli parents whose adult children had perished in two wars 4 and 13 years previously were more preoccupied with the loss, reported more anxiety, and experienced more somatic symptoms. And the passage of time failed to differentiate the two bereaved groups.

In contrast to the phase theories of grief, Worden (2009) has proposed four basic *tasks* that need to be addressed in adapting to the death of a loved one. Task I is to accept the reality of the loss, that the death is final; Task II involves experiencing the pain of the loss in its physical, emotional, spiritual, cognitive, and behavioral manifestations; the varied adjustments that need to be negotiated after the death of a loved one (e.g., learning new roles, searching for a sense of meaning and purpose, redefining a sense of self, and rebuilding one's assumptive world) are included under Task III; and the final task is to establish an enduring connection with the deceased that facilitates reengaging with life. It is noteworthy that both Rando and Worden refer to aspects of ongoing attachment or continuing bonds with the deceased—and not to detachment or disengagement.

Attachment theory, which Stroebe (2002) declared "the most powerful theoretical force in contemporary bereavement research" (p. 127), has also provided insight into how we weather the death of loved ones. Based on the work of Bowlby and his colleagues (Ainsworth, Blehar, Waters, & Wall, 1978; Bowlby, 1969, 1973, 1980; Parkes, 2006), this theory postulates the operation of an innate psychobiological system (the attachment behavioral system), which motivates infants and children, when stressed or frightened, to seek the proximity of attachment figures for comfort, security, and protection. Situations that threatened the parent-child bond (e.g., when the attachment figure was unavailable or unresponsive) elicit bond preserving or restoring protests in the form of crying, anger, or clinging behavior. If the attachment figure does not reappear or respond in a more sensitive manner, separation anxiety fuels grief and despair. As a function of repeated proximity-seeking throughout infancy/childhood, a set of often-unconscious assumptions about self-identity and relationships is forged. Patterns of attachment are actively constructed and reconstructed, with increasing complexity, as one ages, yet they tend to be moderately stable from infancy/childhood through early adulthood (Fraley, 2002; Main, 1995).

When parents respond sensitively and in a timely fashion to their child's needs, a *secure* attachment style results (i.e., children are able to tolerate brief separations and reunions are uneventful). A parenting style discouraging closeness and attachment fosters an avoidant attachment style in which children appear uncaring and detached during separation and avoid or ignore the returning caregiver (*anxious/avoidant* attachment). An *anxious/ambivalent* attachment style eventuates when parents are anxious, overprotective, and discourage exploration; separations lead to marked perturbation and reunions are characterized by ongoing distress, anger, crying, and clinging. A fourth attachment style, *disorganized/disoriented*, was suggested by Main and Solomon (1986, 1990). This attachment style results from unpredictable and inconsistent parenting, often resulting from a history of depression, trauma, or unresolved loss(es) in the family. Consequently, children develop feeling helpless, unhappy, and without a coherent strategy for handling the ebb and flow of separation and reunion. In this context, separation leads to disorganized behavior and reunion is met with unusual reactions such as "freezing" (standing motionless), approaching the parent but with gaze averted, or exhibiting stereotypical behavior.

What, then, is the relationship between attachment style and bereavement, the ultimate form of separation? Individuals with secure attachments, those who are generally comfortable in intimate relationships and who can tolerate and express intense emotions, are able to befriend the pain of their grief, develop healthy continuing bonds with the deceased, and begin to reconstruct their lives. The course of adjustment to loss is thought to be much more precarious for those who exhibit "insecure" attachment styles, i.e., anxious/ambivalent, anxious/avoidant, or disorganized/disoriented. In his study of bereaved adults, Parkes (2006) concluded, "… people who make anxious/ambivalent attachments in childhood tend to have very conflicted relationships in adult life and this contributes to the lasting grief and loneliness that follows bereavement. Their tendency to cling remains a problem and has important implication for those who set out to help this group of people" (p. 88). In struggling with loss, anxious/avoidant individuals, minimally attached and prizing independence and emotional distance from others, may show few if any symptoms of loss. And they are not likely to seek out self-help groups, professional support, or reach out to friends and family. Finally, individuals with disorganized/disoriented attachments experience a rocky grief course that includes anxiety and panic, depression, substance abuse, feelings of helplessness, social withdrawal, anger, and often self-destructive urges (Parkes, 2006; Worden, 2009).

The *Dual Process Model of Coping with Bereavement (DPM)* (Stroebe, Schut, & Stroebe, 1998) is an example of a more recent theory of grieving that acknowledges and accommodates variability, context, and active responding. The DPM outlines two broad orientations, loss and restoration. In loss-orientation, an individual is "concentrating on, dealing with, and processing some aspect of the experience" (Stroebe et al., 1998, p. 91). Dealing with emotional reactions and focusing on the lost relationship are the primary aspects of this orientation. Alternatively, the restoration-orientation involves adjustment to the secondary consequences of loss. "It means establishing new routines, fulfilling new roles, developing a new identity, and adjusting to an environment without the deceased" (Stroebe et al., 1998, p. 92). Both, then, are sources of distress and anxiety and are attended to in varying degrees (based on individual, gender, and cultural differences) (M. S. Stroebe & Schut, 2001).

A critical component of the DPM is the oscillation process between the two orientations. It is hypothesized that the bereaved alternate between the loss-orientation and the restoration-orientation, and that this oscillation is necessary for adaptive coping (W. Stroebe & Schut, 2001). Furthermore, in the early days of bereavement, there is typically more loss-orientation and as time goes on there is a move towards more restoration-orientation (Stroebe et al., 1998). The DPM suggests a modification to the traditional grief work hypothesis; instead of conceptualizing engaging one's pain as good and avoidance as maladaptive, a simplistic view unsupported by research, the model focuses on the regulatory function of oscillation. (Rando [1993], in her three-phase model of avoidance, confrontation, and accommodation, and Worden [2009] also stress the importance of oscillation or cycling among the phases.)

The final model to be reviewed is Rubin's *Two-Track Model of Bereavement* (TTMoB; Rubin, 1999). Early in his career Rubin noted that the two most influential approaches to bereavement adjustment emphasized either the severing of the emotional bond with the deceased or conceptualized bereavement as one of a number of significant and stressful life experiences with concomitant and various repercussions, e.g., behavioral, physical, cognitive, and emotional. Where Rubin acknowledged the importance of including basic indicators of human distress in a comprehensive model of adjustment to loss (e.g., psychological distress, physical well-being, and family adaptation), he rejected the notion that bereaved individuals sever the relationship with the deceased; rather, his research and clinical impressions led him to believe that they renegotiated, reorganized, and transformed a continuing connection with their lost loved one.

The TTMoB adopts a bifocal perspective on bereavement based on the impact of the death on biopsychosocial functioning (Track I) *and* the quality and nature of the evolving relationship with the deceased (Track II). Each of these multidimensional axes or tracks has 10 relevant domains. More specifically, Track I assesses a wide range of physical, emotional, and interpersonal distress including symptoms of anxiety and depression, somatic and health concerns, posttraumatic indicators, spiritual dimensions of loss including one's meaning structure, family relationships, self-esteem and self-worth, and the ability to manage interpersonal relationships including work. Track II captures the prominent qualities of the interpersonal relationship with the deceased including the emotional closeness or distance from the deceased, preoccupation with the loss, the impact on self-perception, idealization of/conflict with the deceased, positive and negative effects associated with recollections of the deceased, and features of loss (i.e., shock, searching, organization, and reorganization). The final Track II dimension is the memorialization process, which refers to "... the way in which the bereaved has transformed the relationship with the deceased into something more, whether in ways of identification or formal or informal memorials ... the loss of a person has been transformed into something beyond grief and mourning and shades into the life fabric" (Rubin, 1999, p. 687).

The usefulness of the TTMoB has been demonstrated in a number of publications (e.g., Malkinson, 2007; Rubin, Malkinson, & Witztum, 2003) and Rubin et al. (2009) have designed the Two-Track Model of Bereavement Questionnaire (TTBQ) to assess the interactive processes of biopsychosocial functioning (Track I) and the complex relationship with the memories, images, thoughts, and feeling states associated with the deceased (Track II). This model provides the clinician with assessment tools and guidance (e.g., delineating components of each track and their interaction over the course of psychotherapy) along with suggestions for intervention to deal with one or both of the domains of the bereaved's response.

☐ Grief and the Family

In defining "family," we agree with Bowen (1990) that "... family is not merely an assemblage of individuals; it is those same individuals inextricably intertwined in ways that are constantly interactive and mutually reinforcing. And family, in the fullest sense of the word, embraces all generations—past, present, and future—those living, those dead, and those yet to be born" (p. 8). The death of a child sends an emotional tsunami throughout the family unit and no member remains untouched by its force. Individually and collectively, the family struggles with the loss of the child; the loss of preexisting roles, routines, rituals, and relationships; the search for meaning; the reconstructing of assumptive worlds; the incongruent grieving styles; the destruction of the preexisting family unit; and the seemingly insurmountable task of restoring family equilibrium or homeostasis.

A comprehensive assessment of a family's response to the death of a child (or the death of any member) must take into account the complexity, diversity, and constant fluctuation of the family landscape in discerning factors that impede adjustment and increase the risk of dysfunction. Walsh and McGoldrick (2004) have documented a number of variables that impact a family's adaptation to loss including the manner of death (e.g., protracted dying, sudden death, violent death, or suicide); family functioning and family relationships (including the social network and extended family) prior to and following the death; family organization including the flexibility of roles, rules, and boundaries, family connectedness, the availability of a social support network, extended family and economic resources, and the ability to communicate clearly and openly with one another; sociocultural influences (e.g., grieving stigmatized deaths from HIV/AIDS or the loss of a gay/lesbian partner, gender-based expressions of grief which can further stress the marital dyad, cultural prescriptions for mourning); and the stage in the family's life cycle when the loss occurs (e.g., the family with young children, or with adolescent children, or the family launching children and entering the "empty nest" period).

With the death of a child, the family is confronted with numerous challenges to its organization, identity, and purpose (Nadeau, 1998; Shapiro, 1994). Mirroring Worden's (2002) model of individual adaptation to loss, Walsh and McGoldrick (2004) have identified four family tasks that "... promote immediate and long-term adaptation for family members and strengthen the family as a functional unit" (p. 9). Families actively engage in acknowledging the reality of the loss and the unique grief of its members, sharing the experience of the loss through meaningful rituals, open communication and the expression of feelings, reorganizing the family system and reestablishing equilibrium, and a reinvesting in other relationships. (Walsh and McGoldrick do not address the issue of continuing bonds or ongoing attachment with the deceased as part of their fourth and final task.) Families that tend to complete these tasks share a number of characteristics including the ability to communicate openly, respectfully, and sensitively; the establishing of meaningful, shared rituals; the acceptance of differences in approaching the loss and the appreciation of differing styles of grieving; and a positive view (i.e., the ability to positively reframe aspects of the individual and collective response to loss) (Gilbert, 2001).

Just as individuals can get "stuck" in the grieving process, so too can families. However, a thorough discussion of maladaptive family responses to loss and the variety of available treatment modalities is beyond the scope of this book. The interested reader is urged to consider the following resources: narrative therapy (Nadeau, 2008), Milan family therapy (Nadeau, 2008), transitional family therapy (Horwitz, 1997), family-focused grief therapy (Kissane & Lichtenthal, 2008), or family systems approaches designed or modified to address PTSD and complex traumatic stress disorders (Ford & Saltzman, 2009).

☐ This Book

There is so much to contend with after the death of a child. The loss impacts the individual parent, the family, and the surviving children. Everything is changed. "Bereaved parents have crossed a threshold across which they can never return ... they experience themselves in relationships with their children and with each other as different than they were, adapting to changing family contexts in a variety of ways" (Grout & Romanoff, 2000, p. 97). How, then, in the face of all of this devastation and upheaval, does one continue to parent one's surviving children? The chapters to follow will assist the reader in answering this question.

Each chapter will deepen the understanding of the process and experience of parenting surviving children after the death of a child. Chapter 2 will outline the method and procedures used to collect and analyze the data that provided the foundation for the theory of "bereaved parenting." In Chapter 3 the devastation of this overwhelming and catastrophic loss will be demonstrated in detail through the metaphor of the "house of refracting glass," including the immediate shatter, the aftermath, and the effect of time. We will then turn to regeneration, starting with self (Chapter 4) and family (Chapter 5). Chapters 6, 7, and 8 will explore the dual tasks of parenting and grieving; parental conceptions of control, protection, and altered priorities; and the unique challenges of parenting bereaved children. In Chapter 9 we will outline the implications of this theory of "bereaved parenting" for clinical practice, future research, and the advancement of knowledge about this unique and devastating loss.

CHAPTER 2

Discovering the Theory of Bereaved Parenting
Method, Participants, and Overview of Results

After the death of a child, how does one continue to parent surviving children? A question such as this begs understanding, exploration, and holism. A complex question demands a complex answer and the research method best suited to explore this intricate query is the qualitative approach. Within the past two decades qualitative research has been gaining momentum and acceptance in a variety of disciplines including psychology (Rennie, 1996; Rennie, Watson, & Monteiro, 2002). Qualitative methods provide access to subject areas that are complex and generally impervious to quantitative research methods. With its focus on the achievement of understanding, the recognition of collaboration with participants, and the emphasis on holism, qualitative methodology, under the domain of human science, has much to offer the researcher interested in the vast complexity of human experience (Rennie, 1994, 1995a, 1995b).

Researchers within the area of bereavement have also embraced the qualitative approach stating that it may more appropriately and adequately represent the experiences of the bereaved than quantitative, modernistic methods (Fleming & Robinson, 2001; Riches & Dawson, 1996; Silverman & Klass, 1996). Some examples of the application of qualitative methodology include an investigation of parents' experiences after perinatal death (Grout & Romanoff, 2000), the long-term grieving patterns of families following a death from childhood cancer (McClowry, Davies, May, Kulenkamp, & Martinson, 1987), the continuing relationships or continuing bonds with deceased loved ones (Silverman & Klass, 1996), the impact of parental bereavement on the lives of parents as a couple (Rosenblatt, 2000a), and meaning-making within family systems after the death of a loved one (Nadeau, 1998). Significantly, in April 2002, the journal *Death Studies* dedicated a special issue to qualitative research, exploring theory and application in the thanatology domain. The qualitative approach to bereavement research makes possible the exploration of questions regarding meaning, experience, and understanding after the death of a loved one, the results of which contribute to ever-developing models of grief that focus on the complexity of human relationships and the connectedness of individuals to those living and to those who have died (Neimeyer & Hogan, 2001; Silverman & Klass, 1996). Such an approach, therefore, is well suited to the present systematic exploration of the experience and process of parenting surviving children after the death of a child, a perspective that is notably absent from the existing research literature.

Methodology

This study was conducted using the grounded theory approach to qualitative research (Glaser & Strauss, 1967) as understood through the methodology of methodical hermeneutics (i.e., the marriage of hermeneutics and method) (Rennie, 2000).

Grounded Theory Method

Concerned that much of the theory in sociology was derived from rational theorizing and, therefore, not rooted in the systematic evaluation of data, Glaser and Strauss (1967) developed a discovery-oriented approach that conceptualizes theory directly from the data. Since its inception, the grounded theory method has been further developed, clarified, and adopted by numerous social science disciplines, including psychology (Rennie, 1998), but not, however, without confusion regarding the application of the approach.

Some of this confusion is attributable to Glaser and Strauss (1967) themselves. In their original monograph, *The Discovery of Grounded Theory*, they failed to clearly specify the procedures of the approach and, consequently, left much room for interpretation (Rennie, 1995c). Another factor contributing to this confusion is that the founding methodologists, Glaser and Strauss, have each independently taken the method in divergent directions. (For a more detailed analysis see Glaser [1992], Rennie [1998], and Strauss and Corbin [1990, 1994].) Based on Rennie's (1998) critical review of the developing differences between Glaser (1992) and Strauss (Strauss & Corbin, 1990), the present study is more consistent with Glaser's (1992) emphasis on interpretive analysis than with Strauss and Corbin's (1990) attempt to unduly formalize the methodology. In an attempt to avoid further confusion regarding the approach, it is important to note that the method employed in this study, as described below, is based on the Rennie, Phillips, and Quartaro (1988) modifications to the original grounded theory methodology of Glaser and Strauss (1967).

The goal of the grounded theory approach is to stay immersed in the data so that the resulting theory is accountable to the data from which it was conceived. This systematic exploration and representation of the meaning of data is accomplished through a set of procedures originally outlined by Glaser and Strauss (1967) and further clarified and refined by Rennie et al. (1988). These procedures, titled "theoretical sampling," "constant comparative analysis," and "theoretical memoing," are the methods by which theory is extracted from data.

Theoretical Sampling

In a grounded theory study, the researcher simultaneously collects and analyzes the data. This approach, titled theoretical sampling, with its vacillation between data collection and analysis, ensures that the researcher remains grounded in the data and has the opportunity to respond, with further data collection, to any questions that may arise (Glaser & Strauss, 1967). This simultaneous process of data collection and analysis to inform further data collection must begin somewhere; therefore, it is important to be clear in one's focus when selecting the initial participants. Rennie et al. (1988) state that it is necessary to focus on learning what is central and crucial to the phenomenon early in the analysis; initially, then, participants should be selected based on their similarity and likelihood of providing insight into the main question of interest. In so doing, the researcher maximizes the possibility of the early emergence of core aspects of the phenomenon under investigation.

Even after the emerging theory has been derived, this interaction between data analysis and data collection continues through the application of theoretical sampling. For example, a researcher might use theoretical sampling of comparison groups to extend the generalizability of a theory derived from a relatively homogeneous sample of participants. In this instance, comparison groups are included in an effort to clarify the impact of the variability among respondents' characteristics on the emerging theory; therefore, selection of these groups is informed by the initial analysis.

Constant Comparative Analysis

It is through constant comparative analysis that reduction in the complexity of the data is achieved; the embedded purpose is to force the analyst to stay close to the data and thereby discourage subjective, a priori, rationally derived theorizing (Rennie, 2000). These constant comparisons are made between units of text, and through this process the theory emerges. Glaser and Strauss (1967) recommended that data should be analyzed line by line; therefore, units of analysis consist of lines of text. Rennie et al. (1988) refined this recommendation and, through their application of the method, found it to be more manageable to break the data into "meaning units," or fragments of text, that have a sensed theme or meaning. These meaning units can be as lengthy as one page or as short as one line (Rennie, 1995c).

Once meaning units represent all the relevant data, the constant comparative analysis can be implemented. This analysis compares the meaning units for differences and similarities, and allows the researcher to conceptualize categories from this process of comparison. The categories are representations of the similarities noted across several meaning units. Meaning units can be assigned to as many different categories as is deemed appropriate. At the outset, as Rennie and Fergus (2006) have noted, generated category names tend to be overly cautious, reflect literal descriptions of the text, and frequently produce far too many unwieldy categories for a meaningful analysis. As the analysis continues, and indeed as the researcher gains both experience in the application of the method and understanding of the phenomenon, the category names tend to evolve to include metaphors, similes, and images that are much more inclusive of meaning and thereby contribute to a rich, eloquent, grounded analysis (Rennie & Fergus, 2006). In any case, as the category names evolve so too does the list of categories, and as the analysis progresses this list is continually revisited as additional meaning units are derived. New meaning units are either subsumed under existing categories or new categories are created to represent the meaning unit, which are added to the existing category list. This process of constant comparison continues to the point of saturation, that is, the point at which relatively few new categories are required to represent the meaning units of new data derived from the chosen theoretical sample (Rennie et al.,

1988). At this juncture, data collection ceases and the analyst applies another constant comparative analysis across all the derived categories.

This conclusive round of comparative analysis is completed in an effort to clarify the relationship between categories and highlight emerging similarities and differences. The core category, which represents the central theme of the study and organizes the theory, emerges from this final analysis (Rennie et al., 1988). The remaining categories, which help to further define and clarify the core category, become the properties of, and are subsumed by, the core category.

Theoretical Memoing

The final procedure in the grounded theory approach, theoretical memoing, addresses the interpretative nature of the method and it is conducted simultaneously with theoretical sampling and constant comparative analysis. Through theoretical memoing, the researcher's subjectivity is explicitly recognized (Rennie et al., 1988). These memos contain the honest reactions (or as honest as can be comprehended about oneself by oneself) of the analyst throughout the process of the research and include such reflections as developing theories, biases, assumptions, previous knowledge, and reactions. As this represents a transparent attempt to stave off the internal influences of the researcher and remain grounded in the data, the memos are influential in the formulation of the emerging theory and the documentation of the returns of the study.

Methodical Hermeneutics

Methodical hermeneutics is the methodology put forth by Rennie (2000) to support the grounded theory approach to qualitative research. At the crux of this methodology, or logic of justification, is the notion of a balance between realism and relativism. Addressing the tension between the realism of the object being studied and the relativism inherent in the subjectivity of the researcher, the aim of qualitative research, specifically the grounded theory approach, is to develop an understanding that is acknowledged to be based on the interaction between the object of investigation and the perspective of the researcher. It is accepted that the researcher's perspective influences the understanding of the research object, and the research object influences the perspective of the researcher, which in turn alters the understanding of the object (Rennie, 1995b). The result is neither extreme realism to the point of claiming foundational knowledge nor extreme relativism to the point of solipsism (Rennie, 1995a). Instead, the grounded theory method incorporates the balance between realism and relativism and results in a theory based on a rigorous, systematic, and sufficient understanding of the meaning of text.

The rigor and sufficiency of the grounded theory method are hinged on the application and communication of the important ingredients to the rhetoric of this method. These ingredients further address the balance between realism and relativism and include reflexivity, groundedness, a demonstration of procedural rigor, and coherence of representation (Rennie, 1995a, 1995b). Reflexivity is addressed and communicated through the use of theoretical memoing while groundedness is the foundation of the approach as the researcher's understanding is extracted from, and accountable to, the data under investigation. The demonstration of procedural rigor is achieved through a comprehensive description of the operations employed throughout the study. The final written account, which serves to explicate the above factors, is the coherence of representation or how rationally and convincingly these fundamentals are presented. All of these elements come together to form and present the study's results. The plausibility of the assertions rests on the extent to which the reader accepts or resonates with the formulations. Inherent within this method is the recognition that different researchers bring different perspectives to the same object of research and, therefore, may derive different results (Rennie, 1998). These varying understandings, however, are acceptable to the degree that they are grounded and, therefore, ring true to the informed audience of researchers and participants (Rennie, 1995a, 1998).

The tension between relativism and realism in grounded theory is explicitly acknowledged through the logic of methodical hermeneutics. Rennie (2000) has furthered this understanding by presenting the manner in which induction is involved in the method and is consistent with hermeneutic analysis (i.e., deriving understanding from text that stands on its own). Drawing on the theory of inference by C. S. Peirce (1965; as cited in Rennie, 2000), Rennie expressed his understanding of the grounded theory method as an inductive approach to hermeneutics.

Peirce (1965; as cited in Rennie, 2000) posited that the discovery of knowledge is the result of the interaction of abduction (the imaginative creation of the hypothesis) and induction (the gathering of facts). Rennie (2000) extended Peirce's theory to the domain of human science, making the link between abduction and interpretation, coupled with the consensus-building nature of knowledge, as consistent with hermeneutics. With regard to the grounded theory method, derived categories are construed as abductions and further tested by the inductive analysis of the remaining text, so that induction informs the abduction in a cyclical fashion, thus making induction self-correcting (Rennie,

2000), in keeping with the observation made by Tursman (1987). Based on this interplay between abduction and induction through the constant comparative analysis (thereby making hermeneutics methodical), paired with the objectifying returns from theoretical memoing (or bracketing), the grounded theory method is conceptualized as rigorous, systematic, sufficient, and involving the demonstration of knowledge.

☐ Participants

There were 10 bereaved parents in this study, five mothers and five fathers. These parents were unrelated except for two mothers and two fathers who were spouses. The latter two sets of parents were interviewed separately, and no mention was made of the interview with the other parent except to acknowledge that both parents were participating in the study. These couples, individually and spontaneously, stated that they had not discussed the interview with their spouse prior to participating. The focus of the research was an in-depth evaluation of bereaved mothers and fathers separately; the impact of one spouse on another is accounted for in many of the themes, whether the spouse was involved in the research or not.

Each bereaved parent (age range: 40 to 51 years, mean age: 44.5 years) had at least one surviving child who had experienced the death of their sibling; the number of surviving children in each family ranged from one to four. Five of the surviving children were now only children as a result of their siblings' death. The age of surviving children ranged from 2 to 30 years (mean age = 14.1 years). Surviving children and their parents were members of intact families at the time of the death to the present. The length of time married ranged from 13 to 31 years, with a mean of 18.5 years. Additionally, both the bereaved parent and his or her spouse were the biological parents of the deceased child and surviving children. There are data to suggest that perinatal death (i.e., fetal death beyond 20 weeks' gestation through infant death within the first month of life) presents parents with a unique set of challenges to their resourcefulness and resilience, and involves different issues and reactions (Bennett, Litz, Lee, & Maguen, 2005; Grout & Romanoff, 2000; Oglethorpe, 1989). As a result, parents suffering perinatal loss were excluded from this study.

The deceased children ranged in age from 1 year 6 months to 20 years 6 months; 7 were male and 1 was female, and the time-since-death varied from 3 to 8 years (mean = 5.5 years). Three of the children died at the scene of fatal automobile accidents, while the remaining five children succumbed to illnesses. In the latter group, parents classified the illnesses as sudden and unexpected. Of the 10 parents, two discovered their children had died when they went to rouse them in the morning; seven were with their children when they died (either in the accident, called to the hospital, or engaged in activity with the child); and one was informed by telephone of the accident that had claimed the child's life.

All of the participants were Caucasian and had been living in Canada for most, if not all, of their lives. Nine of the 10 parents identified their ethnic background, and the ethnic background of their spouse, as North European (e.g., English, Irish, Dutch). The 10th parent described her and her husband's ethnic background as Eastern European (e.g., Polish, Bulgarian). The highest level of education of each female participant (and her spouse) ranged from the completion of high school (participant $n = 0$, spouse $n = 2$), college (participant $n = 4$, spouse $n = 2$), or university (participant $n = 1$, spouse $n = 1$). The highest level of education of each male participant (and his spouse) ranged from the completion of high school (participant $n = 2$, spouse $n = 2$), college (participant $n = 1$, spouse $n = 2$), or university (participant $n = 2$, spouse $n = 1$). While all of the fathers were employed on a full-time basis, the mothers' work status varied with some working part-time ($n = 3$), full-time ($n = 1$), or working inside the home ($n = 1$). Finally, all of the participants were recruited through Bereaved Families of Ontario (BFO), a mutual-help organization established in 1978 to assist families who have experienced the death of a child (Fleming & Balmer, 1995). Please refer to Appendix A for more information about the characteristics and mandate of this unique organization.

The criteria for inclusion were as follows: the individual had to be a bereaved mother or father, the time-since-death had to be at least 1 year, the families had to be intact before the death to the present day, and there had to be at least one surviving child. Both the deceased child and at least one of the surviving child(ren) had to be between the ages of 1 and 21 years and living at home when the death occurred. Furthermore, at least one surviving child had to be living at home when the interview occurred.

The participants in this study, derived principally from a Caucasian, middle-class sample of individuals, tended to be more homogenous than heterogeneous along many dimensions (e.g., education, employment status, race). The data, then, are based on an in-depth analysis of those who volunteered to participate in this research; it would be presumptuous to assume that the experiences of these bereaved parents are generalizable to those from different racial, cultural, or even socioeconomic backgrounds. Awareness and respect for diversity must not be overlooked as these factors have the potential to define and shape the experience of loss and influence our attempts at support and intervention.

In quoting participants throughout this book, we have changed or omitted identifying information. We have assigned each parent a pseudonym to assist the reader in identifying a bereaved mother or father. Each quote is a verbatim representation of the words of the participant.

☐ Procedure

Interview

The interviews, between 1.5 and 2.5 hours in length, were conducted by the first author (JB) over a 9-week period. After obtaining a signed, informed consent to participate in the study, she asked a series of demographic questions, explaining the need for background information to "situate the sample" (Elliott, Fischer, & Rennie, 1999, p.221). These demographic questions elicited information about the individual, his or her spouse, the deceased child, and the surviving child or children. Each participant was informed that this was the only part of the interaction in the more familiar question-and-answer format as the remainder of the interview was discovery-oriented. An open-ended, in-depth approach best represents our position that each participant is an expert in his or her own experience. This was overtly expressed before the interview and further reinforced by the exploratory style of the interaction.

With the recording device activated, each interview began with the query, "Do you feel that _____'s (child's name) death has affected your parenting of your surviving child(ren)?" All participants answered "yes" to this question, which was followed by, "Can you tell me about its effect on your parenting?" Subsequent questions and comments were determined by the participants' responses. One question, however, was prepared in advance and requested that parents take the perspective of their surviving child(ren). The question asked was, "If you could speak from the perspective of _____ (name[s] of surviving child[ren]), what are the changes in your parenting that s/he would have noticed since _____'s (child's name) death?" This "circular questioning" or "mind reading" technique was inspired by Nadeau's study of meaning-making in families after a death (1998, p. 43). Nadeau noted that her use of circular questioning in individual interviews yielded almost as much information about family dynamics as her interviews with multiple family members present. Given the profitable results realized by Nadeau, circular questioning was included in the interviews with each bereaved parent in the present study.

Toward the end of the interview, participants were offered the opportunity to add anything they felt was noteworthy, to ponder the content of the interview, and to contribute any information they felt may have been overlooked. At the conclusion of the interview, each parent was invited to reflect on the experience of being interviewed and to provide feedback. Within 24 to 48 hours, each participant was contacted by telephone to determine the impact of the interview; they were also given the opportunity to clarify issues or events, to expand on their reflections, or request the removal of any information they had provided. In addition to asking for suggestions or comments on how the interview process might be improved, the first author, once again, provided her contact information and encouraged participants to communicate with her should they have any concerns or questions. The anticipated date of availability of results was provided and the conversation was concluded by thanking participants for their valued participation.

Within 24 hours, the first author listened to the tape recording of the interview, made notes about its content and any salient reactions, and recorded the nascent themes and concepts to be explored in subsequent interviews. These themes and concepts were embodied in probe questions introduced in subsequent interviews. For example, after reviewing the second bereaved father's interview, it was realized that both parents had discussed the importance of instilling a sense of independence in their surviving children. Consequently, in subsequent interviews, if this topic did not come up during the course of the discussion, it was introduced in the form of a probe question such as, "Some fathers have mentioned a sense of the importance of instilling independence in their surviving children. Is that something that you have ever thought about or does that fit with your experience?" The introduction of widely experienced phenomena previously introduced by other bereaved parents provided insight into the degree of similarity or dissimilarity among individuals.

This use of probes is consistent with the concept of theoretical sampling (Glaser & Strauss, 1967) as the researcher simultaneously collects and analyzes the data, and then allows those data to influence the manner in which subsequent information is elicited. In its formal application, theoretical sampling involves the thorough analysis of one interview before initiating the next interview, and the knowledge gleaned from the previous interview guides the researcher in choosing an appropriate participant for the ensuing interview. Although we attempted to adhere to this procedure, two amendments were made to accommodate the constraints of working with a community sample within a community agency. It has been noted by previous researchers that making minor modifications to the grounded theory method is acceptable if one is explicit about any adjustments that were made (Annells, 1996; Stern, 1994).

The first of these amendments to strict theoretical sampling involved the scheduling of interviews. There were three factors to be considered in arranging a meeting time—the schedule of the participant, the schedule of the first author, and the availability of an office at the BFO location. Given these constraints, there were limited opportunities for the three parties involved and, therefore, a time that suited all had to be exploited when available. Despite this condition, however, there were always at least 2 to 7 days between each interview, allowing time to review the previous interview in preparation for the next.

The second amendment to strict theoretical sampling procedures was dictated by the constraints of engaging a community sample of bereaved parents through a community agency. The number of bereaved parents willing to participate in a study such as this is limited given the nature of the loss and the interview format requiring a substantial time commitment. Furthermore, this pool of participants was further narrowed by the wisdom of the staff at BFO as to individuals who fit the outlined criteria and would be capable of attending an interview and discussing the topic of focus. Given these various considerations, which through necessity narrowed the potential pool of participants, strict theoretical sampling could not be implemented.

Having said this, however, we feel that the principle or essence of theoretical sampling was followed. The meticulous and thorough appraisal of each interview prior to subsequent contact with participants facilitated the emergence of themes and areas of future inquiry that, in turn, informed ensuing interviews. This vacillation between conducting and reviewing interviews ensured that the first author remained grounded in the data and allowed her to respond to questions that arose in the subsequent interviews. Furthermore, the sample of participants was purposely not homogeneous. Although the initial participants were more homogeneous than heterogeneous, this expanded as data collection continued and fathers were introduced. Likewise, further heterogeneity was introduced by the varying ages of deceased and surviving children and diverse causes of death (e.g., illness versus accident). Through these elements, we believe the spirit of theoretical sampling prevailed.

Ethical Considerations

Given the emotional and sensitive nature of this study, there were a number of ethical considerations to be addressed. First, it was explicitly communicated to each participant that involvement in the study was voluntary and they could withdraw at any time. In addition, to facilitate making an informed decision, potential participants were provided with a description of the research and an explanation of the nature and content of the interview. All participants were assured that our utmost concern lay with their welfare, not the welfare of the research.

Second, potential participants were told that confidentiality would be protected in a number of ways, including the removal of identifying information from the interview transcripts (which were typed verbatim from the audiotapes), the secure storage of all audiotapes in a separate location from the transcripts (devoid of any identifying information), and the presentation of only short excerpts and not complete or full stories of the parents' encounter with loss. Replacing the individual's name or initials with an unrelated pseudonym further protected confidentiality.

Third, as previously mentioned, participants were provided with the name and telephone number of the first author and were encouraged to contact her should they have any further questions or concerns arising from their participation in the study. If the interview raised any disturbing or troublesome issues for participants, and they wanted to receive additional assistance or counselling, appropriate referral information was available upon request.

Finally, although it is often part of the grounded theory research protocol to invite participants to review the researcher's understanding of the text upon completion of the analyses, that component was not implemented in the present investigation. This exclusion was the result of discussions between the authors and the executive director of BFO in which it was concluded that a second meeting would be too onerous and greatly reduce the number of parents willing to participate in the study. This proved to be a correct assessment. It was challenging to coordinate the schedules of parents, the BFO office, and the first author. Furthermore, parents reported that although they enjoyed the interview process, they generally found it exhausting and emotionally taxing. A second interview, therefore, seemed too much to ask of the participants. A compromise was agreed upon that consisted of a follow-up telephone call within 1 to 2 days after the interview and an optional feedback session made available to parents to discuss the results.

Transcription

The first author personally transcribed three of the interviews; a transcriber, who was informed of the sensitivity of the material and signed a confidentiality agreement, typed the remaining seven. Due to the professional training and experience of the transcriber, the impact of exposure to the content of these interviews was not a major concern but it was also not dismissed. On several occasions the first author spoke with the transcriber to ensure that her exposure to the emotion-laden content was not becoming too arduous or personally problematic. Appreciative of the opportunity to discuss her personal response to the material, she reflected that it was periodically distressing to listen to the parents discussing the pain of their grief.

The transcriber was trained in the standards of psychotherapy transcription and preserved all pauses, intonations, and emotional expressions (e.g., laughing, crying). In an attempt to reproduce the complete interview, all incomprehensible expressions, words, or phrases were noted. All identifying details were omitted from the text and pseudonyms were inserted to identify the participants. A legend on the front page of each interview decoded any initials used in terms of their role in relation to the participant or the deceased (e.g., A = sister of deceased, H = spouse, etc.). After receiving each completed transcription and tape, the first author read each transcript while simultaneously listening to the tape recording and corrected any errors or incomprehensible words where possible. A total of 10 transcribed interviews yielded 822 pages of double-spaced text, an indication of the depth of content provided by participants.

Memoing

The task of memoing in grounded theory research addresses the interpretive nature of the method. It is here that the researcher's subjectivity is recognized and reported (Rennie et al., 1988). Through the process of keeping memos throughout the analysis, the researcher, as honestly as possible, records his or her theories, biases, assumptions, and reactions in a transparent attempt to acknowledge and set aside (or bracket) internal influences and to thereby stay grounded in the data.

Throughout the study, the first author continuously kept both theoretical and experiential memos. The former accounted for biases, assumptions, theories, previous knowledge, and new understandings; the latter documented personal reactions to the participants, the research, the analysis process, and the overall impact of the study (that is, tracking the experience of "living with" this material for an extended period of time). Theoretical memos proved essential to the final analysis and the understanding of the data as a whole, and their presence is found throughout the following chapters. The experiential memos had a similar effect but, because they are of a more personal and in some ways abstract nature, they are included in the last chapter of this book under Implications for Practice, Future Research, and the Impact of Qualitative Research.

Analysis

Data analysis of the transcribed audiotape interviews was consistent with the modifications to grounded theory methodology by Rennie et al. (1998). Before the formal analysis had begun, each interview was reviewed a second time by listening to the audiotape; by this time, each transcript had been read through at least twice. Beginning with the first interview, participant responses were divided into "meaning units," or fragments of text that had an identifiable theme. These meaning units varied in length from one line to multiple pages. The theme was identified and then the relevant section of text was recorded under that theme, referred to as a category. If needed to encompass all the meaning of that section of text, more than one category was created for each meaning unit. The second step in the analysis was to create "one-liners" to represent the meaning units. These one-liners consisted of a single line of text (either a direct quotation or a concise statement in the researcher's own words) representing a brief summary of a particular segment of text, or meaning unit. The one-liners served the dual purpose of indicating what was represented in a given meaning unit and, in the later stages of the analysis, facilitated working with representations of the text instead of the full text. The one-liners, therefore, served as summary tabs recalling the main gist of a section of text and providing the location information to retrieve that section. Such a system was essential when working with over 800 pages of text.

As analyses continued, a master list of categories was developed and continuously consulted when attempting to categorize the next meaning unit. If no existing category was found to represent the core meaning of the delineated section of text, a new category was created and added to the inventory. As dictated by the constant comparative analysis procedure, every newly developed category mandated cross-referencing previously categorized meaning units in terms of their relevance to the new category. This process of comparing meaning units for differences and similarities continued to saturation, or the point at which relatively few new categories were required to represent the meaning units of new data (Rennie et al., 1988). With the mothers' interviews, saturation was achieved by the fourth transcript. However, the subsequent analysis of the fathers' interviews necessitated new category formation to reflect differences in their parenting experiences. Saturation was also achieved by the fourth transcripts of the fathers' interviews. Achieving saturation marked the end of data collection.

A spreadsheet was then created with the following columns: the category number, the one-liner, whether it was a mother's or a father's transcript, the identifying number of the transcript, and the page number(s) where the meaning unit was located. The first column (category numbers) was implemented in the interest of parsimony as assigning a number to each category on the master list precluded having to type each category name on every line and it allowed for the computer software to sort each one-liner by category. As each meaning unit was categorized, a category number (or numbers, as appropriate) was assigned and a one-liner was created and recorded in the spreadsheet, with the above-mentioned identifying information.

This process of categorizing forces the researcher to stay close to the text at hand, thereby discouraging subjective conceptualizations. Furthermore, as represented by the on-going hermeneutic circle, it engages an exploration of both the whole (between transcripts) and the particular (within transcripts). Although this cannot occur simultaneously, the vacillation between each influenced the interpretations. The particular informed the whole, and the whole informed the particular—a process that eventually led to an understanding that was greater than the sum of its parts.

After the 10 transcripts were analyzed and one-liners were recorded for each meaning unit assigned to each category, the data were sorted according to the numeric value of the first column (category). The result was a complete list of the one-liners across all of the transcripts assigned to each category. Reflecting the emerging gender differences, the final documentation was a list of categories in numerical order (with their corresponding one-liners) for the bereaved mothers and bereaved fathers.

With the master list of categories, every one-liner subsumed under a given category was reevaluated to ensure that the meaning unit it represented was accurately categorized. As a result of this exercise, it was not uncommon for a category to be renamed so as to better reflect the one-liners derived from the meaning units, or for a one-liner to be reassigned to another category more representative of the meaning unit. Nor was it uncommon, where appropriate, for two or more categories to be merged and subsumed under another category, or for a novel category to be created to accurately reflect the merger. All of these changes grew out of the evolving conceptualization of the meaning of the data as the analysis proceeded from the first to the tenth interview. The number of meaning units represented by one-liners (sorted under each category within and between transcripts) was also noted. These frequency data provided further information on the significance of some categories over others.

The clarification of relationships between categories (both similarities and differences) continued in the pursuit of higher-order categories and a central or core category that consisted of the grouping of the most densely related categories—this represented the central theme of the study (Rennie et al., 1988). The process of conceptualizing the relationships among categories was aided through carefully reviewing extensive memos, working with the spreadsheet of one-liners, and, occasionally, returning to the transcripts themselves. As a higher-order organization began to emerge, it was mapped and, through several renditions of these "maps" and discussions between the authors, the core theme of this study was recognized. All other categories were directly related to this core theme and subsumed by it.

Credibility Checks

Qualitative researchers use many different approaches to assess the credibility of their analyses, and, in this study, four specific strategies were employed. First, the first author's analysis was fully and completely reviewed by the second author (SF). Then Dr. David Rennie, a professor and an expert in the method and its supporting logic of justification, acted as an "analytical auditor" (Elliott, Fischer, & Rennie, 1999, p. 222). In this capacity, he reviewed the data and the analysis to ensure adherence to the method and to check for errors, overextensions, or inconsistencies between the data and the resulting categories and theory. The third credibility check, having bereaved parents scrutinize the results, occurred in a number of different guises, e.g., in a feedback session for the participants, conference presentations to various bereavement and mutual-help groups, invited addresses and workshops, and in psychotherapy sessions conducted by the second author with other bereaved parents. Finally, the fourth credibility check rests with you, the reader, for throughout this book the presence of the unaltered words of each participant offers the opportunity to check the credibility of each category or theme.

Bereaved Parenting: Living the Duality of Devastation and Regeneration

The core category, under which all other categories are subsumed, is the "key concept that organizes the theory" (Rennie, 1998, p. 103). The uncovering of this key concept was not an easy process. From the interviews and analysis, we struggled with the relationship between the unimaginable death of a child and the attention to life demanded by surviving children who continue to require parenting—perhaps now more than ever. These two concepts, and all of the categories representing them, seemed wholly separate, bringing to mind contrasts of death and life, darkness and light, pain and joy, past and future. What could these two extremes of existence have in common? What could possibly link these polarities of experience? The term we feel best reflects this duality is *bereaved parenting*.

Bereaved parenting is an active process: one continues to parent and one is continuously bereaved. This is the duality that bereaved parents and their surviving children must face; it is the duality that is a lived, daily experience between the death of one and the life of another. The core category reflecting this experience is titled, *Bereaved Parenting: Living the Duality of Devastation and Regeneration* (see Figure 2.1).

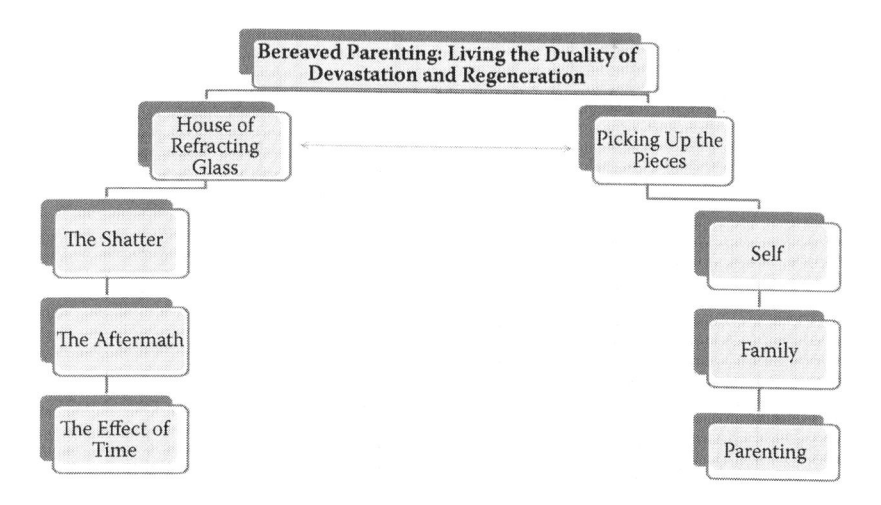

FIGURE 2.1 Hierarchical Category Structure*

---

* The reader is referred to a more detailed version of the model in Appendix B.

To devastate is to "cause great destruction to, to overwhelm with shock or grief" (*Oxford English Reference Dictionary*, 1996). It is clear that the death of a child devastates like no other, affecting every moment, every cell, every breath—tearing the very fabric of a parent's being. This unspeakable tragedy, represented by the "House of Refracting Glass," is explored in detail by these courageous parents so that others may know the utter and complete annihilation following the death of a child.

The "shatter," the "aftermath," and the "effect of time," all subsumed under this category, detail the complex, ongoing and often-overwhelming response to the death of one's child. These are the aspects of the experience that the participants described in relation to their grief and within the context of continuing to parent surviving children. The destruction of the House of Refracting Glass informed all aspects of life, and especially the continuation of parenting.

It is clear that although bereaved parents reside in this devastation, they cannot stay there forever, even if they wanted to. They have surviving children who need them, who require them to step back into their roles as parents, to reclaim the very functions they've been forced to relinquish with their deceased child. Especially in the early weeks or months following the loss, this seems to be a particularly cruel paradox. This beckoning world, starkly antithetical to the devastation that characterizes their current existence, does not even remotely resemble their life prior to their child's death—that has been forever destroyed. Instead, they are being pulled into unknown and uncharted territory—a new world they must struggle to create amidst the unacceptable and abhorrent reality that life as they knew it has been irrevocably altered. This is a process of regeneration.

To regenerate is to "bring or come into renewed existence; to generate again; to impart new and more vigorous life to; to regrow lost or injured tissue; to invest with a new and higher nature" (*Oxford English Reference Dictionary*, 1996). It is clear that bereaved parents engage in an act of regeneration. They "Pick Up the Pieces" (see Figure 2.1), they renew and revive their lives and the lives of their surviving children. It is not in defiance of death, but informed by it. Changed to the core, their existence now is more intense, more focused, and more cherished. Although bereaved parenting is an act of regeneration, it is not an act of acceptance, resolution, or moving on. Rather, it is an act of Picking Up the Pieces in the face of demoralizing devastation, forever reverent to its presence.

Picking Up the Pieces, the regeneration following devastation, not only occurs at the individual and family levels, but it also occurs between parent and surviving child(ren) through parenting (see Figure 2.1). Just as each individual shatter is different, so too is each individual regeneration unique. As will be documented throughout the following chapters, parents varied in their level of regenerating a sense of individual and family identity following the crushing loss of their child. Regardless of the degree of regeneration, however, the shards, cracks, and missing pieces are always and forever present, influencing each parent's sense of self, family, and parenting.

Bereaved parenting is living the duality of devastation and regeneration. It is not a discrete duality in which a parent is functioning solely in one capacity and then solely in the other. Rather, it is a continuous duality where one informs the other, and one can take precedence over the other at any time. Bereaved parenting is an ongoing, often puzzling and disconcerting fluctuation between the two extremes that speaks of the integrated nature of loss and continuance. The devastation, detailed under the House of Refracting Glass, and the regeneration, detailed by Picking Up the Pieces, are two principles that are not wholly independent but rather are coupled in the dynamic, lived, vacillating duality that is bereaved parenting.

CHAPTER 3

The Devastation of Parental Bereavement

During the course of the interviews, each parent exhaustively explored the nature and extent of their loss, some beginning at the moment of their child's death, others further along in the narrative. In their thoughtful descriptions of the crushing tragedy that had befallen them, parents described the devastation that accompanied the death of their child as they referenced the regeneration of their lives and the lives of their surviving children and families. To understand how one currently parents, and the changes that have ensued, it is necessary to understand the delicate and ongoing interplay between the devastation of a child's death and the unrelenting demands of living. Both pieces come together to form the dynamic whole that represents parenting surviving children after the death of a child.

Bereaved parenting is an active process in which one continues to parent and one is continuously bereaved, and the duality of these two extremes is constantly negotiated and debated. It does not represent a series of distinct and progressive stages where a parent completes the grieving phase and then reclaims the parenting role. As previously discussed, whether one refers to the oscillation between loss-oriented and restoration-orientated perspectives (Stroebe and Schut's [1999] Dual Process Model), or to the impact of loss on the domains of biopsychosocial functioning and the quality and nature of the continuing attachment to the deceased (Rubin's [1999] Two-Track Model of Bereavement), we feel that adjusting to the loss of a loved one is a fluid, dynamic process and the resulting interpersonal and intrapersonal reactions represent the blending of both orientations or domains. To focus only on the devastation is to miss the regeneration; likewise, the regeneration is meaningless and fragmented without an awareness of the devastation. We begin with the devastation.

The House of Refracting Glass

All of the parents generously shared what it means to lose a child and they detailed the lived experience of this unique and terrible devastation. They exposed the sheer enormity of the loss and the unrelenting and insidious repercussions that continue daily. From the most routine or insignificant activity to the core structures and beliefs from which they derive a sense of meaning and safety, reverberations of their loss continue to echo into the recesses of their lives. The metaphor that captures the essence of their experience is the House of Refracting Glass.

To fully appreciate the House of Refracting Glass, one must be familiar with the notion of the "assumptive world." In navigating our lives we are only dimly aware of the pervasive influence of our assumptive world, those organizing beliefs about trust, safety, control, and self-esteem (Janoff-Bulman, 1992; Parkes, 1988). Such assumptions, largely unquestioned or unchallenged, operate at a subliminal level and organize our experiences and expectations about the world and our place in it, and they provide a sense of reality, meaning, or purpose to our experiences, past and present. Janoff-Bulman identified three core assumptions that shape our view of the world: the world is benevolent (i.e., it is a good place, people are kind and well intentioned, and events usually end well), the world is meaningful and makes sense (e.g., one can control the outcome of events, good things happen to good people), and the self is worthy (i.e., we perceive ourselves as good, decent, and moral individuals).

We are soothed by the presence of these core assumptions of benevolence, meaning, and self-worth. If stripped of this protective and omnipresent buffer, we would not plan for a future, we would only trust the present, and we would never be completely convinced that the next moment would not end in misfortune or death. Such assumptions allow us to live with little consideration of what might potentially happen, and allow us to say a routine farewell to our loved ones without the wrenching fear that this may be the last goodbye; we can assuredly reject the likelihood of trauma impacting our lives—such dreadful events happen to others and certainly not to my family or me. Bad things don't happen to good people!

These assumptions are so fundamental we liken them to a house of glass that continuously and seamlessly encloses our very existence. This glass is both transparent and refractive. As light rays are bent and distorted (or refracted) on passing through the glass, our perceptions of the external world are tempered and misshapen by unrealistic and unsupported beliefs about the world and our place in it. In essence, then, these unsupported, unrealistic beliefs are illusions—but, for many of us, they are necessary illusions as we cannot exist with the horror of our vulnerability stalking us. We do not see the world as it truly is, with vulnerability inherent; rather, we see it as it is filtered through our house of refracting glass, distorting and reinforcing the illusion of safety and protection.

There are moments, however, when our illusions of safety, security, and invulnerability are challenged and, in the process, we are confronted with the unpalatable and stark reality of the ubiquitous dangers that lurk on the horizon. Instances of a near-collision in a motor vehicle, or anxiously awaiting the late arrival of a loved one, or fretfully anticipating the results of diagnostic testing for a potentially life-threatening disease force us to recognize the House of Refracting Glass and confront the knowledge that, although strong in its present form, the very material of its construction speaks of fragility. This moment of clarity generally causes apprehension and fear—and we don't want such threatening thoughts or events lingering in consciousness. So, with a facile and quickly embraced change of perspective, we abandon the veridical perception of the world and, once again, lapse into the illusionary unconsciousness the refractive glass affords. We assure ourselves of its strong properties, we convince ourselves of its clarity, and we rationalize our safety and invulnerability. We live our lives as though they will not end, and we love those dear to us as though we will never part.

Another defining feature of the House of Refracting Glass is how thoroughly habituated we are to its presence. Constantly influencing our perception and interpretation of events, we acclimatize quickly to its comforting illusions that contribute to the monotony of constancy in our lives. As the saying goes, "you don't know what you have until it's gone." Many of us live privileged lives, taking for granted all that is cherished, all that is wonderful, and all that is currently perfect in our lives. So, we strive, compete, experience stress, overlook the fragility of our good fortune, and look ahead with anticipation—not dread. The wonder of all we are, and all we experience in this moment, is represented by fragility and illusion, and by the metaphor of the House of Refracting Glass.

Analysis of the interviews with the bereaved parents in this study revealed that the death of a child triggered the destruction of a parent's

House of Refracting Glass as all that was known, familiar, and comforting irrevocably collapsed. Their reflections not only yielded a wealth of information about the immediate chaos and devastation (what we termed the Shatter) but also about the long-term impact, individually and collectively, of such a traumatic event (referred to as The Aftermath).

☐ The Shatter

For a bereaved parent, the death of their child is The Shatter. At this moment, with the explosion of their House of Refracting Glass into innumerable fragments, all that is recognizable and reassuring is irretrievably destroyed. In addition to the incomprehensible loss of their child, their assumptive world is also in ruins—the world is definitely not a benevolent place, life seems meaningless, and one's self-worth is threatened. The inconceivable has happened, the imperceptible safety and perfection of what was is now horrifically displayed in pieces—utterly shattered and in shambles. Consider the following parent reflections:

> Our life changed just with a snap of the finger. It hasn't, well, it's never been the same since. (Gary, 16-year-old child died, two surviving children)

> Life just kind of fell apart for us. It literally fell apart. It really did. (Anna, 1-year-old child died, two surviving children)

> It impacts every, every part of your life … and I realized fairly early on that things would never be normal again. (Diane, 4-year-old child died, three surviving children)

It is only in the shards of The House of Refracting Glass that one fully recognizes, on a visceral level, all they had, and now, all they have lost. It was the *perfect life until …*

> We had the ideal life. You know what? We had the perfect life. We had it all. (Anna, 1-year-old child died, two surviving children)

> You know, you are not aware until it happens to you. You think you are, but you just don't know what you have … I didn't and none of us do. (Becky, 4-year-old child died, two surviving children)

In the weeks and months following the death, the exploding shards that penetrated and deeply wounded a parent often threaten the parent's physical and emotional well-being. During this time, survival is the mode of operation and merciful numbness enables the grief-stricken parent to function. Parents described a *numb survival* that stayed with them from weeks to months.

> For the first month or three months or something, or even six months, it's like, life is surreal, oh a numbness. (Elliot, 10-year-old child died, one surviving child)

> You lose a child it's like ripping the total insides out of you. Absolutely everything is gone. You're numb; you really are numb for a long period of time. (Frank, 12-year-old child died, one surviving child)

> You feel a fuzziness for the longest time, you feel that this is your little protective, um, as if you're in a cavity, and you've got this protective element around you ... kind of in a cotton ball, it was all muffled, it was all very muffled, peoples' voices were very much like they were talking through a mask. (Becky, 4-year-old child died, two surviving children)

> I think nature is very kind to you and provides you with this incredible numbness ... it's like you're in a coma ... you're here in a coma because it's nature's way of protecting you ... it's quite amazing when you think about it. As the numbness starts to wear off and reality, it's like you have this coating of numbness and then that starts to dissolve and then you get this, the taste of the grief starting to, the reality of what happened to you, you start to taste that ... at about six months the realization hit, the numbness was gone. (Diane, 4-year-old child died, three surviving children)

In the immediate shatter after a child's death, parents often employ avoidance/distancing maneuvers to dissociate from the pain; these strategies are construed as an adaptive and effective survival strategy that facilitates functioning amidst the pervasive sense of devastation and chaos (Barrera, et al., 2007; Talbot, 2002; Uren & Wastell, 2002).

☐ The Aftermath

In The Aftermath of the destruction of The House of Refracting Glass the numbness eventually recedes only to be replaced by the painful awareness of the multiple manifestations of loss. These include perspectives on the lack of personal and collective safety, the emergence of trauma symptoms, feelings of guilt and remorse, physical and emotional exhaustion, the varied secondary losses concomitant with the child's death, and an awareness of spousal differences in grieving.

Vulnerable and Unprotected

With the death of their child, and in contrast to their prior state, parents now feel deeply unsafe in the world; they have a powerful and pervasive trepidation that extends to all of their loved ones, and especially to their surviving children. The world no longer looks or feels familiar. Instead of the refracting and reassuring illusions of what was, bereaved parents now look clearly through the shards and edges of the shambles that remain—and they feel defenseless and exposed. There is no longer the shelter of illusions protecting loved ones from a threatening and unsafe world. All of the fathers interviewed reported feelings of vulnerability as the following excerpts attest:

> I know I'm not here for a long time; it could happen tomorrow, it could happen on the way home. (Elliot, 10-year-old child died, one surviving child)

> We worry all the time [about surviving child] … it's anxiety all the time, it's always there. (Gary, 16-year-old child died, one surviving child)

> I'm more cautious around what's going on around me, realizing what the results of accidents are. (Frank, 12-year-old child died, one surviving child)

> It's almost every morning, I wake up and I think, you know, the world isn't such a benign place and there's [sic] a few monsters lurking out there and one of them is going to find me today. (Harris, 2-year-old child died, one surviving child)

> We could lose another child. It happened once, it could happen again … you thought nothing was ever going to happen to you and when he died, you realized it can happen to you anytime and it can happen again. That's the fear, because it happened once doesn't mean it won't happen again. (Jake, 4-year-old child died, three surviving children)

The Devastation of Parental Bereavement   47

Without exception, the mothers also reported similar feelings of vulnerability, insecurity, and threat.

> My first thought is a negative thought because I know it doesn't always go nice and hunky-dory and I hate being like that but it's there ... anything could happen ... in four years, I probably have never first jumped to the positive, it's always to the negative. (Anna, 1-year-old child died, two surviving children)

> The fear sets in faster now ... you become very aware of little dangers even ... God forbid, this can't happen again, because you know, it's happened. (Becky, 4-year-old child died, two surviving children)

> My son's death was one in a million, so, it could happen again, it can definitely happen again ... the world is hard. (Carol, 20-year-old child died, four surviving children)

> There are absolutely no guarantees, you don't have that protective bubble around you anymore, it's not like it happened to somebody else that you'd watched on TV, it's happened to you ... the worst case scenario is just always there, every second of every day. (Diane, 4-year-old child died, three surviving children)

> Always a fear that something could happen ... you just feel very vulnerable, your sense of safety in the world isn't there anymore. (Isabelle, 2-year-old child died, one surviving child)

Although all the participants commented on the sense of increased helplessness and lack of safety in the world, the mothers referred to this uneasiness three times as often. This difference was echoed by a father who stated that it was his wife who moved quickly to entertain thoughts of fret and foreboding following their son's death.

> Now my wife, she probably became more negative. More than before, I think she would be the more protective of the two of us now. (Elliot, 10-year-old child died, one surviving child)

One of the mothers stated that her husband thought the same of her.

> He [husband] says that I'm always looking for disaster. He teases me about it, and I guess I do worry, I do worry more. (Isabelle, 2-year-old child died, one surviving child)

In conclusion, mothers in this study referred more frequently to a sense of helplessness in the face of anticipated, lurking danger. Succinctly stated, if one child can die, it can happen again. The infrequent occurrence of such tragic events did little to assuage the all-encompassing and all-consuming dread that they were, and are, helpless in protecting their children and ensuring their survival. Another dimension of this theme has been noted in the second author's psychotherapy with bereaved parents. Although certainly not indifferent to their own well-being, and acutely aware of the finitude and the precariousness of life, obsessive concerns are for the safety of their children—not themselves. Where a parent may have acknowledged elevated levels of personal death anxiety in the past, this is quickly eclipsed by the clear view that they could never survive the death of another child and, for those who believe in an afterlife, the soothing hope that they will "see" their child again.

A casualty of the collapse of feelings of safety, predictability, and security was the reputation of those perceived as allies in shoring up this illusion, i.e., members of the medical and nursing professions, law enforcement personnel, emergency and ambulance staff, and insurance representatives. No longer were these bereaved parents able to sustain the belief that such professionals can offer protection from harm, they were now perceived as merely reinforcing the security myth. Almost all of the parents expressed disappointment and anger toward those involved in their child's care or in the post-loss medical/legal/rehabilitation proceedings. Whether blaming third-party insurers for being "insincere" in the provision of rehabilitation services, or paramedics for not saving their child's life, or the courts for failing to convict in an impaired driving death, it was not uncommon for parents to be outraged at those associated with the disintegration of their assumptive world. Consider the following comments:

> You know they would have died anyway, and maybe that's true because the paramedics were there and they couldn't do anything, but who knows how much they did? And again, you get the trust thing, because you know, it's a vicious circle. (Becky, 4-year-old child died, two surviving children)

> There are other things I'm not 100% comfortable about. The coroners. How I was treated. You know? Where do you get off? Coroners putting down this [incorrect cause of death]. Now I did get an apology. I got a

follow-up call from him [coroner] and he did apologize ... so, now my biggest worry is for my daughter and I'm annoyed that the doctors don't want to see her again. I had thought that they would do follow-up. (Carol, 20-year-old child died, four surviving children)

To this day, I really believe that she [a nurse] wasn't very careful. And whether that's true or not, that's in my mind, she's the reason that he died ... now there's been a change [in hospital procedure] and it's kind of like, feeling like you're the person ... where you know, the doors have been closed after the horse has already gotten out. And that hurt, I thought, if they had done that before, would he be here now? (Isabelle, 2-year-old child died, one surviving child)

I was really mad at the prosecuting attorney or the crown because they just wanted to make it go away. They didn't want to do anything with the case. So, I'm very cynical now of the justice thing in Canada. (Elliot, 10-year-old child died, one surviving child)

Thinking about the ambulance service, very disappointing [length of time it took for the ambulance to arrive]. (Gary, 16-year-old child died, one surviving child)

It may not have been, it might have been, I think it was flawed procedure [at the hospital], I think a flawed procedure played a role in it [child's death] ... It makes me furious that it was ever allowed to happen ... the bacteria that killed him is basically a product of inadequate housekeeping ... it is too much to take, I mean you would like to come to some catharsis about this, but I'm not sure that I ever can. (Harris, 2-year-old child died, one surviving child)

Definitely the police at the scene needed a lot more knowledge of people, in terms of death and grief ... they need to know how to deal with people better in terms of when there's a child who's died ... and the legal system, it's just something else, so, our experience in the legal department wasn't the greatest, insurance companies wasn't good ... insincere, the way they treated you. (Jake, 4-year-old child died, three surviving children)

In the midst of this pervasive sense of loss and devastation, Beder (2005) notes, "For the bereft, there are no answers, safety, logic, clarity, power, or control" (p. 259). And, understandably, mental health professionals may share this sense of powerlessness in the face of overwhelming and unspeakable tragedy. But there is much that can be done, especially in the realm of encouraging nascent feelings of empowerment, influence, and control —and, ultimately, survivability. A case example will illustrate this point. A bereaved mother, Judy, was seen in therapy (by SF) following the brutal rape and murder of her 16-year-old son. As the three accused were prosecuted individually, Judy contemplated separate pre-trial procedures, anticipated numerous court delays and legal maneuvers and, eventually, the individual trials of the perpetrators. Feeling compelled to attend the court proceedings and represent her deceased child, the objective of early intervention was to help Judy reach the seemingly unattainable goal of attending three separate legal proceedings.

An initial focus of therapy was her entrenched belief that the trial would result in "justice" being done. Convinced that the evidence was incontrovertible, and that each of the accused would receive life sentences (there is no capital punishment in Canada), Judy was incredulous on hearing that the defense attorneys would mount legal challenges to this expectation. To avoid further devastation, it was imperative that she replace this cornerstone of her assumptive world with a belief that more accurately reflected the legal arena she was about to enter. Gradually, Judy was able to abandon her unsubstantiated notion that the judicial system inevitably leads to "justice" and fairness; in its place was substituted a more painful, but more accurate reflection, namely, "there is no justice, only law." With the begrudging acceptance that case law not only governs legal proceedings but also the admissibility of evidence and the sentencing of convicted criminals, Judy approached the court proceedings embracing a set of veracious expectations faithful to the re-traumatizing reality she was about to encounter.

In addition to introducing a psychoeducational focus, reinforcing or strengthening adaptive beliefs ("there is no justice, only law"), relaxation training, and anxiety management, the therapist also introduced elements of safety and control into the seemingly incomprehensible and uncontrollable legal process. When the criminal justice system is involved, bereaved parents are confronted with a legal process that is foreign to them, and over which they have little or no influence or control. In this instance, where Judy was determined to attend the trial(s) of her son's murderers, it was imperative that she be prepared for the horrific images and testimony that would confront her in court. As part of a complex treatment process essentially based on cognitive-behavioral therapy principles, the therapist exposed Judy, in a graded fashion, to the police reports of the assault on her son. In addition, as the first trial approached, he worked with the prosecuting attorneys, the defense lawyers, victim witness personnel, and the judge, to establish some sense of control for Judy in the midst of an alien and intimidating process. For example, she was informed in advance of what would transpire during the next court date and, during the proceedings, when gruesome material or testimony was to be presented, the judge offered Judy the option of leaving the courtroom or staying to hear the evidence. The promise of some control over the proceedings dampened her feelings of powerlessness and terror, and enhanced the belief that she might physically and emotionally survive the grinding judicial process. In perhaps her final act as a mother, Judy was able to represent her son in all three trials and witness the conviction and sentencing of the perpetrators.

Trauma

Virtually all of the parents made reference to the trauma associated with their children's deaths. Some parents referred to unsettling and haunting images associated with being present at the moment of death, others referred to external cues that triggered painful reminders of what happened, and yet other parents avoided places or activities that were associated with their losses. Consider the following fathers' comments:

> Every weekend I drive past the accident site, so that's my little gates of hell every weekend ... when I shaved every morning I had scars from the accident, so I was everyday, it still bothered me [he now has a beard] ... it was a pretty gruesome accident, when I came out of it, I had to look across and he was there ... and so, I checked for vitals on my son. There were no vitals. (Elliot, 10-year-old child died, one surviving child)

> When they took him by on the gurney, I knew he was dead then ... I could, there was a look in his eyes, I could tell ... so, it was a lot of trauma. (Frank, 12-year-old child died, one surviving child)

> When you lose one, it's really traumatic ... you're just looking at your son lying on the stretcher there and it's tough ... that's why we don't like going to the cottage [where the death occurred]. No, I mean, that was bad. (Gary, 16-year-old child died, one surviving child)

The mothers, all of whom either witnessed their children's deaths or were first on the scene, responded with:

> Who in their right mind would think that you would go to the crib and he's dead? I still get flashbacks ... I still have a hard time going to the girls' room [in the morning]. I can't touch them ... I'll look and until I see her move, my first reaction is, she's dead. I still get that after four years. So, it's like every morning for me I wish somebody else was there to wake them up. (Anna, 1-year-old child died, two surviving children)

> I said to my husband, I don't ever, ever want to drive again, I just don't want to be in a car, I'm not safe, I think I'm going to be killed in a car, and I was convinced. I didn't drive for about a year after ... every single thing that you do there's a reminder of what you've already lived ... they walked me through the scene to this other police cruiser and they walked me between two ambulances and there was a big orange tarp on the ground and as they walked me past, I saw her hair, it was underneath the tarp, so she was still there. So, then I knew that she had died. (Becky, 4-year-old child died, two surviving children)

> Because my son died in his sleep, I became, where I had to check to see if somebody was going to wake up ... I did it with everybody in my house. (Carol, 20-year-old child died, four surviving children)

> When he died and because of the accident, because I was part of the accident, and I think the trauma of what had happened, I really, I don't think I was in my right sense. (Diane, 4-year-old child died, three surviving children)

Furthermore, the trauma was not limited only to those parents who had witnessed the death. One father, not present when his child died but haunted by horrifying images, reflected:

> There are certain things that, um, you don't go there anymore. It's more the trauma of it all, and there's still images I can't get out of my head ... but you learn to cope with that ... but there are times when you're really down and if you let your mind go, you can really lose it very quickly. It's always there. (Jake, 4-year-old child died, three surviving children)

Nearly all of the mothers and fathers commented on the trauma that envelops parents after the death of a child and, as this father has experienced, one need not witness the child's death for this to eventuate. They may have similar reactions to those directly involved due to their close relationship and identification with their child (Kagan, 1998). For some, the impact of the trauma had subsided over time; for others it had remained present and harrowing. For virtually all, it was an important aspect of their grief.

As we briefly discussed in Chapter 1, when mental health professionals refer to "trauma" (or, more formally, posttraumatic stress disorder [PTSD]) a number of symptoms need to be present including the persistent reexperiencing of the traumatic event (e.g., unbidden images, thoughts, perceptions), persistent avoidance of stimuli associated with the trauma (e.g., avoiding thoughts, feelings, conversations about the traumatic event), and increased symptoms of anxiety and arousal (e.g., anger/irritability, concentration difficulties, and increased concerns around safety and security) (DSM-IV-TR; APA, 2000). Although we did not systematically assess for PTSD in this study, it was obvious that trauma symptoms were an integral and worrisome aspect of processing and assimilating loss.

With a host of symptoms common to both grief and PTSD, including the intrusion of memories, sleep disturbances, concentration problems, hypervigilance, irritability, anxiety, avoidance, and clinically significant distress and impairment of functioning, it is incumbent upon clinicians to thoroughly assess for symptoms of PTSD when treating someone who is grief-stricken. Muddying the clinical waters somewhat are those whose symptoms reflect "partial" PTSD, i.e., they do not meet the full diagnostic criteria for a diagnosis of PTSD but who, nonetheless, struggle with disruptive, disconcerting symptoms of intrusion, avoidance, and hypervigilance (Breslau, Lucia, & Davis, 2004). Although subsyndromal, such manifestations of trauma ultimately need to be addressed in psychotherapy. The commingling of grief and trauma has the potential to adversely impact adjustment to loss through intensifying symptoms common to both, inhibiting comforting and supportive social interactions due to posttraumatic estrangement, and introducing painful traumatic recollections when attempting to reminisce about the deceased (Nader, 1997; Rando, 2003). It is imperative, then, that bereaved parents be formally assessed for PTSD and that standard trauma therapies be part of the clinician's therapeutic armamentarium when working with the traumatized bereaved (Tedeschi & Calhoun, 2004a).

In circumstances where PTSD is evident, it is recommended that trauma symptoms be addressed prior to targeting the impact of the loss (Fleming & Robinson, 2001; Figley, 1999; Rando, 1993; Worden, 2009). This is prudent for two reasons. First, traumatized individuals often have difficulty tolerating and regulating intense emotions associated with the traumatic event and, consequently, they may be overwhelmed and destabilized. Second, it is not uncommon for unbidden and disturbing traumatic images to flood one's consciousness when attempting to grieve the loss of a loved one. As bereaved parents are constantly fighting an unseen enemy, increasing one's sense of safety and security, along with distress reduction and affect regulation training, are the first steps in any formal intervention.

The course of psychotherapy, however, isn't always neat, nor does it always evolve according to theory. In the second author's experience (SF), it is not uncommon for psychotherapy with parents who are traumatically bereaved to proceed along both avenues simultaneously, i.e., grief *and* trauma. For example, Lisa witnessed her 4-year-old daughter, Emma, being run over by her school bus. During a therapy session she commented on the dress Emma was wearing the day she died, and how pretty she looked in that particular attire. This led her to reflect, "you know, I used to love going shopping for girl's stuff with Emma—I'll really miss that." The conversation then moved to Lisa's fond memories of mother-daughter "retail therapy" and the secondary loss of such memorable excursions. Then, in the midst of yearning and pining for Emma and remembering the warmth of her daughter's smile, traumatic material presented itself in the form of haunting images of Emma's eyes as she lay in her mother's arms on the road. At this juncture, the therapist chose to move to the exploration of such traumatic images and the "grief" response was abandoned for the moment. Of course, such rapid transitions put the therapist's response agility to the test as he struggled to effectively keep pace with Lisa.

Prior to leaving this section it is instructive to examine the relationship between the circumstances surrounding the death of a child on parental grief responses and trauma. Wijngaards-De Meij, Stroebe, Stroebe, et al. (2008) found that parents who were with their children at the moment of death reported less grief than those who were not present. Furthermore, 2 years post-death, they found that parents who had the opportunity to say "good-bye" to their children (before or after the death) had lower levels of grief than parents who did not have this parting opportunity. Likewise, Woodgate (2006), in a qualitative study of 28 bereaved parents, noted that all of the parents focused on being present at the moment of death as a critical aspect of their parenting role. The parents who were present discussed comforting their children in these last moments. The parents who were not with their dying child reported that their parental role had been taken away from them when their child was in greatest need and they had been robbed of their last parenting opportunity. Fletcher (2002) analyzed two case studies of families grieving the death of a child and placed the parents' desire to be present with their dying child under the heading "parental responsibility/duty" (p. 65).

In the clinical experience of one of the authors (SF), parents have frequently expressed a powerful need to be present when their child dies, even when the death is violent and sudden. In the previously discussed case of Lisa who had witnessed the death of her 4-year-old daughter, when the therapist gently asked her, "Would you rather not have been present when Emma died and be free of such images?" Lisa unhesitatingly responded, "No, I'm grateful I was there ... Emma died knowing she was in her mother's arms, and that she was loved." Other parents have responded in a similar manner; suffering the traumatic images is the emotional price they pay for being with their child, and it was important for them to be present during their child's final moments. The compelling desire to be present at what is arguably one of life's most painful and devastating experiences does not characterize other types of traumatic events. And it ultimately enables parents to perform acts that others find overwhelming and paralyzing, e.g., bathing and clothing the deceased child prior to burial.

The bereaved father's comment above, and the results of the study by Wijngaards-De Meij, Stroebe, Stroebe, et al. (2008), inform clinicians about the importance of assessing for grief complications *and* traumatic responses not only with bereaved parents who have witnessed the death of their child but also with those who did not witness the death or discover their child's body. Further to this point, when working with bereaved parents it is important to explore if they had the opportunity to say good-bye to their children either at the moment of death or in their own way after the death. Given the literature illustrating that saying good-bye is beneficial (Gamino, Sewell, & Easterling, 2000; Schut, de Keijser, van den Bout, & Dijkhuis, 1991; Wijngaards-De Meij, Stroebe, Stroebe, et al., 2008), interventions to encourage this component, either symbolically or literally, may be helpful to the overall grief experience of bereaved parents.

We feel there are qualitative differences in trauma associated with the death of a child that differentiates it from other trauma types (e.g., combat, sexual assault, motor vehicle accidents) and that different traumatic experiences may result in varied clinical presentations. For example, in a study of college students, Kelley, Weathers, McDevitt-Murphy, Eakin, and Flood (2009) compared PTSD symptom profiles in three distinct types of civilian trauma: sexual assault (SA), motor vehicle accident (MVA), and the sudden, unexpected loss of a loved one (SUD). Although they did not look at the death of a child specifically, they concluded that victims of sexual assault reported higher levels of PTSD symptom severity, and the bereaved were more distressed on the majority of PTSD symptoms than those who survived motor vehicle accidents. The authors added, "Symptoms conceptually related to interpersonal loss—such as restricted range of affect/inability to love close others, avoidance of thoughts/feelings, detachment/estrangement—were significantly more severe in SA and SUD than in MVA" (Kelley et al., p. 233). The authors speculated that this was a reflection of the challenge to one's assumptive world and the revision of beliefs about interpersonal loss and the benevolence of others. Such symptoms may be present in those who survive MVAs, but they are fundamental to trauma stemming from sexual assault and sudden, unexpected death. Preliminary results suggest that different trauma types lead to distinct trauma profiles, and they may be a function of different etiological factors requiring different treatment approaches.

Guilt

The Aftermath also entails profound guilt. Parents described a sense of failing at their most important job—protecting their child. This guilt is invasive and consuming. It is noteworthy that while the majority of mothers discussed their feelings of guilt, only one of the fathers mentioned guilt. The mothers shared the following:

> He was dead. He's the one I needed to take care of ... What kind of a mother am I? ... I did my job with the girls. I didn't do my job with him ... I've experienced the worst guilt that you can have, you can't have any worse guilt than feeling guilty about your child dying ... so, I figure, you know what? I'm not feeling guilty for anything else. Forget it. (Anna, 1-year-old child died, two surviving children)

> Maybe Mommy didn't do such a good job with him otherwise, why did he ...? Something happened to him right? Cause I was taking care of him when it happened. You know, I took him out, chose to take him in the car that day. (Diane, 4-year-old child died, three surviving children)

> And that day [day of accident] it was the wrong decision to make so therefore you double-check all of your decision making ... so, that comes back on me. (Becky, 4-year-old child died, two surviving children)

The sole father to make reference to guilt commented:

> Especially in my case where maybe I was responsible, right? Yeah. I went through that too ... It eats you. It eats you. (Elliot, 10-year-old child died, one surviving child)

Miles and Demi (1984, 1994) proposed a typology of the ubiquitous guilt experienced by parents following the death of a child. They posited various dimensions/causes of parental guilt, including the parent's belief that they somehow caused the child's death (causal guilt); the feeling of having failed to protect their child or having treated him/her badly in the past (relationship guilt); the notion that the child's demise occurred as a result of a parent's previous moral transgression (moral guilt); remorse over having survived your child, a violation of the natural order (survival guilt); the experience of guilt for not feeling the appropriate emotions or exhibiting socially prescribed behaviors during grieving (grief guilt); and, finally, as a parent begins to laugh again, to enjoy a family outing or anniversary, or engage in other life-related activities, they often experience recovery guilt.

In wrestling with issues of guilt and self-blame, bereaved parents often indulge in counterfactual thinking, that is, they generate imagined and more positive alternatives to events that ended disastrously. These counterfactual thoughts are often preceded by "what if" or "if only" statements; for example, a patient of one of the authors (SF), Doug, whose 23-year-old son was murdered, reflected: "To this day, I still wonder if only I had kept Sam at home for just a few more minutes ... he never would have met his killer, and he would still be here. If only I could've known; could've prevented it somehow ... I have held in my heart for many years, a guilt for not being able to prevent it, for not talking to him just a few minutes more ... not preventing him from walking out that door. I can't help but wish I could turn back time." Counterfactuals are exceedingly common with 48% of those who had experienced the death of a child or spouse in a motor vehicle accident entertaining thoughts of "if only" 4 to 7 years post-accident (Davis, Lehman, Wortman, Silver, & Thompson, 1995). Interestingly, the counterfactual thoughts were not directed at undoing the perpetrator's behavior but rather at changing their behavior or that of the deceased.

Davis et al. (1995) concluded that undoing one's own behavior (or that of the deceased) was a function of the perceived mutability or modifiability of the pre-accident circumstances. Since the behaviors and actions of the perpetrator are relatively unchangeable or immutable, the focus of the counterfactual process shifts to others whose acts are mutable and, although not *causally* involved, could have *prevented* the tragic event from happening. In the preceding example, unable to influence or change the behavior of the perpetrator, Doug chose to reflect on what *he* could have done to prevent such an overwhelming tragedy from unfolding.

Although one may be tempted to dismiss such ruminations with an instinctive "don't go there, it's not your fault, you didn't cause the accident," it is often instructive to explore such expressions of self-blame. There may well be a relationship between the nature of one's counterfactual thinking and qualitatively different affective experiences. Once again, a case example is illustrative. A vehicle fails to stop at an intersection and collides with a van, fatally injuring a 4-year-old child. The mother of the deceased child (Brenda) commented, "if only I had been driving a safer van, my son (James) would still be alive." If this counterfactual leads Brenda to conclude that she was a terrible *person* for not driving a safer vehicle, this process of changing unpalatable outcomes by condemning one's *self* would result in feelings of depression and self-loathing. In contrast, if Brenda's attempts at undoing focused on her *behavior* and not on her sense of self, then the issue is the choice of a motor vehicle (a behavior) and the resulting emotion is less obstructive. Janoff-Bulman (1992) referred to the former as characterological self-blame and the latter as behavioral self-blame. In a discussion of the these forms of counterfactual thinking and their repercussions, Fleming and Robinson (2001) noted, "with its focus on persistent, distorted, and negative perceptions of self, experience, and the future, characterological self-blame may well lead to clinical depression. In contrast, behavioral self-blame is likely to result in a more benign affective disturbance without cognitive bias" (pp. 662–663).

Brenda's inaccurate cognitive processing of causal inferences can be gently challenged by the therapist; probing issues of foreseeability, knowingly putting James in danger, and hindsight bias can facilitate the emergence of a more objective analysis of perceived responsibility, the avoidance of characterological self-blame, and the reestablishing of a sense of control (e.g., by the purchase of a "safer" vehicle). While recognizing that the exploration of such counterfactuals has the potential for amplifying and elaborating themes of self-blame, cognitive intervention strategies aimed at incorrect causal analyses encourage a sense of control (and the rejection of the randomness of events), foster resiliency, and encourage posttraumatic growth.

Depletion

Another aspect of The Aftermath of the death of a child is the omnipresent physical and emotional depletion reported by all of the parents interviewed. It was a theme that came up throughout the interviews, signifying the incredible strain and drain of living with the death of a child. Fathers described it as follows:

The loss of a child took a lot of the strength out ... because what you're doing you're actually burning up all of your energy inside to look good on the outside. (Elliot, 10-year-old child died, one surviving child)

The way I feel right now, I don't have enough energy to put into anybody else. I don't have enough energy for myself ... the energy levels are very, very much lower ... I was probably about 140% [before the death] but, I'd say on average my energy levels are probably about 70% [since the death]. (Frank, 12-year-old child died, one surviving child)

I feel as if I've aged about 15 years in the last 5. (Harris, 2-year-old child died, one surviving child)

Too much, and then you're thinking about the death still, so it all just builds up and you think God give me the strength to endure another day. (Gary, 16-year-old child died, one surviving child)

I don't have the same energy level that I used to, I know that ... it's at a lower level ... my 100% effort now may be equivalent to 75% of what I did before, and that's all I can give ... there's energy required for grief, just to carry on and get up every day, and it's draining. (Jake, 4-year-old child died, three surviving children)

Mothers also focused on this intense and pervasive sense of depletion.

And I don't have the energy, your energy level really is not as high as everybody else's, because you know, part of your energy is dealing with the fact that one of your children is not physically with you, and, so I really have to pace myself ... and so energy, it all comes down to energy ... because I literally don't have the energy. (Diane, 4-year-old child died, three surviving children)

I feel my energy level is lower. (Isabelle, 2-year-old child died, one surviving child)

Everything is dramatic after you've had a loss, everything is bigger, every problem is bigger because you don't have the fight. Normally something that would be quite small is now, it's a mountain. (Carol, 20-year-old child died, four surviving children)

We're tired [her and husband], I think we're tired of grieving for ourselves. (Becky, 4-year-old child died, two surviving children)

It tires you out ... I'm just tired ... It's just too much for your psyche to take. (Anna, 1-year-old child died, two surviving children)

It is not uncommon for those grieving many types of losses (e.g., the death of a spouse or a parent) to experience fatigue (Worden, 2009). Generally, survivors report this sense of diminished energy to be most pronounced in the early weeks/months following a significant loss. In contrast, bereaved parents spoke of a depletion of energy, a "bone-weariness," that appears to be more chronic and intense. For each parent in our study it had been a minimum of 3 years since the death of their child, and, for some, it had been as long as 8 years. Regardless of the time since death, these parents clearly remained depleted—this was not a passing or temporary aspect of their grief. Barrera et al. (2007), in a study of parents who had lost a child to illness or drowning in the previous 19 months, quoted a bereaved mother: "It's just I'm tired all the time ... I wake up and I'm tired ... lately I'm tired all the time, I can sleep 15 hours a day ... I can sleep all the time" (p. 156). Barrera et al. labeled this mother's experience "symptoms of fatigue" (p. 156); however, when the length of time since the death and the deep level of her exhaustion is considered, it seems more closely related to the notion of depletion—ongoing, all-encompassing, and immune to restorative rest. Rosenblatt (2000a) wrote of bereaved parents being sapped of energy and used the metaphor of their grief as "draining" (p. 77) to depict the deep, pervasive loss of energy limiting a parent's ability to function in all aspects of their lives. It appears that the protracted sense of energy depletion is yet another characteristic illustrating the distinctive nature of grieving the death of a child.

Levels of Loss

The levels of loss also become apparent in The Aftermath. The thousands of penetrating shards that was The House of Refracting Glass were slowly and painfully found over time, some small, some larger. The parents stumbled upon these pieces and they hurt, pierced, and cut again. These are the levels of loss—the painful discoveries that emanate from a life lived without their child. As some of the mothers described it:

The Devastation of Parental Bereavement

> I'm thinking if he had been here, if he had gotten married, then the son always dances with the mother, but I'll never have that ... the girls, they're going to be doing things that he will never do, never, ever, ever. (Anna, 1-year-old child died, two surviving children)

> He's a fabulous dad [her husband]. It was just amazing to see him with the two boys ... to have [deceased child] taken away from him really hurt, that's hard for me to have seen that happen to him ... the loss extends into everything. (Isabelle, 2-year-old child died, one surviving child)

Two of the fathers sensitively discussed the complexity of the loss of a child in a family of two children where the surviving child has physical and/or mental challenges.

> He's a handful. He has ADD and he's always been a handful since the day he was born ... his ADD put him on a different path. I mean he was harder to deal with. He didn't have as many friends. One walked early, he walked late. You know, one was reading early, the other wasn't. One was achieving higher marks at school without having to work really hard, where he does. So, the kids are very different. (Frank, 12-year-old child died, one surviving child)

> When he was alive, like he was an island of salvation ... he would take his sister and play with her and it was like, we had down time ... but with his loss, there was no down time anymore ... he was the more gifted of the two children, I have to, I hate to, I don't like to differentiate between the children ... that's the biggest thing, you know. You look at, so where would he be today? (Elliot, 10-year-old child died, one surviving child)

As a result of the uniqueness and the centrality of the attachment between parent and child, there are numerous secondary losses associated with the child's death that serve to complicate and intensify a parent's attempts at integrating such a loss. These include the loss of a sense of self, the demise of one's assumptive world, the evaporation of hopes and dreams associated with the child, the loss of a sense of parental identity, and the diminution of the family subsystem that predated the child's death (Rando, 1993).

Spousal Grieving Differences

Although both parents have suffered an identical loss, that of their beloved child, the Shatter is unique. No two panes of glass splinter in exactly the same way and spousal differences in grieving became apparent to many of the parents. Mothers noticed the following differences between their experience and that of their husbands':

> My husband and I are very close and we discuss things, but again he's a man, and he's going to, there's [sic] certain things he sees differently. (Anna, 1-year-old child died, two surviving children)

> He hadn't been in the accident I was in. I don't think even he realized just how quickly something can happen ... I don't know if he goes through the same things because he's suffered the same loss. But he wasn't involved, therefore, is it so, you know? (Becky, 4-year-old child died, two surviving children)

> Well my husband to this day, I will not talk with him about [deceased child] ... he's very uncomfortable when I talk about him, and still is ... there are big time differences that made it more difficult ... and I think he had thought, okay, you grieve a year and that's it. Forget it. There was no way anybody was telling me that you do that. (Carol, 20-year-old child died, four surviving children)

> You know to start with, I think I was more traumatized, having been in the accident myself. (Diane, 4-year-old child died, three surviving children)

Fathers also noticed differences and described these discrepancies as follows:

> But my wife was going through really hard cycles, and like, I would go so far down the curve with her and I'd say, I don't like this roller coaster ride, so if you want to ride it right to the bottom, you're welcome to it, but I'm taking off from here. There's no sense both of us being in the pit at the same time ... this is self-preservation, I'll deal with you so far ... if one person can pull themselves up and keep sanity without self-destructing, then why not do that? (Elliot, 10-year-old child died, one surviving child)

> Her grief had taken her in a different direction than what mine had at that time ... and I think that happened probably twice to us, that we were on

different roads. The other times I think we were fairly close on what was going on. (Frank, 12-year-old child died, one surviving child)

Well I grieved too, but in a different way than my wife grieved. She still needs a lot of help. It's a tough go. I try to be as supportive as I can ... she grieved really bad. It really hurt to hear that ... she's still having a tough time, I mean, I'm having a tough time too but you know, I don't know, maybe just don't show it as much, or as my wife. (Gary, 16-year-old child died, one surviving child)

I think we were quite fortunate. We grieved similarly, not exactly the same, but we didn't go off in different directions, we were sort of on the same wavelength and I think we helped one another with our grief. (Jake, 4-year-old child died, three surviving children)

The majority of parents in this study commented on spousal grieving differences, a theme that frequently resurfaced in their reflections and one that will be explored further in the following chapters. From the mothers' perspective, these differences ranged from generally being on the same path with minor departures in experience, to feeling alienated and challenged by a noncommunicative spouse. The fathers also recognized differential spousal reactions, which varied from general harmony with few experiences of discord, to feeling their wives grieved much more intensely and longer than they did.

With their social support network threatened, and well-meaning friends and acquaintances frequently distancing themselves from the palpable and painful evidence of a parent's loss, they are often isolated and thrust back on each other—at a time when their lives are in chaos and when they are least capable of communicating wishes and needs clearly. In an examination of marital adjustment following the death of a child, Riches and Dawson (1996) noted:

... bereaved couples have *both* suffered traumatic loss. Two pendulums will be de-stabilized. Two parallel and interdependent, but not necessarily identical, self-narratives will be struggling to address major disruption to each other's identity. Mother and father may share a marital and family paradigm and a common history with the lost child, but each has possessed a unique relationship with that child ... mothers and fathers adopt very different strategies, and hence exaggerate each other's sense of isolation from reality and from each other. (p. 12)

There are numerous studies to suggest that mothers and fathers grieve the death of a child differently. Mothers tended to report a more intense, long-lasting grief than did fathers (DeVries, Dalla Lana, & Falek, 1994; Fish, 1986; Schwab, 1990, 1996); they reported more severe and more diverse grief reactions including depression, despair, guilt, social isolation, somatization, rumination, and meaninglessness when compared to their male counterparts (e.g., Barrera et al., 2007; Bohannon, 1990; Lang & Gottlieb, 1993; Moriarty, Carroll, & Cotroneo, 1996; Parkes, 2002; Rubinstein, 2004; Vance, Boyle, Najman, & Thearle, 1995; Varney Sidmore, 1999–2000; Wijngaards-de Meij et al., 2007; Wing, Clance, Burge-Callaway, & Armistead, 2001); mothers seemed to feel the loss more intensely and reported greater difficulty adjusting to the world without their child (Rando, 1986a); and mothers were also more likely to characterize the death as a loss of a core aspect of themselves and ignore other aspects of their lives that were now deemed unimportant (Riches & Dawson, 2000). It has also been found that bereaved mothers were at increased risk for both natural and unnatural deaths, and showed an overall elevated risk of cancer (Li, Johansen et al., 2002; Li et al., 2003). In contrast to bereaved mothers, who frequently cited inadequacies in spousal communication as a source of distress, bereaved fathers often referred to the lack of intimacy as the principal contributor to spousal tension (Fish, 1986; Lang & Gottlieb, 1991).

Coping strategies also differ between bereaved mothers and fathers. Mothers were more likely than fathers to report experiencing the loss as isolating, to seek support, and to confront and share their emotions (Conway & Feeney, 1997; Klass, 1988). Fathers, on the other hand, tended to report experiencing the loss as a void and sought solitude, describing their grieving as a private matter (Klass, 1988; Sprang & McNeil, 1995). Additionally, fathers tended to resume regular activities sooner and were more likely either to keep busy or to distract themselves from the pain (Lang & Gottlieb, 1993). Fathers also reported that they felt a need to continue to provide for and protect their families (DeVries et al., 1994), which often involved controlling affective expression, intellectualizing grief, and employing problem-focused strategies (Lang & Gottlieb, 1993; Rosenblatt, 2000a). In essence, they felt a need to be "strong" for the family's sake, often neglecting their own grief (Bohannon, 1990; Schwab 1992).

It is hypothesized that the relationship between gender and grieving patterns is a function of how men and women are socialized in our society, more specifically, a woman's socialization, emphasizing values such as nurturing, self-disclosure, and "rapport" talk over "report" talk, predisposes her to express grief intuitively (Martin & Doka, 2000). The intuitive pattern is one in which individuals experience and express grief in an intensely affective manner, with coping strategies that are oriented toward the expression of feelings. In contrast, with its stress on autonomy, self-sufficiency, and competency, a male's socialization experience is thought to eventuate in an instrumental grieving pattern (Martin & Doka, 2000) in which grief is experienced cognitively, with moderated affect, a desire to master feelings, and a tendency to avoid the open exchange of painful feelings associated with the child's death (Kamm & Vandenberg, 2001).

This discrepancy was clearly demonstrated to the second author when seeing a bereaved father in psychotherapy following the death of his 17-year-old daughter in a motor vehicle accident. He referred to coping style, which might best be described as cognitive, instrumental, and solitary, he described in the following manner:

> As a father, with both a wife and other children depending on me, the death of a child left me little to do than "cope" (mostly on my own) and survive until the others were somehow back to being able to live day to day—a number of years later. (We are at well over 5 years and that is just starting to happen).
>
> "Coping" meant the most basic of things, like having the financial resources we needed to keep moving forward (we were very fortunate, but a lack of money when your family needs it the most must be a devastating heartbreak for those not so fortunate). It meant seeming to be strong and reliable—the rock of the family. For a man, keeping a brave face is important, but it is not easy with a wife who cries all day and looks like it when you get home, a son who seems to deal with his grief by being stoned and angry, and a daughter who continues to excel and work herself hard while not talking much about her life.
>
> For some reason, it did not seem right to grieve publicly, even in front of my family. I talked to some friends, but most quickly moved on and many did not know how to deal with the death of a child so they stayed away. Only a few friends really understood that we just needed them to be there and that we knew that there was no way for them to "understand" what we were going through.
>
> Privately, I tried to have "time" with my dead daughter. Music in the car on the way to work in the morning would lead to tears and sometimes hardly being able to see driving on the expressway, wondering what I would look like to my staff when I got to work. I wrote my daughter letters in journals as a way to keep our lives together and for her to know what I was thinking and what was happening in our lives, and wondering what was happening in hers. I found ways to work hard for causes that were important to her, went on boards, made speeches, gave money, and did anything I could to give some kind of meaning to her 17 years of life.
>
> I found new hobbies to keep myself "busy," to learn new things and to be physical. I worked hard at my job—long hours doing interesting

things—all to try not to focus on the devastation that our family life had become. At the same time, I took up running much more seriously than ever and ran two half marathons, privately in my daughter's memory.

Our family relationships are much different than they might have been, but then again maybe not. Life with my spouse is different, but we still love each other and are moving closer together after many years of being in completely different places. Our children are moving on, back at school and apparently well adjusted, but always on edge it seems.

Intuitive and instrumental grieving styles, according to Martin and Doka (2000), are ends of a continuum; although men are more likely to be found at the instrumental end, while women are more likely to exhibit an intuitive pattern, because grieving is not determined by gender, this is not the case for all men, or all women, and one must be constantly aware of individual styles of responding to loss.

Wijngaards-De Meij, Stroebe, Schut, et al. (2008) documented the intrapersonal and interpersonal processes relevant to parents grieving the death of their child, through the lens of the Dual Process Model. In a study of 219 couples 6 to 20 months post-loss, they found that wives were more loss-oriented than husbands and both husbands and wives had a reduction in loss-orientation over time. While the restoration-orientation of husbands was high at the start, for wives it was lower to start but rose somewhat over time. Interestingly, the more a wife was restoration-oriented, the lower the levels of grief and depression were in a husband. Wijngaards-De Meji, Stroebe, Schut, et al. (2008) interpreted this finding to be an indication that when a woman engaged in a coping style that was generally more frequently used by men, this was beneficial for the man married to her. The same did not hold true for the women in the study—their husbands' coping orientation was not related to their own grief or depression.

It is valuable to bear in mind that despite the differences, there are often commonalities noted between coupled mothers and fathers. For example, Wijngaards-de Meij et al. (2005) in a study of 219 couples, found that while there was variation within a couple in grief reactions, there was greater variation between couples. Kamm and Vandenberg (2001), in their study of gender differences in communication after the death of a child, reported both convergence and divergence among spouses. They concluded, "women who valued open communication were likely to have husbands who also valued open communication, but women also had significantly more positive attitudes about open grief communication than their husbands" (p. 579). These authors also found more intense responses in the early days of grief for those bereaved parents endorsing the open expression of their loss; however, over a longer period of time, these couples reported less intense grief reactions. Perhaps a couple's open exchange of feelings shortly after the death intensifies their grief and, conversely, censoring conversation immediately following the death may initially serve as a buffer or antidote but, long-term, may lead to complications in the grief response. This finding suggests that gender differences between spouses are present but may not be so dramatic as to obscure marital harmony. Rather, bereaved partners may be able to live with one another in a manner that respects, if not satisfies, their somewhat differing needs and experiences.

Our findings, then, are consistent with the literature delineating the differences in the grief experience of mothers and fathers, while also acknowledging that these differences are generally not so extreme as to cause serious problems in the relationship. The death of a child can precipitate a rupture in a parent's sense of identity, can destroy individual/parental/family assumptive worlds, demand the joint reconstruction of self and family paradigms, and inflict intolerable stress on the marital relationship—but it need not mean the inevitable ending of the marriage. This point needs elaboration. Although there are no conclusive data that such a cataclysmic event inevitably causes the dissolution of the marriage, the myth persists that this is indeed the case. Sadly, bereaved parents not infrequently expect their marriage to end following the death of their child. Although there are methodological problems in the research, most marriages not only survive the death of a child, but couples often report enhanced relationships, improved cohesion or closeness, and increased resiliency post-loss (Dijkstra & Stroebe, 1998; Oliver, 1999). Clinicians need to work diligently in disabusing parents of such a destructive and potentially self-fulfilling expectation.

☐ The Effect of Time

Parents never "get over" the death of their child. Additionally, the adage that "time heals all wounds" does not apply. Time, however, does play a role in the trajectory of parental bereavement. To a bereaved parent, time is bittersweet. While it often brings a degree of relief from the consuming intensity of grief, it also brings greater distance from the physical relationship with the beloved child. Ultimately, as much as time brings change, for bereaved parents there is the constant that time does not affect—their child has died and they must continue to live with that unchanging reality. The properties of the category The Effect of Time explicate this role.

What Time Gives

Although conceptualized in different ways, all of the parents spoke about an easing in the intensity of the grief with the passage of time—but it never dissipated completely. Each parent spoke of grief spikes, where the intensity of pain came flooding back as in the early days. What time gives is increasing space between these grief spikes, so there are fewer consecutive days of wrenching agony. The pain no longer consumed every minute of every day; rather, the spasms of pain became intermittent, but no less intense. The fathers described it as follows:

> It comes back at different times and different severities. I would say, if you talk about the roller coaster ride, the roller coaster ride was like very, like in amplitude it was up and down and the cycles were really close together so it was like zoom, zoom, zoom, zoom. And as time goes on, usually what will happen is the roller coaster ride is now, the amplitude is much further apart so the cycle could be two months where you and the amplitude are very low. So you may still have a low one day and you know, I'm not feeling too good, but I know what it is. But it's not like in the old days where it was like, where you went down huge swings. (Elliot, 10-year-old child died, one surviving child)

> The pain will go away, but the hurt never stops, I mean, so, you've got to get through that to deal with it ... you have to keep your mind focused, because really, as we all know, those are all emotions and we can't change the facts and our emotions are going to change. Some days hurt more than others ... the pain is starting to go away and I need to refocus. The last two years have been like a 10,000 piece jigsaw puzzle that fell off the shelf and trying to put it together. So, there's still missing pieces, but, I have to get back to having a full picture. (Frank, 12-year-old child died, one surviving child)

> Well right after he died, to look anymore than a few hours ahead was almost impossible. The first few weeks I couldn't even think of the next day, and it took us a long time before we even planned something even a week down the road or a month, we couldn't think that far ... now as time's gone on, we can see further down the road, we can plan trips and things like that ... You cope. You get through the days. And there's still days that, I think we all get it, where the emotions are right up there, the day he died. There are triggers that can set it off. There are definitely triggers. (Jake, 4-year-old child died, three surviving children)

The Devastation of Parental Bereavement 69

The mothers described a similar experience of what time gives in the grief process. Like the fathers, they commented on the notion of grief spikes, but they also focused on the concept of increased functioning as time progressed.

> It gets easier in that I am able to function every day ... I'm amazed at where I am ... when I think of how far we've come ... you know, one day you think you're doing so great and then the next day, you've had it, it falls apart in a breath. (Anna, 1-year-old child died, two surviving children)

> When you lose a child and the initial grief is that, just that, like a concrete block of time where they never leave your mind. And I'll always remember the first morning that I got up and went down to the kitchen and I'm not, I think I had dressed, and I had done quite a bit, and *then* thought of him. And was actually feeling really guilty, why this morning had I not?? There had to have been 20 minutes and then I thought, that's healing. You know, those spaces ... It's nothing near as frequent. No, I function well now ... I still think of him an awful lot now. But it's different. It's not the intensity of the pain ... you still miss them terribly, but, your missing doesn't hurt as much ... but there are triggers ... you know, you think you are doing okay and then you're quite surprised by the emotion, it's powerful. (Carol, 20-year-old child died, four surviving children)

The Effect of Time is not always perceived as benevolent and inviting as some of the parents remarked on what time takes:

> In a lot of ways it doesn't get easier. Because now you have to deal with the forgetting, I can't remember what he sounded like. You know? What did he look like? Did he, you know what? It doesn't get easier. It doesn't ... there are days I just don't want life to go on because the time is getting farther away ... A lot of times it hurts harder inside because you don't have that outlet anymore. Nobody wants to discuss it, nobody really wants to talk about it, get on with it. (Anna, 1-year-old child died, two surviving children)

> I really felt that I had progressed, but there was sort of an emptiness in a sense, it was almost like I'd left a part of him somewhere but I wasn't quite sure where. But I knew in a sense I was moving on. (Carol, 20-year-old child died, four surviving children)

> The intensity of feeling that went along with earlier grief, I don't ever think I felt a wish for it to be over ... I'm not in a real hurry for this grieving to subside, because in grieving I feel connected and I'm not looking

forward to the moving on part because along with moving on feels less of a sense of connection. (Harris, 2-year-old child died, one surviving child)

Sometimes you want to bring it all back. I don't know why, but, you want to bring it all back. But, you pay a price for it. It's very draining. (Jake, 4-year-old child died, three surviving children)

Throughout the interviews, there was a clear sense that although time impacted aspects of the grief, the grim reality of the death stood impervious to The Effect of Time. It is the constant. It is a loss that will never be forgotten or resolved as it is stitched into the fabric of the lives of these parents, ever present. Interestingly, it was the mothers who described the constant presence more frequently than did the fathers.

I just want him back. I just want him here. I don't think that ever goes away. (Anna, 1-year-old child died, two surviving children)

The loss is always going to be there ... it's with you all the time though, it's with you from the time you get up. (Becky, 4-year-old child died, two surviving children)

I almost look on grief as a living entity in itself, and it's got so many facets and personalities and moves to it. It's like something that I lug around ... you're living with this all the time, it's not going to leave, that's how it is. (Diane, 4-year-old child died, three surviving children)

You never get over it ... it's always there in our head, all the time. (Gary, 16-year-old child died, one surviving child)

It's always there. You learn to deal, learn to cope with it I think. (Jake, 4-year-old child died, three surviving children)

The Shatter, The Aftermath, and The Effect of Time collectively detail the complex, ongoing nature of the devastating loss of a child. It is important to note that The Aftermath is ongoing and the properties of it are not discrete; rather, they are continuous, in that there are no clear distinctions between the beginning of one and the ending of another. The properties of The Aftermath detail the impact of the death of a child. Although not an exhaustive list, it is a representation of the most salient experiences of the bereaved parents interviewed. The collapse of The

The Devastation of Parental Bereavement 71

House of Refracting Glass and the loss of (necessary) illusions left these parents vulnerable and confused. In the face of the multidimensional nature of such a loss, their efforts to survive individually and collectively were courageous and Herculean—although none felt particularly brave or courageous. It is to this individual and family resilience in the rebuilding of assumptive worlds, and meeting the demands of parenting at a time when they felt depleted, devastated, and demoralized, that we now turn our attention.

CHAPTER 4

Picking Up the Pieces
Regeneration of Self

Picking up the Pieces speaks to the regeneration after the devastation. This regeneration occurred on the level of the individual, the family, and between parents and surviving child(ren) through parenting. Just as each individual shatter was different, so too was each individual regeneration. As we will document in the following chapters, some parents, with considerable effort, were ultimately able to rebuild their lives and reconstruct shattered assumptions of the self and the world; others were not. Some were able to return to the touchstones of their sense of self and re-establish meaning; others struggled to create anew from what was left after The Shatter. Regardless of the level of regeneration, the shards, cracks, and missing pieces were always and forever present, affecting each parent's sense of self, family, and world view.

Picking Up the Pieces is an active process, it demands attention and, as we will illustrate, one must *engage* in regeneration. This painful, exhausting process of rebuilding not only involved the examination of minor, day-to-day activities, it extended to the most profound organizing principles, values, and meaning structures in a parent's life—and it continued indefinitely. Living with a "new normal" (i.e., the death of a child and its impact on one's self and family), bereaved parents were pressed to reestablish new meaning, new awareness, and new ways of being in the world—at the worst possible time of their lives. In the midst of self-doubt, personal devastation, and often trauma, they were constantly confronted by the intrusion of life and parenting demands that exposed their vulnerability and fear. Literally at the moment of the death, parents often reluctantly and without much enthusiasm or conviction began the process of Picking Up the Pieces, of regenerating their lives and the lives of their families and remaining children.

The process of Picking Up the Pieces will be explored at the level of the self and the family, as both inform and culminate in parenting. In this chapter, we discuss this process of Picking Up the Pieces as it relates to changes in the self as expressed through one's identity, relationships, and spiritual/religious beliefs and practices. Subsequent chapters will deal with the regeneration of the family including the relationship with the deceased child (Chapter 5); the dual tasks of simultaneously parenting and grieving (Chapter 6); the lack of control, protectiveness, and the struggle for balance (Chapter 7); and the challenges of sensitively parenting bereaved children (Chapter 8).

☐ Self

All of the parents in the study shared their personal experiences of Picking Up the Pieces of their lives, including regenerating their identity, reevaluating their relationships, and questioning their spirituality and religious beliefs in the aftermath of the death of their child. As will be seen through exploring each ramification, the death had a pervasive and profound impact on self-definition.

☐ Identity

All but one of the parents spoke of the profound changes in their identity after the death of their child. Some of these changes were almost instantaneous, while others evolved over time. All referred to a process of regeneration, of consciously examining infrequently contemplated personal questions about one's life, and recognizing what was lost forever and what was created anew. The fathers highlighted the following changes in their identity:

> It's a real soul-searching. You look inward a lot when you have the loss of a child ... in some ways it boosts your self-awareness. (Elliot, 10-year-old child died, one surviving child)

I'm a very high achiever, or was anyway. I was the leader in our field. I had a very strong commitment [to work], I mean 60-, 80-, 100-hour weeks were nothing. I realized after his death that there's really no value in that. I don't need that success anymore. It means nothing to me. Not anymore ... I really restrict the amount of time I put in to that now. I'd rather be at home. (Frank, 12-year-old child died, one surviving child)

We're probably stronger for going through what we've gone through ... I think I took on a lot of values after my child's death, like, relax and take it easy, instead of getting all bent out of shape about things. It's not worth it ... I've been actually more tolerant ... I have more patience I think. (Gary, 16-year-old child died, one surviving child)

Do I have the strength of will now when inevitably it's tough to pursue a dream? Do I still have enough to just keep on picking myself up and going on ... I don't know what's missing now. I think it's motivation though. (Harris, 2-year-old child died, one surviving child)

I'm a different person now ... I find it easier to say "no" now, and say, "sorry I can't do that" ... I remember a sense of feeling a little, of being freed because there's nothing worse that could happen to me than my son dying, there's nothing worse anyone could ever do to me. And I think that's kind of freeing and it made it easier to say to someone, "sorry, this is the way it is." (Jake, 4-year-old child died, three surviving children)

Mothers also reflected on the post-loss changes in their lives and, consistent with the fathers' responses, commented on what was lost and what was gained in the slow, painful reconstruction of their personal sense of identity.

It's changed me and what I feel is important ... I'm just not the same. I'm just totally different ... Before I was much more wishy-washy, but, you know what? There's better things to do with your time ... You have to stick up for yourself and once you've decided what you think is right or wrong, don't keep going back and trying to reevaluate everything. (Anna, 1-year-old child died, two surviving children)

That day [day child died] it was the wrong decision to make, so, therefore you double check all of your decision making ... Insecurities ... but, you think, look how far I've come since, look at what I've learned since. (Becky, 4-year-old child died, two surviving children)

> I didn't realize how submissive I had been ... I had always been the type, the person to do anything to keep an even balance ... it [the death] brought out a side of me, but it was a side of me that needed to be brought out ... I felt like a turtle. I would retreat. And I would come back out and I'd go back in and I would keep going ... I'm not usually confrontational. I'm not. No. It meant enough to me in this case. (Carol, 20-year-old child died, four surviving children)

> The way you are as a person changes. I changed from the inside out. Absolutely ... This is who I am now, and I can't even remember what I was like before. I really can't ... Physically, you look the same, but, you're not because your personality, your whole psyche has undergone a huge, huge change. Nor would any of us want to be the same after that. Would you want to have a child die and be the same person you were? Not in a million years ... you learn really early on to listen to yourself ... part of the change in your psyche is not that you turn into a pessimist. Because I don't feel by nature I am. But, I think being an optimist is somebody that thinks well, if something really bad happens, then maybe we can make something good come from it ... I don't have rose colored glasses. I have bifocals. (Diane, 4-year-old child died, three surviving children)

Although both fathers and mothers talked about the significant changes in their identity as a result of the death of their child, some also commented on the limits of this change.

> The basic person of who you are is still there, I don't think you do this dramatic character change. But, I think if there was something underlying, when this magnifying glass comes down on you [the death], I think everything just gets magnified. So, if you had a tendency to be depressed before, I think maybe afterwards that would just magnify. (Jake, 4-year-old child died, three surviving children)

> You can't change your character too much ... I mean how can you change all of that? (Gary, 16-year-old child died, one surviving child)

> I just don't have it in me to be like that [to hold someone liable], but I wanted answers. (Carol, 20-year-old child died, four surviving children)

Living presently was another aspect of identity change as participants discussed both a foreshortened sense of time (with no guarantees) and a heightened appreciation for the present moment. In the regeneration of their lives, living presently, in many ways, had become a guiding principle for these parents.

> We [bereaved parents] are more tuned into life. We treasure more things in life. Nothing is taken for granted. I live in the present far more. Little things mean a lot more than they ever did. It's all so precious. (Diane, 4-year-old child died, three surviving children)

> I treasure the time, the age he is [surviving son], each day, very definitely. (Isabelle, 2-year-old child died, one surviving child)

> Time has another meaning, it goes away too. What matters? (Elliot, 10-year-old child died, one surviving child)

> I try to cram too much in because I know that I have limited time left on this earth, so I try to cram too much in one day. So I feel good about, hey, if I die tomorrow, I did something good today. That's the way I think now. (Gary, 16-year-old child died, one surviving child)

> You enjoy every day, you don't take anything for granted ... you enjoy every minute and you savor every minute ... definitely I would say you live in the moment, not to the point of being extreme, but you would live in the moment much more than looking down the road. Before we'd be looking quite a way down the road. Now we don't look as far down the road as we used to. (Jake, 4-year-old child died, three surviving children)

Related to the notion of living presently is the concept of *reordering priorities*. Parents spoke of a fundamental shift in their values, a change in perspective after the death of their child, a reordering that came from the act of Picking Up the Pieces and regenerating new meaning and purpose. The mothers shared the following regarding their reevaluated priorities:

> It [child's death] has caused me to look at my life a lot. You sort of realize, my family is what's really important ... Material things aren't of the same importance ... I'm not really concerned about that. As long as we have a comfortable place to live. If we have a car that's comfortable and reliable and that type of thing. I don't care whether it's new ... No, the small things aren't, you know, they'll be there tomorrow. (Isabelle, 2-year-old child died, one surviving child)

I am very, very, very possessive about my family time now. I am very protective over it. And I don't apologize for that. (Diane, 4-year-old child died, three surviving children)

You don't sweat the small stuff anymore. It doesn't matter. It's not important anymore. Everything has changed ... We didn't have a lot, but you know we had enough. Nothing else mattered. (Carol, 20-year-old child died, four surviving children)

It definitely makes you see your priorities and it makes the important things really, really important. It just puts life into perspective ... How precious life is ... the special things. (Becky, 4-year-old child died, two surviving children)

Things don't matter anymore, certain little things and material things ... I don't want life to be about things. That has no meaning anymore ... I've also become much more generous. I've given a lot more money to charity for things that are important to me. (Anna, 1-year-old child died, two surviving children)

The fathers also referred to the reordering of priorities and how the death of a child changed what was important to them and how they conducted their lives.

It [the death] totally turns life around. Nothing's important. The only thing that's really important is family ... Your priorities are totally reordered. You get rewired very quickly. Everything is different. You see things differently. (Elliot, 10-year-old child died, one surviving child)

I leave more space now. I take my time ... Your focus in life changes. Nothing is a rush to me anymore. (Frank, 12-year-old child died, one surviving child)

It's a whole different focus now. (Gary, 16-year-old child died, one surviving child)

Bereaved parents were confronted, then, with the task of rediscovering or regenerating a recognizable sense of self amid the shattered remnants of their house of refracting glass. Some felt that their former self died with their child, and a completely new identity was forged in the regeneration process. Others felt that the basic foundations of identity survived and the resultant alterations in character were more subtle or circumscribed. Whether they experienced significant identity change or more limited identity revision, challenges to their self-perception were the norm rather than the exception. As the parents in this study had been at least 3 years post-death, these significant revisions in assumptions and beliefs appear to be enduring. While demonstrating the cataclysmic impact of the death of a child on a parent's identity there was also evidence of positive personality changes, or posttraumatic growth, stemming from this horrific experience. Tedeschi and Calhoun (2004b) defined posttraumatic growth broadly as "positive psychological change experienced as a result of the struggle with highly challenging life circumstances" (p. 1). They argue that posttraumatic growth does not eventuate from simple exposure to a trauma; rather, it is the struggle with the repercussions of "psychologically seismic" events that threaten or destroy one's assumptive world that will determine the nature and extent of growth (p. 5). Tedeschi and Calhoun have identified a number of domains of posttraumatic growth including the prospect for a change in life's direction or path, the realization of more fulfilling and intimate relationships, an increased sense of personal empowerment, an increased appreciation of life, and changes in the realm of religious or existential beliefs. Research has begun on the correlates of posttraumatic growth in bereaved parents. For example, Riley, LaMontagne, Hepworth, and Murphy (2007), in a study of 35 bereaved mothers, found that personal growth was associated with an active coping disposition (i.e., planning and problem solving), support-seeking behavior, and positive reframing. Although not strictly a study of bereaved parents (the sample included the loss of child, spouse, parent, sibling, grandparent, and friend), Gamino, Sewell, and Easterling's (2000) results showed that personal growth was correlated with the ability to conclude that good resulted from the death, the opportunity to say good-bye, intrinsic spirituality, and the capacity to reflect on positive memories of the deceased.

There is much debate on the definition of "posttraumatic growth" and disagreement with Tedeschi and Calhoun's (2004b) emphasis that such growth is a function of successfully extracting a sense of meaning or purpose from the loss (Davis, 2008). For example, Janoff-Bulman (2004) suggested three models of growth through (a) awareness of one's new strength, courage, and self-confidence as a result of having survived an indescribable loss; (b) psychological preparedness for future distressing events as a result of surviving the current trauma; and (c) "existential evaluation" (similar to Tedeschi and Calhoun's increased appreciation of family, friends, and life). Regardless of the controversy in conceptualizing and defining the concept of posttraumatic growth, that bereaved parents often report such outcomes is not in dispute. Clinicians need to be cautious, however, in the introduction and exploration of this topic since, presented prematurely, such reflections may be interpreted as minimizing the impact of their child's death. And, as one bereaved father reflected, "yes, I've changed and become a better person ... but I was a pretty good dad before and it sure as hell wasn't worth the price."

☐ Relationships

In Picking Up the Pieces parents also regenerated relationships with others outside the immediate family (relationships within the family will be addressed in the next chapter). The majority of parents noticed significant changes in their relationships with others, a finding to be expected given the reported profound changes in identity. This finding is also not surprising given the widespread societal discomfort with death, especially the death of a child. Rather than continuing to nurture friendships characterized by avoidance, fear, or discomfort when their child's name was mentioned, parents often opted to curtail their contact with such friends, or simply discontinued the friendship. While they initiated the termination of some friendships, parents also reflected that friends often abandoned them. Fortunately, some parents also reported the development of new friendships and the deepening of existing ones.

Fathers described some of the changes in relationships as follows:

> Your true friends come out. Friends that you didn't think were close friends may become your close friends, and friends that you thought were close friends just vaporize ... Well, I can understand it because psychologically I guess, sitting where they are, the fear factor. They're afraid because they don't want that to happen to their kids ... and it's just too painful to associate with. So, that's when you know you have a good friend 'cause even if a good friend knows it's painful, they sit and listen to you, while other people, they sort of put the wall up. And that's very hard when that happens. It's like you have the plague. (Elliot, 10-year-old child died, one surviving child)

> You really start finding out who your friends are. You know people that were very close to you, some of them you don't associate with anymore. Some of them that we had nice relationships with are now very close friends. You tend to look at people in a different light. I'd say more discriminating ... what I do now, if I'm not comfortable with the person or if I don't believe in their ideals and things, I just will avoid that situation and

go on and find somebody else to talk to or deal with. I'm more selective now. (Frank, 12-year-old child died, one surviving child)

These fathers are not alone in their experience of reconfigured relationships and perceived rejection from others. Sanders (1980), in her study of the death of a child, parent, or spouse, found that the former produced the most pronounced feelings of isolation, lack of support, and stigma. Oliver (1999), in documenting similar findings, noted that bereaved parents were not particularly supported by society, and were often met with fear and impatience. It is not uncommon for relationships, especially friendships, to change significantly after the death of a child. Bereaved parents, like the fathers in this study, have frequently reported the secondary loss of friends after their child's death (Barrera et al., 2007, 2009; Brabant, Forsyth, & McFarlain, 1995; Klass, 1997; Knapp, 1986; Peppers & Knapp, 1980; Rosenblatt, 2000a; Sanders, 1980).

Bereaved mothers also referred to some relationships deepening while others, unfortunately, did not survive. However, mothers referred less frequently to people avoiding them, and more consistently mentioned *their* dodging or shunning friends with whom they did not feel comfortable or validated. Consider:

> I found I can't expend that energy on being around people that don't, that you can't be yourself with and relaxed ... you know, because I can't let the mask down ... and so I don't get into people that are judgmental. I just can't go there ... when you've been with really good friends, you can relax with, I would feel so rejuvenated because I've spent a good time with good people. (Diane, 4-year-old child died, three surviving children)

> The people we've cut out of our lives ... I'm not willing in some ways to include them because they will not talk about [deceased child] ... Like I won't try anymore. I'm the one in my family who always gave in. Who always tried again. And now I don't try and I always have, for my whole life I was that person they could count on and now that's no more. And that's it. (Anna, 1-year-old child died, two surviving children)

The comments of this last parent are illustrative. The literature has consistently shown that bereaved parents experience a persistent desire to discuss the life and death of their child (Murphy, 1996; Rando, 1986a, 1988). There are many reasons for doing this; such discourse keeps the child's memory alive, facilitates making sense of the loss, provides comfort when hearing their child's name, exercises the ongoing attachment or continuing bond to their child, and encourages an exploration of the child's legacy. If thwarted in their efforts to engage others in discussions of their deceased child, bereaved parents feel invalidated and they are confronted with the dilemma of maintaining such relationships or terminating or curtailing them. Uniformly, parents find comfort and solace when friends and family members have the courage to engage them in conversations about their child.

The impact of changes in identity, especially living presently and the reordering of priorities, had a salient and negative impact on some relationships. Bereaved parents exhibited little tolerance or patience for superficial comments and what they perceived to be insignificant or unimportant issues. This superficiality now stood in stark contrast to their on-going attempts to restore a sense of purpose and meaning in the context of their child's death. For example, parents reflected:

> Don't get into stuff that's stupid. I find it insulting. Because they are equating things that are not even at the same level. And I don't like that anymore. I don't give that the time of day. (Anna, 1-year-old child died, two surviving children)

> You know I've sat in conversations, I did last week, about a mom talking about two of her daughters who she told to clean up [their bedrooms] and I wanted to just say, "Would you shut up about this?! I don't want to hear this. This is such a stupid conversation. It's not important anymore." (Carol, 20-year-old child died, four surviving children)

> I've got a lot less patience for what I call not really important things. (Diane, 4-year-old child died, three surviving children)

> One of the biggest things I found that really bothered me, people would be petty arguing about things at work and I felt like just jumping up and going, "Listen you assholes, this is not important!" ... very low tolerance to stupidity or pettiness ... and I found with some of the Bereaved Families men's things, a lot of the guys became that way. They were very impatient. They don't like stupidity, or ambiguity, they really couldn't handle it. The tolerance was gone. (Elliot, 10-year-old child died, one surviving child)

> Patience for people that say, what I would consider stupid things, you put them straight pretty quick. (Jake, 4-year-old child died, three surviving children)

The experience of these bereaved parents, becoming much more discriminating in their relationships and having lower tolerance for

Picking Up the Pieces 83

superficiality, is consistent with what Rosenblatt (2000a) termed "sorting" (p. 168). This sorting referred not only to bereaved parents noting people who faded or disappeared from their lives, but also those from whom they actively disengaged as they found the contact was aversive, unsupportive, or uncomfortable. It is clear that sorting occurred in both directions.

Although the bereaved parents in this study became less tolerant of what they deemed insignificant and superficial in relationships, they also reported feeling more open, caring, and actively supportive of others experiencing loss or emotional difficulties. They discussed being "tuned in" and wanting to reach out to others—feelings of altruism in the midst of depletion and emptiness. The fathers described it as follows:

> Probably a contradiction, sometimes you are less patient with people and other times you have a lot more empathy and patience with people, for certain situations. When it comes to people emotionally, you can certainly see where they're coming from. (Jake, 4-year-old child died, three surviving children)

> So, when there is a death, I watch the person, and I go over to them and say, "Listen, when you want, just give me a call. I'm here and I'll listen" … you become a little bit more compassionate in certain things. (Elliot, 10-year-old child died, one surviving child)

> One thing I do now, understanding more about death and loss, I too try to lend a lot of support to people who are going through similar things. I always try to contact them right away. And say, "I'm here if you want to talk. Here's my phone number, or here's my home number, or whatever." And then you know, stay fairly close, make sure you phone once a week to see what's going on. So, I feel I might as well take some of my experience and I mean if it can help somebody else a little bit, do it. (Frank, 12-year-old child died, one surviving child)

Always a "touchy kind of person" and concerned about the well-being of others, one bereaved mother now felt more confident in her ability to comfort the distressed.

> I could just tell from the way that she got out of the car, and walked across the car park, that something had happened. I got up and I said, "Okay, let's talk. What happened?" … it seems like you sense when other people have this same kind of thing … I don't know if it's more now, I think I was always a touchy kind of person, like I was always the one who never hesitated and

put my arm around somebody or whatever if they were upset. I feel now that I can probably do it because before when I used to do it I used to think, "oh, have I done the right thing?" Now I feel they don't have to talk about it if they don't want to, but, at least I'm there, and at least I've made that move to show them that I understand a little bit. (Becky, 4-year-old child died, two surviving children)

This reflection might well represent the reality of other bereaved mothers but they did not offer such contemplations—and, consistent with the grounded theory method, the first author (JB) did not lead the conversation in this direction. Perhaps their orientation toward others was consistently altruistic, and there was no change post-death. The answer to this will have to await further research. It was the bereaved fathers, however, who consistently reflected on their newfound tendency to respond more empathically to others, particularly those who were suffering. The regularity with which they commented on this embryonic reaction leads us to believe that it will not be a transient dimension of their personality.

The mothers did refer to feelings of *separateness* in some of their relationships, and indeed, in their interactions in general. It was a sense of not being 100% engaged in the world anymore. The fathers did not mention this experience.

He [deceased child] should be grown and the girls are going to be up here and I'm going to be living here [with deceased child]. (Anna, 1-year-old child died, two surviving children)

We moved as part of a subdivision but we're on the outside of a subdivision. So I guess it's even happened as far as our moving ... when you're grieving, you really don't live a life because you're so wrapped up in your grief. (Becky, 4-year-old child died, two surviving children)

Just the rest of the world goes on ... that's why I like the Loving Memory Tree [BFO activity] at Christmas time. Because if the rest of the world is having Christmas, we can at least have one day for [deceased child]. (Carol, 20-year-old child died, four surviving children)

You have this split, where part of you is with [deceased child] and the other part of you is with [surviving child]. (Diane, 4-year-old child died, three surviving children)

Another area where relationships were impacted by the death of a child involved *rejecting expectations*, particularly those of one's family of origin. Bereaved mothers, but not bereaved fathers, reflected on how they were parented as children and their determination to alter their parenting/family style to more accurately reflect their changed priorities and values. They were determined to respond in a more therapeutic, supportive manner.

> In my family, they don't talk about anything, they don't discuss anything, they're totally the opposite of what I am. I could have gone that way too ... But you see, I've gone the other way ... part of my upbringing and what I saw my parents do, I think in that respect it was a conscious choice to say I'm not going to do it, to do that here [with child's death] because look what it did to them. (Anna, 1-year-old child died, two surviving children)

> We want him [surviving child] as he's growing up to be very comfortable about having his friends in our home and I want it to be a place where he's comfortable bringing them. I never really, growing up, felt that it was, they [her friends] were really welcome to just knock on the door and come in you know ... my mom wasn't like that. And I guess I'd like to, if I've learned anything from what's happened is I really want other children to feel that our house is a very warm, friendly place to come ... everything that's happened has made me look at how I was parented, and things that I didn't like ... with my family that's what I want to change and be different. (Isabelle, 2-year-old child died, one surviving child)

A final impact on interpersonal relationships which virtually all of the parents discussed was the *powerful support* they received after the death of their child. As previously noted, although parents experienced distancing and rejection in some relationships, there were those who remained present and supportive in profound, meaningful, and nurturing ways. In a very real sense, this social contact was life sustaining. Mothers referred to it thus:

> I don't think we would have survived without the friends that we had ... without those people there, doing stuff for us and being there for us, I think we would have been, I don't know where we would have been to be honest with you. (Anna, 1-year-old child died, two surviving children)

> My family were just pretty much there. They were there because somebody needed to be there for [surviving child] ... we had a lot of support from the people in the neighbourhood ... you felt that everybody was there to

comfort you, everybody was there to make things okay. They were doing their best to make things okay. (Becky, 4-year-old child died, two surviving children)

I have very good friends. I have a good friend that has supported me through all of this and we've talked about [deceased child] 24-7 ... we were very fortunate, we had a community that went behind us. It was powerful. (Carol, 20-year-old child died, four surviving children)

We had so much support, I don't know how we would have done it otherwise. (Diane, 4-year-old child died, three surviving children)

In echoing these sentiments, fathers also acknowledged the comfort of human contact:

We had a lot of support, a very good family, [mother-in-law] spent weeks and weeks and weeks, my parents came up, we had a lot of other family, we had a lot of friends, so we had a good support network. So in the early weeks I can't even remember cooking a meal, or even thinking about cooking a meal ... They were all very supportive of us and helped us tremendously ... Everyone was just so supportive to us. (Jake, 4-year-old child died, three surviving children)

Tons, tons [of support] neighbors and friends were outstanding ... We constantly had, somebody was always there, whether it was our neighbours or one of our family members, or the minister coming over ... the kids in the neighborhood were really good, they were coming over and seeing [surviving child]. (Frank, 12-year-old child died, one surviving child)

The significance of social support, whether in the form of empathic listening or an open acknowledgment of a parent's anguish and forlornness, has also been reported by Rosenblatt (2000a). In addition, Riley, LaMontagne, Hepworth, and Murphy (2007), in a study of 35 bereaved mothers, found that the perception of adequate social support was strongly correlated with the perception of personal growth, including positive changes in self and improved relationships with others. Finally, bereaved parents who expressed a "balanced integration of grief reactions," i.e., grief responses (intense pain, sadness, crying, pining) balanced by an optimistic outlook about life and a sense of personal growth from the loss, reported meaningful social support from family and friends (Barrera et al., 2007, p. 151). In contrast, those parents who were "overwhelmed" by their grief (and who also reported symptoms of depression) felt abandoned, alone, and isolated as they struggled to cope with the death of their child (Barrera et al., 2007).

☐ Spirituality and Religion

Whereas none of the bereaved mothers made reference to spirituality and religion, fathers consistently introduced these topics if not during the interview itself then at the conclusion when invited to introduce any issue that had not been discussed. Religion was distinguished from spirituality in this analysis. Religion was discussed in terms of activities and ideas associated with an established or organized system of faith. Spirituality spoke more to an individual incorporeal or immaterial quality or influence that was not tied to any one system of faith. From the analysis, it was clear that although many questioned religion and declared a reduction in their commitment to a specific system of faith, all spoke of increased spirituality since the death of their child. These questions often took the form of "why?"

> Maybe we're just intended to have one child and focus all our resources on her. So, who knows? I'll ask him when I get there ... you have to say well, in the big plan in life, well, why was he recalled? ... you look for why? How come me? What did I do wrong? What could I have done different? ... And I had a hard time with the church cause you know, well if God is so benevolent, why is he taking children? So that really pushes your faith. I was really never a strong believer. (Elliot, 10-year-old child died, one surviving child)

> I struggle on matters of faith about why was he toyed with? ... And this all feeds on the notion of why was he, you know, why wasn't he just left to fight the battles he was born with, and I've had some success in not sort of continually dwelling on this question, but the question remains unanswered ... I sit here and I go, you know, the odds of those two things happening are about, you know, they're one in billions, there haven't been enough people born in North America to sort out what the likelihood of those two events happening in one individual, so I say, I struggle with matters of faith ... did God simply decide he was going to pick on this kid? (Harris, 2-year-old child died, one surviving child)

For fathers, themes of struggle, crisis, and betrayal of faith or religion emerged with the death of their child. A relatively common experience among bereaved parents (Rosenblatt, 2000a), this shatter of religious beliefs led to Picking Up the Pieces of their spiritual selves. These unique, individual conceptions, strong and comforting, were born of their devastation and reflected new ways of appreciating the world, reconnecting with their deceased children, and living with profound and penetrating loss.

> I'm a believer if there is, because of being trained in physics and that, energy can neither be created or destroyed, it goes somewhere. I'm more of a believer that way that people can, because it's like two dimensional, we're in the third dimension. People in the fourth dimension can see the third dimension, you can see backwards but you can't see forward. And life, you just, as you die, and you go through a number of series of planes, so. But that's my sense of what's happened, so that he [deceased son] can see what's going on, but I can't see him ... I'm a firm believer in he's here anyhow. He's around us somewhere. (Elliot, 10-year-old child died, one surviving child)

> I don't know what your spirituality is, but, we've had some signs. We've had some really neat things happen over the last two years and we've had a couple lately that have been very unique ... It's neat to know ... I've always been a sceptic and I feel that I was always sceptical and my own experiences have led me to start believing a little different. (Frank, 12-year-old child died, one surviving child)

> I'm not an irreligious person. I probably spend more time thinking about matters of faith than most people. It's just that I'm thinking about it in a way that's perhaps a little more, "Right, get down here, I have a bone to pick with you." And yet, without any effort to sustain it, and possibly an intellectual process that argues against it, I still find that I have an expectation, I wouldn't call it a belief because it's not something I spend any time trying to put anything, any substance to. I have an expectation that I will be with [deceased child] again. (Harris, 2-year-old child died, one surviving child)

From the words of these fathers, the death of their children may have shattered a religious faith, or called into question that which had been taken for granted. However, they have since engaged in a process of regenerating their spiritual selves, informed by their loss, in a manner that now affords them a more intimate, and perhaps more satisfying, sense of spirituality.

This was an area where mothers and fathers differed. As previously noted, fathers universally questioned religion and reported a heightened sense of individual spirituality, while none of the mothers mentioned this topic. Spirituality or religion was not specifically queried in any of the interviews, but all of the fathers spontaneously introduced this topic. This consistency is intriguing, as is the contrast with the mothers who did not mention it. This was a surprising finding as there is evidence to show that issues of spirituality and religion are important to both bereaved mothers and fathers, although the impact of these factors on coping with grief remains ambiguous (Stroebe, 2004). For example, there is research to suggest a positive relationship between religion and bereavement outcome (e.g., Bohannon, 1991; Sherkat & Reed, 1992; Walsh, King, Jones, Tookman, & Blizard, 2002), no relationship between these two variables (e.g., Anderson, Marwitt, Vandenberg, & Chibnall, 2005; Higgins, 2002), or a worse outcome for those identified as religious (e.g., Wijngaards-De Meij et al., 2005).

As we considered the discrepancy between mothers and fathers regarding religion and spirituality in our study, a number of possible explanations came to mind. First, it is possible that the mothers did not experience a spiritual crisis and, therefore, had no reason to introduce the topic. This possibility is, however, strictly a conjecture. Second, it is also possible that the majority of the mothers focussed on the details of day-to-day parenting (because they were the primary caregivers), leaving little time left to discuss other issues such as spirituality or religion. Again, this is speculative as there was no evidence that mothers felt they had exhausted their interview time. At the conclusion of each interview participants were asked if there was anything further they wished to discuss. Some mothers added information while others did not, but none mentioned spirituality or religion. Conversely, many of the fathers' additions were elaborations on this topic.

There appears to be a substantive difference between mothers and fathers on this issue and research corroborates it. For example, Lohan and Murphy (2002), in a study of parents' perceptions of adolescent grief responses after the death of a sibling, found that bereaved fathers listed spiritual issues as salient, while mothers did not. Schwab (1990) reported that mothers often turned to reading and writing on loss and grief, whereas bereaved fathers endeavoured to help others who were bereaved, attempted to keep busy, and sought solace in religion. Likewise, it has been noted that men tend to conceptualize their loss in more broad religious or philosophical explanations of life or fate than do women (Cook, 1988; Das, 1993). The reexamination of spiritual and religious beliefs may be an important component in the cognitive quest for meaning and the reclamation of a sense of control in an otherwise incomprehensible and uncontrollable event (Doka, 2002; Matthews & Marwit, 2006; Sherkat & Reed, 1992); it is also consistent with an instrumental pattern of grieving

(Martin & Doka, 2000). The saliency of spiritual and religious issues for the fathers in this study corroborates previous research and appears to unearth yet another nuance in the grief process of men and women.

Picking Up the Pieces
Regeneration of Family

Although attempts at understanding bereavement reactions overwhelmingly reflect an individual and intrapersonal perspective, Picking Up the Pieces was also evidenced at the family level as the impact of the child's death reverberated through each individual member and, ultimately, the family collectively. The family is a unit defined by the presence of each member; the death of a child, therefore, heralds the loss of the family as it was. How a member grapples with the shatter and the aftermath of a child's death is mirrored by the family's struggle with this painful reality. A number of factors are influential in determining a family's response including the extent of emotional sharing and self-disclosure, the cognitive appraisal of the event and the collective struggle with meaning, the extent of family cohesion, the degree of family conflict, and the family's coping skills (adaptive or maladaptive). The parents in this study discussed changes and acts of regeneration in relationships within the family after the death. These changes occurred in two main areas: the ongoing relationships with surviving members of the family and the continuing or ongoing relationship with the deceased child.

☐ Family Relationships

The majority of the parents in this study thoughtfully reflected on an increased closeness that resulted from coping with the death. Although individually buffeted by numerous and onerous stressors (e.g., the collapse of one's assumptive world, physical and emotional depletion, legal procedures, spousal tensions) and ongoing individual/family differences (e.g., spousal dissimilarities in grieving, financial pressures), there was a feeling of emerging family cohesion and increased sensitivity to one another. Born of the pain of their communal loss and still fragile, this unexpected but comforting development was a source of strength to the parents.

> It has made me closer to them and it will make me closer to them forever ... that bond will be there because of [son's] death. I think it's very different. (Anna, 1-year-old child died, two surviving children)

> I think we're probably more sensitive of each other's feelings than we would have been if we hadn't gone through that experience ... I think because of what's happened we appreciate [surviving child] more than what probably we would have with two, and not that you don't appreciate every child, every child is a lot different but I think that bond with him is stronger ... I think there's a real bond there now between all of us. We've been through this together. (Isabelle, 2-year-old child died, one surviving child)

> I think we gained strength from one another ... It certainly brought [wife] and I very close ... she's great. She's been a lot of strength for me and I for her. (Jake, 4-year-old child died, three surviving children)

This increased closeness may be a function of time-since-death as parents were at least 3 years post-loss. There was now a strong and enduring bond resulting from continuing to go through this devastating experience together. Detmer and Lamberti (1991) noted that this move toward togetherness in a grieving family relieves anxiety, but cautioned that it may become problematic if there are dramatically different grieving styles among family members.

Although the general sense from most parents was that family relationships had deepened and become closer because of the anguish they were enduring, this was not the only comment on regenerating the family relationships. As is clear in the themes that follow, the family system had been dealt a fatal blow and the regeneration in the face of such devastation was a complicated, wrenching process. We recognize, too, that the surviving children may not share this perspective as they witness their parents' individual and collective emotional turmoil; the resolution of this issue awaits further research into the children's perceptions of family closeness following the death of a child.

Quiet Home

Immediately following the child's death, parents noted a dramatic change in atmosphere—their homes became "quiet."

> You know, just sort of the rough housing play that happens? You know, you're making dinner and the kids are doing something. Now it's one of us who is doing something with him a lot of times as opposed to just going off and playing, or he's doing something on his own. Which again, is not a bad thing to learn how to entertain yourself, but it is just a different dynamic than a lot of families. (Isabelle, 2-year-old child died, one surviving child)

> We were getting used to the dynamics in the family ... the house is not noisy. The house is very quiet. There's not an interaction going on between kids. (Diane, 4-year-old child died, three surviving children)

> The house was very, very, quiet ... it was really, really quiet. (Becky, 4-year-old child died, two surviving children)

> It's not the same, it's quiet. (Gary, 16-year-old child died, two surviving children)

> That was the biggest change. And it still is. It is a quiet house. Very quiet. (Frank, 12-year-old child died, one surviving child)

For families with one surviving child, the source of this "quiet" was the sudden and dramatic termination of sibling banter. Interestingly, parents with more than one surviving child also commented on their now quiet home. It appears that death had hushed the din of family life, irrespective of the number of surviving members.

Routines

With the reluctant recognition of the reality of their child's death, parents gradually realized the pervasive and penetrating impact of this unspeakable tragedy—it permeated every aspect of family relationships and functioning. One major area of accommodation was in family routines. Parents found they could no longer engage in many of the traditions and habitual patterns of their daily life, old behaviors didn't seem to work any more. They were constantly confronted with the pain of absence and, in response, changed aspects of the family's routines and traditions to reclaim a level of family functioning. It was just too painful to engage in everyday tasks the same way, so parents modified these routines in an effort to survive the devastation. Change can be difficult, even at the best of times; now, in the midst of the pain and pandemonium that had become their lives, parents were forced to alter their routines to accommodate the devastation. The fathers described this transition as follows:

> I guess the biggest impact no matter what was, you know, Christmas times, birthdays, or whatever, when we were having a group sitting. There was like, one chair always missing, because it was like Christmas dinner we were always wanting to leave a setting for him. (Elliot, 10-year-old child died, one surviving child)

> We changed quite a bit. I mean we'd still eat. We ordered in quite a bit for a while. Instead of eating at the kitchen table, we started eating in the den, we were watching TV and stuff. The routines changed quite a bit. (Frank, 12-year-old child died, one surviving child)

> I think we consciously just tried to carry on doing a lot of things that we had done before but in a different way. You know, I think we realized very early on that you can't duplicate what we had, so we started our own routines that were different. (Jake, 4-year-old child died, three surviving children)

The mothers described a similar experience and the need to reconstruct or alter preexisting family routines and practices.

> This is how it is and we're not going to get back to normal. We might as well quit trying to be like other families because we're not. We were getting used to the dynamics in the family. You're starting to get into a new routine. We started doing things differently, because we couldn't do them the same because the same would be with [deceased son] so we changed

routines a little ... We couldn't keep doing those same things because we needed him to make it work. (Diane, 4-year-old child died, three surviving children)

When you lose the youngest, the fun things are not as much fun anymore because the little one is not there anymore to enjoy it. So we used to go camping and we used to go to Ontario Place and Wonderland and all these types of things and you know, a year after the accident we did it, but it wasn't the same. And it wasn't the same for the kids either, even though they enjoyed it, it wasn't the same. And then we kind of stopped doing it. (Becky, 4-year-old child died, two surviving children)

My husband's birthday was [shortly after the death] and I remember saying to him, "We have to have our family over because that's what we do and we have to make it normal for the girls." It was a total ruin. We should never have. And so consequently we've stopped that, they thought I was just going to continue these nice big celebrations for their benefit so that the family could get together. Well, I realized I couldn't do it anymore. (Anna, 1-year-old child died, two surviving children)

The death of a child, often traumatic and sudden (regardless of the forewarning), frequently ruptures the family's established routines and activities. At a time when it is most needed, the comfort and stability of family routines and structure are in disarray (Shapiro, 1994). As Jordan, Kraus, and Ware (1993) have noted, altering the day-to-day life and ongoing functions of a family threatens its well-being, stability, and cohesiveness. For example, as we have illustrated, the reliability and consistency of caregiving behaviors can be changed or abandoned, there may be increased marital conflict and a diminution of supportive and mutual pleasure-giving activities, and families may face financial hardship as a result of the cost of medical services, funeral expenditures, or the fiscal consequences of extended work absence. Family income, or the lack thereof, often determines which routines and activities are feasible, whether vacations will be realized, which children's sports teams will be joined, and when a parent decides to return to work. Shapiro (1994) asserted that a family's first priority after a death is to reestablish the stable family conditions required to support day-to-day functioning. This priority was perspicuous in the early parental strategy of rescripting routines and patterns of behavior, which, in turn, contributed to the regeneration and continuation of the family system.

Roles

Parents soon realized that not only were there significant changes in routines as they Picked Up the Pieces of their family relationships, there were also significant changes in roles. The death of a family member taxes the resources of the surviving members and alters their ability to fulfil their usual roles (Jordan, Kraus, & Ware, 1993). The roles of family members and the changes that occurred after the death have been conceptualized through family systems theory. From this perspective, the family is composed of a set of intimately connected individuals whose relationships with each other are mutually influential in that the action of any one member affects all of the others and vice versa, occurring in a context of past, present, and future (Nadeau, 1998; Shapiro, 1994). When a family member dies, relationships and roles change and boundaries shift in response to the loss and the family's role characteristics (rigidity or flexibility) are influential in determining adjustment (Lamberti & Detmer, 1993).

Roles within a family system are the expectations and characteristics of given family positions, such as parent or child (Broderick & Smith, 1979). Boundaries distinguish the elements belonging to the system from those external to it and serve to delineate subsystems within the family, e.g., the parent or the child subsystem (Broderick & Smith, 1979). The death of a child sets off significant family reorganization of roles and boundaries. These changing roles occurred at all levels of relationships within the family, between mothers and fathers and between parents and children. The change in roles between mothers and fathers saw the fathers *expanding* their roles or fulfilling more tasks within the family. The majority felt they were now assuming more family responsibilities since their child's death and they addressed the varying degrees to which this occurred.

> But she [wife] had her off days where I'd have to look after [surviving child] and do things ... I think it was better for her, because at least there was some sanity and she knew that she could let go and go there if she had to. Somebody was there. She knew she could rely on me, that a least, somebody's not going to be, "could you look after [surviving child], could you make dinner, can you do this," okay, sure, don't worry about it, you just do what you have to do. I would say there were more times that I helped her than she helped me. Is that a man thing? I don't know ... Somebody had to be around to keep the rudder in, okay? There had to be somebody at the helm. (Elliot, 10-year-old child died, one surviving child)

She [wife] still maintained whatever work she would do. I had to be proud of her ... I have to give my wife a lot of credit, she still got out of bed, so she still functioned, but she didn't function, you know what I mean? Like going through the motions ... So, you have to step up to the plate and do whatever it takes to help out and not feel you're doing more than the other, you just have to do it. Maybe a little bit [assumed more roles] ... I went right back to work, I mean, I'm not saying I'm proud that I had to go back or take the man role, like some people say, but I had to do it because otherwise what are we going to do? Lose everything? So I made the sacrifice to go back to work because she couldn't work, and I mean we needed an income to try to maintain the household. (Gary, 16-year-old child died, two surviving children)

In a way I did pick up doing work. I got involved, I started cooking more. I always liked to cook, but, you know. I started to get involved in doing things, you know, going to the market, make up some dinners or brunches or whatever, I did more of that and I think [wife] appreciated that. And the change is something we still do now ... ["Do you feel that you were able to give into your grief or was there a feeling that you had to keep things together?"] Yeah. That's interesting you say that, because I was thinking quite a bit about that in January. My wife needed a lot of help so I grieved when I could. Some days I've wondered if I've grieved enough—but I did. I've done a lot. I had my time alone, but, I did put a lot of effort into my wife and my son ... It had to be done. I wouldn't say it was hard. The fact of life is that it still, everything had to go on. I mean it was a horrible, horrible thing, but, we still have to live and we still have to raise [surviving child] and we still have to go to work and still have to pay our bills. (Frank, 12-year-old child died, one surviving child)

I don't think [wife] ever suffered sort of an inability to function or a death of motivation or anything ... I didn't ever feel as if this, but for me, this household was going to come unglued and I didn't ever feel as if I simply must hold myself together for the good of others. I think we all sort of were holding each other together in a fairly gentle way. I think the only place that would have come about is in not being able to indulge my urge to just walk out of the work environment. (Harris, 2-year-old child died, one surviving child)

Where fathers reflected on an expansion of family roles and responsibilities, two of the five mothers mentioned *relinquishing* roles within the family. One bereaved mother renounced many of her roles and needed to rely heavily on her husband, at least during the initial weeks/months following the child's death. The second parent abandoned aspects of her roles within the family as they related to her husband; she was no longer able to meet all of his needs.

> My husband was good ... He pretty much carried us through ... He was the one who had to do it all. I wasn't doing anything ... I started to realize, he hasn't grieved. I think I started to realize that I had been selfish. (Anna, 1-year-old child died, two surviving children)

> I had sort of been his [husband] caretaker in a sense and he also needed to take on some responsibility himself. So then he finally had to because I backed off completely. (Carol, 20-year-old child died, four surviving children)

In keeping with the differences and similarities in the grieving processes of mothers and fathers, and in contrast to the pre-death family dynamics, the expansion of fathers' roles within the family was a consistent reference—they had to remain in control and assume fiscal and financial responsibility for the family. Even in those families where significant role changes were not evident, fathers reported a sense of urgency in returning to work, whether they wanted to or not. In comparison to bereaved mothers who returned to work 4 to 11 months following their child's death, fathers were back on the job within 2 to 6 weeks. Detmer and Lamberti (1991) commented that it was not uncommon for bereaved husbands to meet their responsibilities within the family and, in addition, to care for their wives and assume their roles as well. Our data show a clear difference on this dimension between bereaved mothers and fathers with the latter acquiring an overall heightened sense of responsibility. Detmer and Lamberti (1991) felt the spouse who assumed additional responsibility was the one most vulnerable to difficulty or dysfunction with the passage of time.

Little attention has been paid in the literature to the financial repercussions faced by bereaved parents; however, as we have shown, they are oftentimes away from the work environment and, consequently, may experience an appreciable reduction or interruption of earnings. Where the resumption of work is motivated by financial necessity (and not a commitment to the employer or the role of breadwinner) bereaved parents may feel they have returned too soon, that their profound sense of loss, uncontrollable crying, problems with focus and concentration, and lack of motivation make full-time employment improbable—at least for the immediate future. The lack of financial resources also determines whether individuals and families seek psychological intervention for the myriad issues and problems confronting them (Corden, Sainsbury, &

Sloper, 2002). Addressing financial issues in therapy is a worthy pursuit as financial difficulty, often shrouded in secrecy and shame, can further impair family functioning (Walsh & McGoldrick, 2004).

Although it appears that many bereaved fathers felt burdened by added roles and pressures, it is important to note the previously discussed relationship between gender and grief expressivity and cultural prescriptions for mourning. Men often adopt a more problem-solving, instrumental grieving pattern than do women (Martin & Doka, 2000). As Dean (2002), a bereaved mother, succinctly stated, "He wants to *do*, I want to *be*" (p. 80). It is possible that although fathers described feeling burdened by the expanded roles, they may also have sought out these additional responsibilities in an attempt to problem-solve and *do* something to manage their grief. Helmrath and Steinitz (1978) found that fathers involved themselves more actively in work, supported their wives, and generally expanded their role identities in an effort to fill the void left by the loss of the parental role.

Although it has been reported that bereaved fathers expressed resentment at feeling the pressure to be strong for the family, they also, without complaint, focussed on the visible distress of their wives and frequently embraced the role of the strong, dependable male (Cordell & Thomas, 1990; Schwab, 1996). A father's sense of heightened responsibility and role expansion must be carefully considered within the cultural context of male socialization in which the expected behavior of a man is consistent with one who is a strong, reliable, problem-solver. One must also be sensitive to a father's inability to fully articulate and express his grief due to his overwhelming sense of family responsibility, his fear of destabilization or dysfunction, or lack of available social support. It is also essential to assess the degree to which these additional roles are embraced by bereaved fathers in an attempt distract from or actively *do* something with their devastating grief.

The second manner in which roles changed was between parents and children. In this case it was almost a role reversal or a blurring of the boundaries between parent and child. This was a common theme for both parents with fathers noticing:

> The relationship [with surviving child] is very loving and very much at ease. But, you know, sometimes I wish that he used us a little bit more as a place of comfort. I'm not sure why that isn't true. I think certainly a possibility [that the surviving child is trying to protect parents] and I think there's likelihood that that's some part of it. (Harris, 2-year-old child died, one surviving child)

Whereas at home, maybe there's a sense that she [surviving child] doesn't want to upset mom and dad. She tries to protect us, which means not saying anything ... she didn't want to see us upset. (Jake, 4-year-old child died, three surviving children)

The mothers noticed similar changes in the roles of their surviving children in the family relationships.

Sometimes I think [surviving child] is too cautious about what he does because he knows he doesn't want to worry us ... I think that he has become protective of us in the sense that he wants to share things with us, but also when he's having a particularly bad day, he's concerned and he'll ask me if I'm okay after we've talked about it. (Isabelle, 2-year-old child died, one surviving child)

She [surviving child] would worry if daddy and I weren't home at a certain time, so, I'd have to remember not to get too sidetracked, and I'd have to be a lot more attentive to her worries and concerns ... And she would treat us a little differently and I think she didn't want to say anything to maybe set us off ... She was very much [taking on some of the parenting roles], with the worrying and protection. (Diane, 4-year-old child died, three surviving children)

He's [surviving child] in a way protective of us. He's turned it around where if we're not home and we say we're going to be home, he'll say, "Where were you? You told me you were going to be home" ... She's [surviving child] become the nurturer. She's become the protective person. (Becky, 4-year-old child died, two surviving children)

They [surviving children] parented me. They took care of me. They definitely took care of me ... Right now they're still worried about me. They kind of sometimes, they take better care of me, in their little ways. (Anna, 1-year-old child died, two surviving children)

Witnessing the devastation and unavailability of their parents is disconcerting and, with the revelation of parental vulnerability and powerlessness, a child's anxiety is heightened. With the resources of the family threatened and members struggling to fulfill their customary roles, the need for family stability and predictability is acute. From the child's perspective, becoming the emotional and physical caretaker of parents contributes in some measure to the stability of the parent, encourages the ongoing functioning of the family and, consequently, the child's survival and development (Jordan, Kraus, & Ware, 1993; Shapiro, 1994). If mom and dad *appear* emotionally stable, the child will be reluctant to upset that stability, as fleeting as it may be, by saying or doing anything that might trigger parental distress. For the sake of maintaining parental/family stability, however, the child may pay a steep psychological price in the form of the inhibition of his/her own grief response (Lattanzi-Licht, 1996; Rando, 1986a). For therapists working with bereaved families, an ongoing assessment of role reversal and the potential for blurred boundaries between children and parents is critical. Parents can come to rely too heavily on the child for support and caretaking, placing an additional burden on the bereaved sibling. Moreover, the child's expression of grief may be inhibited and altered in an effort to stabilize the family, at the cost of the child's own individual adjustment to the loss.

The final manner in which family dynamics shifted involved surviving siblings assuming the deceased's roles and/or personality characteristics. Consider:

> I don't want him to think he's filling the shoes of his brother. And sometimes I think he is. I think trying to fill some of the voids for his mother and myself. Like I think he says, "Well, I know [deceased child] used to do this stuff, maybe I'll do that for mom and dad." He's doing that trying to make everybody feel good ... He'll try to fill some of the roles that his brother used to. (Frank, 12-year-old child died, one surviving child)

> So, he [now youngest child] kind of went back to being the one that needed all of our time and patience and kind of, not a baby, but we did everything for him and we really did protect him from a lot ... [Oldest child] feels that we spoil him and that he's treated like a little baby. And we probably do. (Becky, 4-year-old child died, two surviving children)

> My daughter took on a lot of his [deceased child] characteristics initially ... Our daughter has decided that she wants to go to [school that deceased child attended]. I really do think it's because of him she's doing it. (Carol, 20-year-old child died, four surviving children)

With a death in the family, the remaining family members may attempt to redistribute the roles of the deceased by appointing (or self-appointing) a member to fulfill the now abandoned functions. During this time of role shifting and realignment, it is the surviving siblings who are most vulnerable to assuming the deceased's roles, a phenomenon with significant therapeutic implications. Frequently, the roles of the deceased child will be shared among surviving siblings with no ill effects, just as some of the roles will be forever lost. A practitioner working with a bereaved family must monitor the degree to which role rigidity is present within the family system as Lamberti and Detmer (1993) found that this characterizes less functional families. Family sessions can assist in exploring the roles played by the deceased child and how the family is redistributing these functions or adjusting to their absence (Walsh & McGoldrick, 2004). The key component in assessing this dynamic is noting the degree to which surviving siblings maintain their own identity and individual boundaries despite assuming new roles and responsibilities (Lamberti & Detmer, 1993; Rando, 1986a). Moreover, in conducting this assessment of role redistribution, the practitioner is cautioned against overpathologizing evidence of a sibling's adopting roles or characteristics of the deceased. As we will explore in the next section, assuming aspects of a sibling's role or personality has the potential to be powerfully life-affirming and enhancing. Skilled assessment is required to separate evidence of oppressive role rigidity from evidence of legacy.

It is clear that the family relationships were dramatically altered—from the atmosphere in the home to family routines and individual roles, the impact of the child's death was insidious. The family had to learn to live with the loss and incorporate it into their daily existence in a way that facilitated survival. This incorporation leads to the second main category within the family—the relationship with the deceased child.

☐ Relationship with the Deceased Child

Analysis of the interviews revealed the parental imperative to integrate the deceased child's life and death into the family narrative. Each child was an essential element of his or her family; therefore, Picking Up the Pieces of the family required regenerating the relationship with the deceased child in new terms. It is important to recognize that, although the physical presence of the child had been severed, the relationship continued. Parents repeatedly described how they struggled to maintain a creative and meaningful connection with their children.

Keeping the Child Present

Especially for bereaved mothers, keeping the deceased child present in the family was a prominent theme. They spoke of implementing various strategies to maintain an ongoing connection or bond with their child to ensure that they are not forgotten and that they remain a part of family functioning.

> I need my girls to know that [deceased child] is important and that their brother can be talked about ... He's very much a part of us ... and she'll [surviving daughter] say, "We'll I'm gonna buy, daddy's birthday is coming up first and I'll buy daddy this, and then [deceased child]'s birthday is coming and I'll be able to have this much money to buy for him." So it's already ingrained ... I still need to talk about [deceased child]. I have to have him here. You have to. Because the longer you don't talk about him, the more you forget. (Anna, 1-year-old child died, two surviving children)

> We still have our little one's room, even though we moved, we set up the room exactly the way it was in the old house and we still have all her toys and her furniture and her clothes and things ... we still buy things for special days or whatever. (Becky, 4-year-old child died, two surviving children)

> And [sibling born after child died] is very aware that her brother died. His picture is everywhere around the house and she's very sensitive, and she knows about her brother when we go to the cemetery, you know ... we did different things, we incorporated him into it. He gives her [surviving child] a gift still. It's always something to do with angels ... That's something as a parent I've chosen to do. Because I always say, "I picked it out but it's because, for some reason I picked it out because it's what he would have liked to have given you." And so, he does it with his little sisters. And the girls get him a little something, whether it's to go on his shelf, I mean, I have a shelf under his picture and it's filled with all kinds of bits and pieces that the girls think he would like or things he actually had ... I'm trying to parent her, her relationship with her brother in a way that she can still interact with him. Still have knowledge about him, feel very comfortable doing it and expressing it. (Diane, 4-year-old child died, three surviving children)

Two of the fathers also mentioned the ways in which they were keeping the child present within the family.

> Absolutely a part of the family. Oh yeah. We have a, every Christmas, Easter, Thanksgiving, and things like that, whenever we have a family function where family members are over, we have a candle, an angel candle, we say grace and we always light it in memory of him. To be with us for those special occasions. (Frank, 12-year-old child died, one surviving child)

Because he's not physically here doesn't mean he's no longer with us. And I think that's one thing that we got across to [surviving child] very early. He was always there and we'd talk about him and still do. (Jake, 4-year-old child died, three surviving children)

Ongoing Connection

Whereas "keeping the child present" addressed the outward activities and rituals of explicitly acknowledging the deceased child's continuing presence in the family, the ongoing connection spoke to the individual, personal relationship that parents continued to have with their deceased children. The fathers described it as follows:

He's with me all the time ... he's here ... he's all around me ... he's still here [puts hand over heart]. But, do I have to be sad about it? No. I've made my peace with that. (Elliot, 10-year-old child died, one surviving child)

I think about him even when I go home at night, we've got a tree planted at the school, we did a memorial service there, we planted a tree and a rock and we had a plaque made up there. I go by and I say goodnight when I'm on my way home. (Gary, 16-year-old child died, two surviving children)

The mothers explained their ongoing relationships with their deceased children in the following excerpts:

I'll always have my baby, because he'll never grow up. I'll always have him. He'll always be my baby, just not one that I can hold. (Anna, 1-year-old child died, two surviving children)

I keep a journal for her and I write little letters to her and stuff ... she's not gone anywhere because she's such a big part of my life that she hasn't gone anywhere. It's just that I'm not seeing her grow up. (Becky, 4-year-old child died, two surviving children)

He's with me all the time. He's a part of me. (Carol, 20-year-old child died, four surviving children)

I've learned to be with him. It's just on a totally different level. It's taken me six years, but, I've learned to get there. I still need my time. I need that time

> with him. Whether it's sitting quietly you know, just reflecting. Looking out in the garden, I've got an amazing garden, and I've got lots of things there for him, angels and things. Just looking out there quietly, just for a few minutes, just to be with him. He's always with me. Always ... The grief could push him away, so I felt that I really, doing the things that are really about him, or about my life changing, and you know, allowing myself to love my girls without guilt. And making myself laugh, that is my gift from my son and I feel him very strongly in those moments. It's more of a connection to him. (Diane, 4-year-old child died, three surviving children)

The ongoing parental connection with their deceased children was intimate, individual, and enduring. Clearly the connection of a parent to a child does not die. Such a love cannot be vanquished by death—it remains, deep and essential, in defiance of the devastation. (An example of this is "bereavement math," i.e., a family consisting of two parents and three children will remain a family of five—even after the death of one of the children.)

Legacy

Legacy, that which is changed or altered because the child has lived, also stands in defiance of death. It is the reverberation of a life lived, a life that affects others, and continues to do so even after death. In a sense, the legacy of the child existed in every category under Picking Up the Pieces, for the regeneration of a parent's life was informed by the loss at all times and, therefore, all that eventuated was related to the legacy of the child. For our purpose, however, we wish to narrow the definition somewhat and present specific examples of what mothers and fathers shared about the legacy of their children.

> We did donate quite a few of his organs. There's a boy going to the University of Toronto that has his liver. There's a boy and a girl that each got a kidney. His eyes were used. Two different people have sight, in one eye each now. Heart valves were used. So. I mean, if, I guess the word fulfilling isn't proper but it was, you know. It didn't give us the feeling of a total waste of life. He was very athletic. He was big and he was strong, and at least some people can benefit from what he had to offer. (Frank, 12-year-old child died, one surviving child)

> When my son died, we started a sports achievement award which each year the coach submits some names to us and we pick the name we feel

best suits his [deceased son's] character, achievements, and personality. (Gary, 16-year-old child died, two surviving children)

We started working with the government to try and get standards changed ... We pushed hard for two years or so to get standards changed and I think we had a lot of positive things come from it ... We felt that we didn't want it to happen to another child, if we could do something to prevent another child from dying, then we would and that's what we started off with. And I think we certainly got a lot of things changed as a result of it. (Jake, 4-year-old child died, three surviving children)

He left a beautiful legacy ... He was very much a part of the school ... He had been the first to receive the Principal's Award, which is a humanitarian award ... I did leave a copy of the newsletter [regarding signs and symptoms of illness that killed her son] there [at the school], for them to, first to give to the guidance counsellor and then to just have in the teachers' lounge. Because I want to educate teachers too. If they see things like that, what to do, you know, because it's through education that they'll know about it. (Carol, 20-year-old child died, four surviving children)

We started a fund in his name to provide care for families ... It's a very positive thing and a good thing to feel proud of ... you have families that are depending on you ... how much of a difference it can make to quality of life for [these families who receive the fund]. (Isabelle, 2-year-old child died, one surviving child)

These excerpts address the external or public legacy of each child's life. The following fathers also noted an internal or personal legacy of their child by highlighting the ways in which they are different now, a difference they directly attributed to their child's life.

The power of his example was so immediate to me at those times, I can remember thinking, in the early days after he died, nothing's going to scare me now. And you know, consequently virtually anything is easy ... feeling some sense of determination on behalf of him. (Harris, 2-year-old child died, one surviving child)

We had him for almost four years and he taught us a lot ... He brought so much joy to our life and we wanted to share that joy of him, there's all these good things that this little boy brought to us and how much we learned from him. We gained strength from him. I think he gave us a lot of strength to keep going. (Jake, 4-year-old child died, three surviving children)

I get motivated through him ... to dig down deep. If he could do it, I can do it. (Gary, 16-year-old child died, two surviving children)

As is clear in the words of these parents, their deceased children became inspiring examples and they integrated aspects of their child's personality into their own. These parental responses are very similar to the notion of "legacy" proposed by Fleming and Robinson (1991). Within this context, grief is defined as the transition from losing what you have to having what you have lost. What is lost is the physical relationship with the child, what one ultimately retains is the child's legacy. Fleming and Robinson suggest that legacy is gleaned from probing the meaning of the child's life and grappling with such questions as: "What lessons in living has my child taught me?" "What lessons about loving have I learned?" and "How am I different for knowing and loving my child?" Legacy is not simply a collection of memories, but rather an ongoing attachment that is evidenced in the ways in which the bereaved person is transformed because of knowing and loving the deceased. With the internalization of their child's legacy parents are irrevocably changed, their self-identity is immutably altered, and what is lost is, in some measure, reclaimed and cherished.

Another poignant example of the concept of legacy was provided to one of the authors by Lucy subsequent to the death of her 4-year-old son. Thomas perished, along with his best friend Natalia (also four), when their van was struck by another vehicle whose operator failed to observe a stop sign. Juggling the emotional vicissitudes inherent in a civil suit and contemplating Thomas' legacy, Lucy reflected: "Your child now lives within you. Just as you would never let your child go where you have not gone, you go within. You get intimate with yourself, check out your values, the meaning and purpose of things ... you want your child to live in a warm and nurturing place, not one filled with anger, resentment, and revenge." In other words, as long as she entertained feelings of "anger, resentment, and revenge," Lucy could not appreciate Thomas' legacy as such toxic feelings were incompatible with how his short life was lived. The integration of characteristics of the child into the parents' self-identity is one aspect of the continuing bonds or ongoing attachment between parent and child and often occurs in the form of the parent deriving important life lessons based on the child's life, not solely his/her death.

A number of authors (e.g., Klass, Silverman & Nickman, 1996; Rubin, 1999) have commented on the existence of ongoing attachments or continuing bonds with deceased loved ones—and the parents in this study were no exception. Confronted with the stark reality of physical absence, and disappointed with the woeful deficiency of contemporary cultural practices to provide comfort and solace, bereaved parents used creatively tailored, meaningful rituals to preserve an emotional attachment to their children. This ongoing attachment is also evidenced in the internalization of the child's laudable values, attitudes, and personal qualities. Klass and Walter (2001) have elaborated on the existence and function of such "inner representations" of the deceased. They found that such internalizations serve as role models (e.g., as a parent commented above, "the power of his example"), offer situation-specific guidance (e.g., to be strong in the face of adversity), and clarify values (e.g., not to "sweat the small stuff" but rather live presently).

The evolution of the perspective that it can be normal and healthy to maintain connections with deceased loved ones is evident in the work of Worden who initially stressed the need to disengage emotionally and withdraw from the deceased person (Worden, 1982) and now asserts that the challenge facing the bereaved is to relocate, not relinquish, their relationship with the deceased (Worden, 2009). Indeed, there is a growing literature that offers suggestions on how to do so (e.g., Fleming & Belanger, 2001; Gudmundsdottir & Chesla, 2006; Imber-Black, 2004; Neimeyer, 1998; Rothman, 1997; Vickio, 1999).

The assertion that an ongoing attachment to the deceased is an integral part of successful adjustment to the death of a loved one has been criticized by Field (2008) for its unequivocal endorsement of attachment as invariably adaptive, its oversimplification of the relationship between continuing bonds and adjustment to loss, and its failure to differentiate maladaptive from adaptive continuing bonds. Consistent with Rando's (1993) seminal work on adaptation to bereavement, Field made the distinction between two distinct patterns of continuing bonds: those that focus on establishing *physical proximity* to the deceased and those whose goal is *psychological proximity*. Behaviors aimed at recovering the deceased (establishing physical proximity) include going to the deceased's school with the expectation of reunion or keeping a room exactly untouched (with the expectation of return). A succinct expression of this concept came from a bereaved parent in psychotherapy (with SF) who stated, "I knew my son was dead, I just didn't realize he wasn't coming back." Repeated and fruitless attempts to reestablish physical proximity leads to, "... a gradual revising of the working model of attachment to the deceased in order to accommodate the reality of the permanence of the physical separation. This revision process is contingent on the bereaved person's ability to endure the emotional pain of recognizing the irrevocability of the loss" (Field, 2008, p. 120). It is only with reluctance that the bereaved surrender their desire for physical proximity and *resign* themselves to the permanence of physical separation. We feel that the term "resignation," defined as the "uncomplaining endurance of a sorrow or difficulty" (*Oxford English Reference Dictionary*, 1996), captures this painful and loathsome reality more than the conventional term "acceptance."

Field (2008) emphasized that successful adaptation to bereavement demands relinquishing the hope of physical proximity; this, however, does not mean that survivors must surrender attachment to the deceased. Rather, it is through the deconstructing and reconstructing of the relationship with the deceased that one moves from "losing what you have" (physical proximity) to "having what you have lost" (psychological proximity) (Fleming & Robinson, 1991). Field hypothesized that the occurrence of attempts to establish physical proximity (e.g., the "excessive" use of the deceased's special possessions for comfort) may be common in the weeks and months following the death of a child and not indicative of pathological mourning; their presence much later in the mourning process, however, may represent maladaptive functioning and a failure to integrate the loss experience. Similarly, a continuing bond reflecting psychological proximity (e.g., the solace derived from comforting memories of the deceased, an appreciation of the child's "legacy") may reflect a more successful adaptation to the loss.

In a study of conjugal bereavement, preliminary support for this hypothesis was reported by Field, Nichols, Holen, and Horowitz (1999); however, these results were not replicated by Boelen, Stroebe, Schut, and Zijerveld (2006). Although there may be a connection between time-since-death and the nature of the ongoing attachment (physical proximity vs. psychological proximity), it is important to emphasize that this is not a passive process; it is not simply the time you have to use that's important but rather how you use the time you have (i.e., actively deconstructing and reconstructing the relationship with the deceased).

An essential component of Picking Up the Pieces of the family was the relocation and redefinition of the relationship with the deceased child. Undeniably the child remained an important member of the family as parents grappled with and painfully explored this connection. Ultimately, they succeeded in reconstructing a relationship not solely defined by unbearable pain—a relationship that encompassed the child's life, not only the death. Just as family relationships between surviving members were reevaluated and regenerated, so too was the family's relationship with the deceased child. This finding is consistent with a systemic understanding of family bereavement that values an ongoing relationship with the deceased as an appropriate and useful presence in a manner that supports the family's development (Horwitz, 1997; Shapiro, 1994). Our results provide further evidence consistent with the growing body of literature that documents how bereaved parents in particular find new ways to continue the relationship with their deceased child; they do not detach from the child but rather maintain a deep and continuing connection (Attig, 1996; Gudmundsdottir & Chesla, 2006; Rando, 1993; Rosenblatt, 2000a; Silverman & Klass, 1996).

☐ Family Characteristics

There are a number of variables that influence the manner in which a family accommodates and assimilates the death of a child, and it is incumbent upon practitioners to be aware of how these qualities might complicate a family's adjustment to loss and place its members at risk. It is equally important to recognize the characteristics fostering resilience and adaptation so that these may be supported and unaltered by needless intervention. Family communication, organization, connectedness, and meaning-making have consistently been shown to facilitate or impede individual or collective grief work.

Families with open, clear, ongoing communication are more likely to adapt to the death in a manner that preserves or enhances the overall functioning of the family. This capacity to communicate facilitates the unrestricted and honest expression of grief and respects, even encourages, individual differences (Jordan, Kraus, & Ware, 1993; Kissane & Lichtenthal, 2008; Rando, 1991; Vess, Moreland, & Schwebel, 1985–1986; Walsh & McGoldrick, 2004). Where communication is compromised, discussion of the death and the child can become taboo, family members may become alienated, and the potential for conflict is high (Jordan, Kraus, & Ware, 1993; Kissane & Lichtenthal, 2008).

Families in which the matrix of rules, roles, and boundaries are clearly defined, yet flexible, are likely to face fewer difficulties in integrating the loss and moving to more stable functioning (Imber-Black, 2004; Jordan, Kraus, & Ware, 1993; Vess, Moreland, & Schwebel, 1985-1986; Walsh & McGoldrick, 2004). This flexibility does not denote a lack of structure, however, as structure and appropriate boundaries provide sorely needed stability and continuity. If the family is too flexible, the result is chaos, disorganization, and floundering in the wake of loss. Alternatively, adaptive functioning may be jeopardized if the family is too rigid and the necessary shifts in roles, boundaries, and rituals required after the death are met with strong resistance (Imber-Black, 2004; Walsh & McGoldrick, 2004).

The degree of connectedness among family members, and between the family and external supports, is the third quality in assessing a family's capacity for adaptation to loss. Families with a high degree of connectedness or cohesion are better able to cope with the devastation following the death of a child than families not so defined (Kissane & Lichtenthal, 2008; Walsh & McGoldrick, 2004). These families are present and supportive to one another in a manner that respects the individual while valuing the importance of a close family unit. As with the other characteristics, extremes in this category are problematic; this is especially true for adolescents who are struggling to move beyond the embrace of their families and develop a sense of independence (Fleming & Adolph, 1986). Extreme connectedness or cohesion can result in enmeshment and fusion, leaving the individual consumed by the family's identity and unable to engage in the normal development and functioning that requires separation and individuation. At the other end of the spectrum, a lack of connectedness in a family can result in distancing, fractured relationships, and isolation among its members.

The level of connection to outside supports is also critical for adaptation. Families benefit from the presence and support of strong and enduring friendships and extended family relationships when coping with the death of a child. If a family lacks social support the result can be isolation and overreliance on immediate family members to meet all of the needs for connection. This is especially problematic in the aftermath of the death as family members are least able to provide this for each other. The result can be an insular family dynamic with unmet needs for connection.

The fourth variable, meaning-making, refers to the strategies used by families to make sense of the catastrophic events that have befallen them. Rosenblatt (2000a) noted the prevalence of meaning reconstruction in parental bereavement, and Nadeau (2008) has argued "that a family's ability to engage in meaning-making and the nature of the meanings that families co-construct are powerful determinants of how they will grieve and how well they will adapt to their loss" (p. 521). Of particular relevance to clinicians is Nadeau's contention that negative meanings (e.g., the death was preventable, the death was unfair or unjust, or that no sense can be made of the death) portend potential difficulties in grieving. Support for this position was demonstrated by Murphy (2008) who reported a relationship between certain types of meaning-making and health; parents who could make sense of the deaths of their children 5 years post-loss reported significantly lower mental distress, higher marital satisfaction, and better physical health than parents who were unable to find meaning in their children's death.

It is important to consider the family as a unit and to assess how each member is adjusting in relation to other members, rather than solely focussing on the perspective of individuals partitioned from the family system. Having said that, Broderick (1993) noted that it is the individual who has an understanding or experience, not the family; the family consists of individuals each with their own reality. Individuals grieve the death of a child, which in turn impacts the family.

CHAPTER 6

Dual Tasks of Parenting and Grieving

"Bereaved Parenting: Living the Duality of Devastation and Regeneration" is the core category that organizes and represents all other categories; it also addresses the active process spanning the shattering of The House of Refracting Glass and Picking Up the Pieces. Inherent in this core concept is the recognition that bereaved parents dwell in destruction and reconstruction at various times and in varying degrees. In Chapter 3 we discussed The House of Refracting Glass and parental devastation following the death of a child. Two subcategories subsumed under the regenerative process of Picking Up the Pieces then followed; Chapter 4 was devoted to the reconstitution of Self and Chapter 5 with Family transformation. The current chapter introduces the final subcategory of Picking Up the Pieces, namely Parenting; we will discuss the dual tasks of parenting and grieving (this chapter), issues of control (Chapter 7), and the challenges of parenting bereaved children (Chapter 8).

☐ Dual Tasks of Grieving and Parenting

The parents were unanimous in acknowledging differences in their parenting of surviving children. As a mother stated:

Yes. I think it has [changed parenting]. It's probably had a fairly profound effect ... there *is* a different way of dealing with your children after you've lost one of them. (Isabelle, 2-year-old child died, one surviving child)

We will illustrate how the dual tasks of parenting and grieving intersect and inform one another by discussing the immediate demand to parent surviving children, the various levels of parental functioning in response to the child's death, and the mothers' strategies of concealing their anguish.

Although the bereaved parents shared child-rearing responsibilities, it was obvious from the transcripts that the mothers were more intimately involved with the surviving children on a day-to-day basis, and they had much more to say about the complex and demanding dual tasks of parenting and grieving. With bereaved fathers returning to work within 2 to 6 weeks, it was the mothers, whether working outside the home or not, who were more involved in the direct and constant parenting of the surviving children. Consequently, most of what we've learned about simultaneously grieving and parenting was gleaned principally from the mothers' perspectives; we've included the fathers' thoughts and experiences when available and appropriate.

For a parent, one of the startling and unsettling observations was that the demands of parenting and the demands of grieving collided virtually from the moment of the child's death. Reeling from the unspeakable tragedy that had befallen them, and acutely aware of the pressing needs of their vulnerable, remaining children, parents struggled to reconcile these divergent and conflicting imperatives. A mother's statement following a motor vehicle accident that claimed the life of her child painfully illustrates this contiguity:

They took us to one hospital and we were asked to identify our [deceased child]. When we were there, I received a phone call asking us to give permission for [injured child] to be worked on at another hospital because he had been flown there. (Becky, 4-year-old child died, two surviving children)

Immediately, this mother was faced with relinquishing her parental role with one child while being called to parental action for a surviving child. There is no other loss that requires this engagement in the duality or juxtaposition of life and death. Another mother shared her thoughts on these dual tasks of parenting and grieving:

> You literally can't think how you're going to live yourself, how on earth can you parent somebody who's so dependent on you, is so needy, you know they're in a lot of pain, you know you should be, more than ever in their lives, you should be there for them, and you're not actually capable, you're literally physically and mentally not capable of it. (Diane, 4-year-old child died, three surviving children)

This same mother went on to explain the complex duality that exists in parenting after the death.

> You are sharing your child with your grief. There's no other way to do it. I'd love to turn a switch and go okay, this is the mommy that's not had this happen, this is the mommy who can have boundless energy and isn't the world great, and you know. That's a fairytale ... It's like you are learning to parent with this other thing in your life. It's always living with you ... It's REALLY HARD! Your energy level really is not as high as everyone else's, but, people think because you've had a child die you'd be super, super patient with your children, you find actually you don't perhaps have as much patience as you perhaps should or did before. I had to struggle with this. This was a big thing to me. (Diane, 4-year-old child died, three surviving children)

Another illustration of the duality of parenting and grieving involved decisions around the funeral, more specifically, as parents prepared to attend their child's funeral they also had to make decisions about the level of involvement and exposure their surviving child(ren) would have during this ritual. For some, their decisions are now a source of regret, for others, a source of comfort.

> I did stupid things, like the way I made, you know the whole funeral, the way you want your children to be at that too, I wanted my girls there. I wanted my girls to see him in the casket ... I wanted to hold him and I, you know what? I don't even remember. (Anna, 1-year-old child died, two surviving children)

> She would come to me and say, "What do you think mom? Do you think I should go?" I then said, "Well it's your choice, if you feel that you can cope with it all, and if you feel that's something you want to do, then of course you can do it. But, if you're asking me my feelings on it, then I would prefer you to remember her the way that you did." Because I just felt there was enough trauma without witnessing you know, her little [sibling]. So, she chose not to go. Now, I don't know. I think there are a few questions about,

I think she feels like she missed out on something. (Becky, 4-year-old child died, two surviving children)

Other families have talked about whether taking a child to a funeral at that age, what to do, but, I'm so glad that we took him. And that we involved him in it because he remembers that ... and I think it was important you know for him to deal with the death and learning what happens when somebody dies. I've told other families to involve them because I think they understand. (Isabelle, 2-year-old child died, one surviving child)

The one father who addressed this issue shared similar concerns over the decision not to take the surviving child to the viewing. He stated:

In the early days we struggled with, should she have seen him after he died, because he left, she went to school, and she never saw her brother again. Things like that. She asked a lot of questions about him. We made the right decision, but, in your own mind you think, have I done the right thing? (Jake, 4-year-old child died, three surviving children)

Perhaps the most poignant example of the relinquishing-nurturing apposition happened to Kristine following the death of her 8-year-old daughter in a motor vehicle accident. While greeting mourners in the funeral home, Kristine breast-fed her surviving child, a 4-month-old son, while seated next to the casket containing her daughter's lifeless body. As she poignantly stated to one of the authors (SF) in psychotherapy, "what choice did I have ... when your baby is hungry you have to feed him."

These dual tasks also became evident around special occasions that highlighted all that was lost and yet required a parent to engage in the tradition for the sake of the surviving children. This mother clearly described her conflict in responding to Christmas:

As a parent, I want to give my child a good Christmas. [As a] grieving person, Christmas can fall off the damn face of the earth and Christmas is a stupid holiday and it should be abolished. Sorry God, Jesus, you can just pick a different day. Sure, that's, but, that's where you go, gosh, if I didn't have this other child, and you see other parents or say bereaved parents of older children, they don't have to bother with the lights on the house and they can just say to their other grown up kids, you know, daddy and I are not doing Christmas this year and that's fine. To a little girl? Excuse me, Santa has to come! (Diane, 4-year-old child died, three surviving children)

A father also reflected on the difficulties in balancing one's grief and the pressing and omnipresent needs of surviving children:

> She [surviving child] wanted mommy and daddy to behave the way they were, she didn't like seeing either of us upset, she had never seen that before. She had never seen her father cry. That concerned her and she didn't really want to see it because it upset her ... It's a compromise. You've got to reach a happy medium of what's right for us and wasn't too much for her. (Jake, 4-year-old child died, three surviving children)

The primary issue that confronts the bereaved parent immediately following the death is continuing to meet parental responsibilities while enveloped by grief. As Fanos (1996) described, "the parenting role is not over ... their other children need them, and parents must pull themselves together to function and to give when what they may most want is to be left alone to grieve" (p. 73). Having to cope with one's own pain and simultaneously comfort surviving children may be overwhelming for parents who, therefore, decide to tackle only one task at a time. Parents may emotionally shut off from surviving children until they feel capable of resuming parenting (Rosenblatt, 1996; Rosof, 1994; Schiff, 1977). It is not uncommon for surviving children to be overlooked and not given the attention they require because their parents are traumatized, emotionally preoccupied, or unable to be psychologically available to their children (Arnold & Gemma, 1983; Baker, 1997; Rosenblatt, 2000a; Worden, 2009). There are data to indicate that the long-standing psychological absence of a parent can leave surviving children feeling neglected and unimportant (Schwab, 1997). Alternatively, parents may neglect their own experience completely and devote themselves to gratifying their children's needs (Borg & Lasker, 1982; Rosenblatt, 2000b). Rando (1993) noted that the parental role predisposes parents—especially fathers—to attempt to rescue other family members, often ignoring their own needs for the benefit of others; of course, this also provides an avenue for escaping their own pain.

The reaction to these dual tasks was expressed in terms of the *immediate impact of surviving children*. Parent reflections ran the gamut from surviving children being relatively inconsequential (at least initially) to their providing the sorely needed motivation and impetus to continue living and challenge life.

> Having to parent a child while you're grieving helped me actually because it made me push forward. A child won't just let you stop and do nothing ... And I think if I had been left without him, I probably would have

just wanted to pull the blankets over my head and stay there ... Once I was asleep, I just wanted to stay there. That was my escape, for me, I just wanted to sleep. So, for me, it was a good thing that he pushed me to resume the role because I probably would have crawled in bed, or run away from it in that way. Whereas he kept me doing the usual things that a mom does at home ... I think it helped me get back on track with life and start doing the things that most normal families do. (Isabelle, 2-year-old child died, one surviving child)

Where some parents found surviving children to be the only antidote to demoralization and numbing fatigue, others were largely unaffected by their presence. They shared:

My children couldn't get me out of it. Because people would say, "You have two beautiful children." What's that got to do with the tea in China, you know what I mean? That didn't really have a very, for me? For the first six months? Having those children didn't do a whole lot for me. Now I would say it would ... I can remember how many people said to me, "You have to go on because you have two children." And I said, "No I don't." I remember specifically saying that, I don't have to take care of them ... At that point in time, it didn't matter to me. (Anna, 1-year-old child died, two surviving children)

Because a lot of people, they'd say, "Well thank goodness you have [surviving child], at least you have another child." Like, well, you've got one, so. Because there are some days you don't necessarily think it is a blessing because initially, I'm saying now, because you were so consumed with your own grief. (Diane, 4-year-old child died, three surviving children)

Well, during that time, [surviving child] had no meaning ... So that everything was secondary at that point, even the [surviving] child. (Elliot, 10-year-old child died, one surviving child)

In a study of 20 bereaved parents with surviving children, Barrera et al. (2007) noted similar themes 4 to 19 months after the death of a child. In contrast to those parents who were consumed by their grief and those exhibiting a minimal expression of grief, parents who managed to attain "a balanced integration of grief reactions, due to the loss of a child, with everyday life in a way that grieving does not seem to impair daily activities" (p. 151) identified their remaining children as instrumental in the provision of hope and meaning. But this response was not universal as parents consumed by their grief, i.e., overwhelmed by their loss and with compromised daily functioning, found parenting remaining children to be a burden; they also described deterioration in their relationships with remaining children, increased anger and impatience, and role reversal. Interestingly, Barrera et al. (2007) found bereaved mothers, and no bereaved fathers, felt overwhelmed by the loss of their child.

Another aspect of the dual tasks of parenting and grieving was the emergence of the *level of parental functioning* as a key issue. Initially, it appeared there was a bimodal distribution, i.e., some parents managing to meet their parental responsibilities while others were simply unable to do so. Closer analysis, however, revealed that all parents continued to parent at *some* level. At one end of the continuum were those who, from the outset, mustered the motivation and energy to meet their parental obligations. At the other extreme were parents who enlisted the support of concerned family and friends to safeguard their children, and then relinquished many of their child-rearing responsibilities. Either way, all parented at a reduced level, but there was considerable variation in the nature and extent of meeting their obligations. Exploring these variations in the *level of parental functioning* provides insight into the ways in which parents responded to the dual tasks of parenting and grieving and the strategies used to continue to function in this capacity.

Mothers and fathers who felt unable to continue in their parental role did not abandon their families; rather, arrangements were made and support solicited to ensure the well-being of their remaining children as they retreated. One of the fathers described it as follows:

> Well the first thing I did was, wrongly or rightly, I sent my wife and child away. I sent them to [live] with my parents. So, they went down for two months I think. I sent her away. Almost immediately. Like it was no more than maybe three or four weeks, a month [after the death]. So, she went down there. (Elliot, 10-year-old child died, one surviving child)

One of the mothers described a similar experience in which she did not physically separate from her children but offered little ongoing emotional or psychological support.

> Immediately after he died, we looked for help for the children. So, in a sense that's parenting. So it wasn't that I wasn't aware of helping the children, I think I was more aware of that initially, but for a very short time ... They know I was there for them for the week after, but that drastically changed ... He [deceased child] was all I thought about ... When I saw that they were getting help then I just backed off and went into my own little—I didn't do a whole lot of parenting ... I was useless for a good 6 months, I did nothing for them. And I mean literally nothing ... They know I was not there for them

... Other people did my parenting for me. It wasn't me that did it. I'll admit that ... I didn't parent ... I wasn't really taking care of myself, so, I wasn't parenting. (Anna, 1-year-old child died, two surviving children)

This mother was asked about the turning point for her. What was the point when she resumed parenting her children and what was involved in that process of reclaiming that role? She explained:

That summer [after the death] we went up there [to a park for vacation] and that was the first time really that we had gotten out and they [children] were there and I had to do something. Even though [husband] was there, there was no one else there. It was him and I and I knew it ... I think a part of it too was [husband] had had enough ... I think I thought, you know what, he hasn't grieved ... And it was more for him, not so much for the children. I don't think it was so much for them because I know they were taken care of, instinctively I think I just, but I think I saw [husband] and I thought to myself, now it's time for you to do something. Because he needed it ... Except I still didn't take on very much parenting, like I still wasn't fine. I still wasn't doing the stuff that I would normally have been gung-ho to do. I was still self-involved. He [husband] was still doing the parenting. I still didn't parent. So it wasn't until, it had to be a good year at least until I even had any semblance of what I should be doing. (Anna, 1-year-old child died, two surviving children)

Another variation on the theme of reduced functioning did not involve abandoning one's parenting responsibilities but rather the disconcerting awareness that one was caring for the remaining child(ren)—but just barely. Family routines were maintained, but without enthusiasm, life lacked a sense of meaning and purpose, parents struggled to be consistently physically and emotionally present for their children, and they knew their well-intentioned efforts were woefully inadequate. They described their experience as follows:

I just wasn't functioning well at all ... I was still shopping, I was doing the groceries, but I would do it with him in mind. I would hit the grocery store and everything was a reminder of him. I would drive home and there was always somebody that was like him ... I still went through the motions but everything was a reminder ... you have to keep yourself together for them [surviving children] and you know that ... I don't ever remember feeling that feeling of putting any of my kids on hold ... You actually think at the time that you're doing okay, but, when you look back on it, you weren't doing okay at all. You were doing enough though to, I was doing enough to, my kids were, you know I was feeding my family, and I felt I was there for them and I felt I was doing okay. But, it's when you look back and you see the intensity of it. That you were able to—you could see the progression. (Carol, 20-year-old child died, four surviving children)

Normally your child comes first beyond anything you do. I was very concerned as a parent I wasn't perhaps doing everything I could be doing, you know, her needs, I could barely function myself. I felt very inadequate as a parent to start with when [the death] first happened ... But, I had to manage, I had to learn to manage my grief at a very early part of it, I think, I would sort of realize that she needed her mom there. Even though mentally maybe I wasn't quite there, physically I needed to be there for her ... this incredible numbness that you can perform menial tasks and duties ... So then you can function even if you're not there at all. She sees me there, I'm cooking supper. She doesn't need to know that my mind is on an intersection [where the death occurred], you know. And then at night I would try and focus on her and we'd cuddle and she would get into bed with me many a time and we'd cuddle a lot. Initially, a lot of physical reassurance. (Diane, 4-year-old child died, three surviving children)

Within this category of *level of parental functioning* there were parents who practiced "team parenting" or a sense of handing off to the other when one felt temporarily unable to continue in a parental role.

It's a team, and that's, well, parenting is most times teaming and this is just a higher stress level of teaming. (Elliot, 10-year-old child died, one surviving child)

Well, I think the one thing that's been good for us is that [wife] and I have sort of worked as a team together. I think that's helped. It's made things a lot easier ... It made certainly parenting [surviving child] in the early days in particular, I don't know about easier, but, it certainly helped us through it ... if [wife] was having a bad day, I tended to pick up, and if I was having a bad day, she tended to pick up, so, [surviving child] always had one of us that seemed "normal" that day. So that worked well. And maybe that's what helped [surviving child] through in the early days as well. (Jake, 4-year-old child died, three surviving children)

I think [husband] and I were great in that we, you know, I'm very blessed because I've got a pretty great fellow and I think what we did was we learned to read each other, and if I had, if I was having a really crappy day, I mean really crappy, he seemed to know to take over. So, she always had one parent that was, you know, we learned to split it I think. And vice versa. So, if he was not quite capable, I'd function ... we did a lot of that initially early on, when you can't believe you're breathing after this, kind of feeling, that's what we did. I think we split it up. (Diane, 4-year-old child died, three surviving children)

With many bereaved fathers returning to work it was the mothers who assumed much of the responsibility for child-rearing and who were consistently confronted with their shortcomings in meeting parental obligations. Their grief demanded attention, as did their children. With drastically reduced physical and psychological resources to survive in this quagmire of competing demands, one effective strategy emerged over time. Bereaved mothers developed an impressive ability to inhibit their active grieving, literally to put it on hold, until they could safely allow its full expression. In the face of such extensive personal, marital, and family devastation, this ability is truly astonishing. They explained it as follows:

> I was still able to be okay outwardly, when there were people around. As soon as I had the place to myself, that's when I lost it. But I welcomed that. I welcomed the time to break my heart ... I would get my child off to school and that was it, I would lose it. Those were my moments. I could space out all day and I did. I was spaced out all day until lunch time and I'd think, oh, it's 12 o'clock, I better eat. So, I'd eat. And then I'd space right out again until she came home ... But it was still a 24-7 thing. (Carol, 20-year-old child died, four surviving children)

> Try and parent your existing child and not let your grief sort of, you sort of have to keep it for a time I think when you don't have those other responsibilities. (Isabelle, 2-year-old child died, one surviving child)

> Mommy could just put that on hold for a minute or two, I'll get to that when she's gone to bed. And I'd function, so you have your time ... Well it's overwhelming initially, you don't really have a choice, you can't suppress the tears to start with. You get to be able to do that. Like I literally would time myself, and I'd literally just say to myself, all during the day, if you just hang on until 7 o'clock, just hang on until 7 o'clock and then that was my clocking off time and then I'd sob and scream and do all the things I had to do. (Diane, 4-year-old child died, three surviving children)

Barrera et al. (2007) noted a similar response and interpreted this ability to exercise control over the turbulent and often unpredictable vicissitudes of grief as evidence of an "integrated grief reaction" (p. 151). This pattern reflects the delicate balance between embracing or befriending one's pain and the ability to respond to the needs of one's child and function parentally on a daily basis. Based on our data, we would suggest that this ability to exercise control over grief is less an indicator of effectively integrated grief and more likely a typical expression of adjustment in bereaved parents who seldom feel they have the option of exclusively remaining in their grief. Very early in the grief process, bereaved parents were powerfully motivated to moderate, if not control, the unbridled expression of their pain. There are many reasons why they struggled, not always successfully, to manage the overt expression of their grief. Our data revealed that two of the more prominent reasons included the desire to protect children from witnessing the full intensity of a parent's grief and, as previously discussed, the incompatibility of grieving and parenting. To continue in the parenting role, therefore, they oscillated between the dual tasks of parenting and grieving.

Related to the admirable ability that mothers developed to manage their grief and literally "put it on hold" is a phenomenon we've termed *drowning the tears*. We were struck by how many of the mothers talked of escaping to the shower as a refuge. For these women, for whom private time was a scarce commodity, the bathroom represented the one room in the home where they could lock the door and, in isolation and safety, explore the depths of their pain. The rushing water of the shower or bath muffled their verbal and nonverbal expressions of loss and protected children from the frightening reality of parental disintegration. They said:

> I would give myself time, say in the shower to grieve. Run the water, sob away for half an hour so I could put on this mask and try to be, you know ... I'd get in the shower and scream and do what I had to do. (Diane, 4-year-old child died, three surviving children)

> I didn't have as much private time. The bath, the shower was a great place ... It [grieving] had to be done, so I did it. (Carol, 20-year-old child died, four surviving children)

> So it's a very fine balance. I think sometimes for me, there were times I got in the shower. And turned the water on and cried, because I thought, I'm not hurting anybody, nobody knows ... There were some times, I can remember going in there and just saying, I just want five minutes that nobody wants me for something. And that's very difficult, you know, to feel selfish and think, I need five minutes to cope with what's going on, the only time, sometimes you feel that you know, nobody can bug you when you're in the bathroom. (Isabelle, 2-year-old child died, one surviving child)

The raw expression of parental grief is not only disconcerting to children, it also has the potential to terrify parents who feel overwhelmed and unsettled by the power of their physical and emotional responses. During the course of psychotherapy with bereaved parents one of the authors (SF) witnessed a particularly potent expression of loss marked by the sole presence of pain that suffocates self-awareness and reflection, and the emergence of unrecognizable, inhuman sounds emanating from a place of suffering deep within one's being. Roy (1988) might well have been referring to this response when he wrote, "Our cries ... often carry the thin plaintive notes of deep, organic, biological, even animal, wound" (p. 5). During this time of indescribable torment, memories of their child are absent, there is no reflection on the impact of this tragedy or how one will survive it—there is only pain. With the subsiding of such convulsions of grief, parents are left physically and emotionally exhausted and frightened by what they've witnessed and endured. Of course, the unanticipated emergence of such overpowering emotions and sounds can also unnerve even the most experienced clinician.

Due to the press of time, bereaved parents often find asylum and safety in unlikely and more risky places than the shower. In his research, Rosenblatt (2004) observed that being the sole operator of a motor vehicle presented a welcomed opportunity free of intrusive demands, distractions, and unbidden observation. A bereaved mother stated, "I remember getting into my car every day, crying all the way to work, then getting to work and working, getting in my car and crying all the way home, and taking care of [our surviving son], and when I was alone crying again for I don't know how long" (Rosenblatt, 2004, pp. 681–682). Although a potentially more dangerous location than the shower, this quote not only highlights the therapeutic value of a private and safe time to grieve, it also illustrates the effective management of the dual tasks of parenting and grieving through oscillation between the two, switching parental functioning (and work) on and off in relation to grieving.

This process of rapid cycling through grieving and parenting fits theoretically with both the Two-Track Model of Bereavement (TTMoB; Rubin, 1999) and Stroebe and Schut's (1999) Dual Process Model of Coping with Bereavement (DPM) that were briefly discussed in Chapter 1. To reiterate, the TTMoB describes adaptation to loss as occurring along two multidimensional axes or tracks; Track I refers to the bereaved's functioning while Track II represents the relationship with the deceased. Track I encompasses a wide range of general functioning indicators including somatic concerns, trauma, anxiety and depression, family relations, and work. Bereaved parents in this study, in attempting to reestablish an adaptive reaction (regeneration) to the tragedy that had befallen them (devastation), acknowledged an array of responses that would fall within the Track I domain, e.g., reconstituting one's assumptive world, PTSD, feelings of anxiety and vulnerability with a pronounced concern for the safety of surviving children, overprotection and withdrawal from parenting responsibilities, the depletion of social support, changes in family relationships, and the search for meaning.

Track II, with its focus on the relationship with the deceased, includes such subareas as positive and negative emotional responses to memories of the deceased, preoccupation with the loss, ongoing attachment or continuing bonds with the deceased, and idealization. Our data provide ample evidence of Rubin's (1999) Track II domain as parents acknowledged the relocation and redefinition of the relationship with their deceased child on an individual and family level.

For clinicians, an appealing feature of the TTMoB is its bifocal approach to assessing parental bereavement; one looks for problems or difficulties in biopsychosocial functioning *and* along the dimension of the continuing relationship with the deceased child. Intervention would be dictated by self-limiting or maladaptive Track I or Track II components of adjustment. For example, if PTSD or depression complicates grief (Track I), appropriate treatment is implemented, e.g., cognitive behavior therapy, eye movement desensitization and reprocessing (EMDR), or in severe cases, the prescription of psychotropic medication. Similarly, if maladaptive variants of continuing bonds impede the reorganization of the relationship with the deceased (Track II) they will be the focus of intervention. This would include persistent attempts to establish physical proximity to the deceased long after the death, or as we discussed in Chapter 1, the deleterious influence of insecure attachment styles on the course of adjustment to loss.

The DPM outlines two broad orientations: loss and restoration. The loss-orientation includes dealing with one's affective responses, focusing on the lost relationship or continuing attachment with the deceased, delving into circumstances of the death including the deceased's last moments, reflecting on life with the deceased, exploring circumstances of the death, and yearning and pining. Alternatively, the restoration-orientation involves a different coping strategy, namely, turning one's focus away from the loss and accommodating the secondary consequences of loss. The authors emphasize that the "restoration" orientation refers to the process, not the outcome, of adjusting to secondary losses, e.g., having to learn to drive an automobile or balance a check book; reconnecting with friends, acquaintances, and social organizations to avoid social isolation; and reconstructing a sense of one's self. With the death of a spouse, the transforming identity is from "spouse" to "widow(er)"; with the death of a child, a parent's identity is compromised as they remain parents but frequently apply the adjective "bereaved" to refer to their changed status.

Oscillation between the loss and restoration orientations, the unique and crucial component of the DPM, is necessary for adaptive coping and adjustment (W. Stroebe & Schut, 2001). Oscillation is defined as "the alternation between loss- and restoration-oriented coping, the process of juxtaposition of confrontation and avoidance of different stressors associated with bereavement" (Stroebe & Schut, 1999, p. 215). In a dynamic, fluctuating process of implementing avoidance and confrontation strategies of coping with loss, Stroebe and Schut hypothesize that initial responses will be principally characterized by a loss-orientation; however, with the repeated and painful exposure to a new and demanding reality, adjustment is facilitated by the emergence of restoration-oriented responses.

The results of our research are not only consistent with the predictions of the DPM, they illustrate loss- and restoration-oriented coping styles and extend the generalizability of this model from its partner-loss base to the grief of parents at the death of a child. Bereaved parents tended to oscillate between an orientation of devastation (or "loss") and an orientation of regeneration (or "restoration"). We have intentionally used different descriptors than Stroebe and Schut (1999) to reflect the annihilating impact of the death of a child. It is beyond loss; it is devastation. Furthermore, the antithesis is not restoration, but regeneration. Many of the touchstones of a parent's existence were obliterated by the death of their child; therefore, there was little left to restore. For bereaved parents, the process of reconstructing a sense of self involved more than rebuilding, it involved regenerating. They must find their way into renewed existence, regenerating aspects of what was lost all the while cognizant of the hopelessness of reclaiming what was.

Although the DPM has received wide acclaim, what remains to be fully explored is the nature of the oscillation process itself; empirical verification of the confrontation–avoidance fluctuation, and how these divergent coping strategies affect adjusting to bereavement, is lacking. Our data shed light on this important, but empirically elusive, concept of oscillation. Where Stroebe and Schut (1999) suggest that a bereaved individual oscillates between the two orientations of their own accord, as fits with their personal style, gender, and cultural differences, and in relation to time (loss-orientated early in bereavement, more restorative later in bereavement), our analysis indicated that bereaved parents (especially mothers) were *pulled* into regeneration very early in their bereavement out of the necessity to care for their surviving children. They did not have the option of remaining in their devastated state. They could not gradually incorporate increasingly regenerative aspects of their grief;

instead they had to find a way to quickly accommodate regeneration in the midst of devastation, whether or not they are ready to do so. While, theoretically, there is choice regarding the active engagement of each orientation, bereaved parents frequently reflected "what choice did I have?" and reported feeling forced into restoration, which became the default mode of coping.

Although acknowledging their immediate and unrelenting responsibilities for their surviving children, there was considerable variation in how well bereaved parents met these obligations. Some met their child-rearing duties initially, made arrangements to ensure that their children were safe and cared for, and then retreated from their parenting role (and the regenerative orientation) to grieve. Others attempted to strike a balance between their grief (devastation) and their parenting (regeneration)—a balance that involved a reduced level of parental functioning, but functioning nonetheless. By virtue of their prominent role in nurturing surviving children, it tended to be the mothers who immediately encountered the competing demands of grieving their loss and parenting their offspring. In an admirable balancing act, they developed the capability of managing the overt expression of their grieving; they could inhibit potentially disruptive outbursts of grief until the opportunity presented itself.

It was here that the oscillation between the two orientations became clearest, unveiling the unique circumstances of bereaved parents with surviving children. There was certainly an oscillation between the two orientations of devastation and regeneration, but it was one of deliberate and focussed intent for these mothers. They consciously moved from one orientation to the other, not out of personal style or a timely process, but out of necessity. Of course, there were occasions when they felt overwhelmed and frightened by the uncontrollability of their grief and devastation, but they also had to consistently engage in regeneration. They lived the duality of their experience because of their responsibility to their surviving children.

CHAPTER 7

Parenting, Protecting, and Priorities

Having a sense of control, the assumption that we are essentially safe and can influence what happens to us, is an important component of feeling confident and secure in the world. As discussed in The Aftermath of the shattered House of Refracting Glass (Chapter 3), the disintegration of assumptions regarding benevolence, justice, and purposefulness, bereaved parents faced a minacious world feeling exposed and helpless. Mired in this existential chaos, they struggled to continue parenting and wrestled with complex issues created by their impotence in the face of potential and unthinkable danger—that another of their children might die. This chapter focuses on parental lack of control and reactions to this ominous situation including "controlling all you can," protectiveness/possessiveness of surviving children, the struggle to balance contagious safety concerns with fostering a child's independence and autonomy, a reordering of parenting priorities, and the challenge of effectively managing their surviving children's fear, vulnerability, and perturbation that inevitably follow a sibling's death.

☐ Lack of Control

Having failed to protect or preserve their children's lives, parents were abruptly confronted with an unaccustomed and frightening powerlessness. This firmly entrenched and pervasive articulation of their impotence was made by virtually all of the mothers, but only one of the fathers.

> I remember being at the hospital and doctors would come to me and say, "You know what? There's nothing you could have done." So the more times I heard that, I mean, and it's interesting because now I think about it and I think, there's nothing you could have done—there's nothing. That tells me I have no control over anything. They kept telling me that ... Again, they were trying to help me in that, yes there was nothing you could have done, but, on the other hand you're telling me, there's nothing I could have done, so now, you know [wipes hands], there's nothing I can do with anything. My life is pretty well whatever's going to happen is going to happen and it doesn't matter ... I no longer had control. (Anna, 1-year-old child died, two surviving children)

> There was nothing you could do about the loss ... I was responsible the day of the accident too, and this is what happened ... not that there was anything I could do that day. (Becky, 4-year-old child died, two surviving children)

> I've come far enough now to know that I have no control ... It's amazing how powerless you are. (Carol, 20-year-old child died, four surviving children)

> Because it's not like you weren't looking after him, therefore, something happened to him. (Diane, 4-year-old child died, three surviving children)

> This thought goes through my mind often enough and this is, what's the point of playing it safe? And so sometimes I'll be sitting there and he'll want to go on the top of the deck with his roller blades on or something like that, and I don't know, and you know, my life experience with [deceased child] says, I'll tell him to get off his roller blades and walk down the stair and a limb will fall off a tree and hit him or something, you know? So, it's not like you might expect and say hold him closer and try to protect him, it's like, I can't protect him when I'm doing it full-time, so ... (Harris, 2-year-old child died, one surviving child)

What is the impact of the sudden realization that you have failed the defining task of parenting—safeguarding your child's life—on parenting surviving children? How can you continue in this role, making daily decisions in an unsafe and dangerous environment that could potentially claim the life of another of your children? How can you persist in parenting, all the while feeling ineffectual and flooded with fear? From our data, it appears you cannot. The traumatic rupture of the family did not sever the parenting role; parental decisions still had to be made, even in the face of paralyzing, potential risk. Ultimately, a world characterized by randomness and incapacity was intolerable; however timorous, and perhaps out of desperation, bereaved parents implemented a number of strategies to facilitate reengagement with their parental role. They moved from a feeling of lack of control to controlling all you can.

☐ Controlling All You Can

The ubiquitous sense of having no control was equally repugnant for both mothers and fathers. The mothers described it as follows:

> I'm not a big one for sleepovers. And I will not let her go to anybody I don't know. She can forget it. She's out of luck ... Poor kids are never going to be able to go anywhere because I can't handle that. I think of all the things that can happen to her ... Because you're the only two I have and I'm not going to let anything happen. Or it's not that I'm not going to let anything happen, I don't say it that way, I'll say, "I know the things that can happen and I'm not going to give somebody the opportunity for something to happen that I know I can control. That I might have control over." You know what I mean? The other stuff I can't control. But, there are certain things that I can, see I've gotten some of that back. Initially, I thought I didn't have any control. (Anna, 1-year-old child died, two surviving children)

> You just don't trust anybody anymore. I mean the trust is, the fact that you know how easily things can happen, you lose so much trust but the trust goes everywhere, so you don't trust anybody with them anymore ... You want control. You want to be in control, so if something goes wrong you are in control and you can make everything right ... Well, then I have to make sure that this does not happen, I have to make sure that this child does not get hurt. (Becky, 4-year-old child died, two surviving children)

> I was really funny about letting her go with people. I had to say, "I'm really sorry, but, knowing what I know now, I cannot let you go in the [vehicle] with [friend]." You know those kinds of things. And there would be a little

anger there, but, that's just the way it is. I don't feel safe enough for you to be in that [vehicle] ... There's no easing up with vigilance of any sort. (Diane, 4-year-old child died, three surviving children)

They're teenagers and they want a place, a safe place to hang out, I'd sooner they come and hang out at our house. And that they're welcome there, as opposed to hanging out at the mall. And again, I guess it's because, maybe it's a more controlled environment, and [husband] finished a room down in the basement which is kind of his place where he can take his buddies. (Isabelle, 2-year-old child died, one surviving child)

Fathers also strongly identified with the concept of controlling all you can and shared strategic maneuvers designed to identify, and then avoid, potential threats in order to secure a safe future for their children.

We decided to move to [city] so we'd be closer to the school so there wouldn't be the chance that she would be in a car accident. Because she was being bused for an hour each way every day, so, safety-wise, we were worried about that ... Those are things where I would really put, try to put, some form of control on. (Elliot, 10-year-old child died, one surviving child)

I mean friends are always welcome over, and we think it helps for good parenting, you know, we get to know the kids better that are hanging around. (Frank, 12-year-old child died, one surviving child)

We need to make sure we keep the communication open so we know what's going on ... We've already talked about we're probably better off to have her learn to drive and put her in a car that we know and have her drive rather than have someone else drive her. It's our way of dealing with the driving. Then we have some control over the situation. We're going to put as much control into it as we can. (Jake, 4-year-old child died, three surviving children)

☐ Protectiveness

In the wake of such devastating trauma, a powerful motivation closely related to controlling all you can is that of parental protectiveness. When asked how their parenting was impacted by their child's death, the majority of parents cited assuming a more protective stance with surviving children. The fathers explained:

First of all, the impact of caring for the second child was, of course you become overly protective. You don't want to lose them from out of sight ... It must be really hard on [surviving] children, where you're so overprotective ... You can't help it as a parent because you're afraid of what's going to happen ... I would suggest when she was younger that we were still very protective of her, and that was probably four or five years it took before we started to trust people, or let her go somewhere out of your sight and that with other people. You wanted her nearby. So, it's the fear. If you lose another one, you know. (Elliot, 10-year-old child died, one surviving child)

You're just more paranoid now and maybe a little bit too strict ... And then you get really overprotective on the other side because you know how things can change so quick that you just, watch this and watch that. (Gary, 16-year-old child died, two surviving children)

We probably overprotected her ... She always tells us that her friends can do this and this and this but we won't let her do that. You can never win. (Jake, 4-year-old child died, three surviving children)

Mothers also shared this sense of heightened protectiveness and anticipated threat to their surviving children. They explained:

We became more protective to the point where we asked a lot more questions and we'd have to find out all the facts and then we'd decide whether we were going to drive them ... I think we're just more protective as far as, we're more aware of the dangers out there, we're more aware of how simple things can turn into tragedies ... I think with this, you don't let them out of your sight for as long ... We're not so relaxed about letting her go places ... [Before the death] no, I guess I wouldn't have been as protective because I wouldn't have the fear ... Definitely more protective [now]. (Becky, 4-year-old child died, two surviving children)

I think I was probably a lot more overprotective ... It's really magnified. Absolutely, safety for sure. I have to work on that. Even now [when] she wants to go to the movies or she's with a friend and you know she's going straight from school. It's just there, always there ... you know, it feeds itself. It's like an affirmation that what you're doing must be working. That's how the mind works, I don't know, it's kind of weird. (Diane, 4-year-old child died, three surviving children)

I think now I realize I'm more aware of what could happen and the pain that's involved, and I want to protect myself from that. And to protect him from it and our family. And I think as a result I have to guard against being overly cautious with him ... I don't think it ever totally returns to the way it was. (Isabelle, 2-year-old child died, one surviving child)

Whether one refers to protectiveness, overprotectiveness, or paranoia, there were two foci of parental concern or vulnerability—the safety of their children and their personal survivability should a similar tragedy repeat itself. In a profound and painful manner, these parents had discovered there are no guarantees of survival, everyone is vulnerable and, ultimately, there is nothing you can do to secure the safety of your surviving children. Bereaved parents remained unmoved by the utterances of well-meaning others that "lightning doesn't strike twice" or other, similar arguments citing the statistical rarity of such disasters. Rather, what resonates with their experience is "if it can happen once, it can happen again," and the perceived probability of such an occurrence is 100%. Given the extent of personal and family havoc that had befallen them, bereaved parents expressed the percipient insight that surviving the death of a second child was an impossibility. The stakes were high; everything must be done to prevent such a calamity for, should it eventuate, parental survival would be doubtful at best. These two themes are not dissimilar to those identified by Rosenblatt (2000b) as the origin of heightened protectiveness in bereaved parents.

The post-loss increase in parental (over) protectiveness had the potential to create conflict with children, but this did not seem to eventuate. Not only were surviving children aware of this restrictive proclivity in their parents, they cooperated in the endeavor. Both mothers and fathers noticed this mutual enterprise.

> She's normally very good because she knows how important it is, that if she's not going to be [on schedule] she'll call me. (Diane, 4-year-old child died, three surviving children)

> So I would walk her to the bus stop. I knew she was a little bit too old, but, she never once said she didn't want me to take her there. Never once. So, I would take her ... She understood how I, I would explain it to her and say, "I know if you think this is silly, this is the reason." And I was, she knew it was because of [deceased child]. And she never once questioned it ... She knew I wanted that control and I think she felt protected and safe by it. It helped. (Carol, 20-year-old child died, four surviving children)

> She has learned to realize that we're a lot more concerned and a lot more worried if she's late. (Jake, 4-year-old child died, three surviving children)

Parenting, Protecting, and Priorities   135

> You worry about where they're going, that's why I say, "Give us a call if you're leaving or" you know what I mean? And she's pretty good with that. We got a cell phone for her. (Gary, 16-year-old child died, two surviving children)

From our analysis, there are two possible reasons why surviving children accommodated increased parental protectiveness. As can be seen in some of the previous responses, surviving children were likely aware of enhanced parental apprehension and cooperated with their safety dictates to maintain family stability (similar to the theme discussed in the changing roles explored in Chapter 5). Children may also have acquiesced to reinstate the belief that their parents could indeed protect them and keep them safe. Remaining invulnerable and secure within an atmosphere of heightened but intrusive parental concerns served to restore faith in their parents' ability to immunize them from harm—in effect, rebuilding their assumptive worlds. Although never explicitly conveyed by his parents, a bereaved adolescent, seen in psychotherapy by one of the authors (SF), insightfully and succinctly described two clear post-loss parental dictates—"be good" and "don't die."

While mothers and fathers agreed that the "new normal" in parenting emphasized control and protectiveness, they differed on the ramifications of such a dominant strategy. Fathers voiced concerns about the long-term, deleterious effects of restrictive and repressive parenting; they felt a child's search for independence and autonomy would be compromised.

> As a parent, you have to step back ... if it's something where they're going to get sort of a, or something of life experience, then let them learn. That's all you can do, you know. After all, they are their own being ... Not dependent on the parents ... To be there holding them, I don't think is the right thing to do. Try to let them experience life the way they can without sheltering them too much. (Elliot, 10-year-old child died, one surviving child)

> I don't think it's necessary and I don't think it would be a good result for anybody anyway ... I don't want to alter his life by being too possessive say ... Being male, I know he's going to have to earn his own way, and support his own family and different things, and I believe if you don't give people the opportunity to develop, they'll never reach their full potential. And if I was going to shelter him, then I'm going to be responsible for him for the rest of his life. And I have no intentions of doing that. I don't mind helping or being involved, [but] I don't want to make those decisions. I want him to go and I want him to learn. I want him to learn the trials and tribulations of life. (Frank, 12-year-old child died, one surviving child)

Just trying to educate her more and be more independent, maybe try to prepare her for being a little bit more independent, don't be relying on us. (Gary, 16-year-old child died, two surviving children)

I have every intention of saying, go and find out ... really wanting him to take a flyer [i.e., take a chance] and it would be tragic if he didn't. (Harris, 2-year-old child died, one surviving child)

No doubt, that's definitely a struggle there. We probably overcompensate more than a parent that hadn't lost a child, but, at the same time you make a conscious effort not to smother her and to give her own sense of freedom, make her own decisions. (Jake, 4-year-old child died, three surviving children)

Although the negative impact of heightened protectiveness was not an expressed concern for any of the bereaved mothers, fathers were virtually unanimous in identifying their spouses as the source of this parenting style.

As I'm speaking, that's the one area where I expect that you might hear something a little bit different from [wife]. I would probably still be more inclined to say, you know, jump in and see what it's like. And [wife] is probably more along the lines of load up your tool kit with as many options as you can. They are different approaches to the same anxieties. She says, be as fully equipped as you possibly can before you step out into the world and I guess my approach is, make sure that you are prepared to take a chance. Because if you're waiting for the road to be clear before you, then you're never going to go. And they can lead in very different directions, those two philosophies. (Harris, 2-year-old child died, one surviving child)

My wife sometimes, you know, she babies [daughter]. But I don't really say anything because it's not my place to really say, but I kind of said it to my daughter. With me, I try to let her fend for herself. (Gary, 16-year-old child died, two surviving children)

Putting your child under the umbrella [of protection], I know, [wife] did that quite a bit. I think she's been in it for quite a while. We can't shelter him forever and ever. (Frank, 12-year-old child died, one surviving child)

Now my wife, I think she would be the more protective of the two of us now. (Elliot, 10-year-old child died, one surviving child)

Mirroring these fathers' concerns, Rando (1991, 1993) stated that, although not uncommon, overprotection has negative consequences for surviving children in that they may be robbed of the normal experiences of life, they may internalize fears and anxieties that can interfere with normal growth, and they may be prevented from age-appropriate responsibilities and opportunities. This overprotection may result in resentment from surviving children towards their parent(s) and may represent additional secondary losses for the bereaved parent (Rando, 1993).

☐ Balance

Although parents responded differentially to concerns over the long-term impact of an overprotective parenting style, they agreed, albeit for different reasons, on the importance of striking a balance between concerns for their child's well-being and promoting their happiness. In a reasoned manner, fathers articulated the dangers inherent in being too protective and expressed concern about preserving a good relationship with their children:

> Then realizing she's a teenager and also wanting to live her life and try to find a balance and just try to get along with her and not [be] an overbearing parent. (Gary, 16-year-old child died, two surviving children)

> You know that if you keep it up you'll smother the child and the child will resent it. You have to let them breathe, because if you're too protective, they'll just rebel. (Elliot, 10-year-old child died, one surviving child)

In contrast, the mothers' struggle to find a balance between the child's happiness and their immobilizing fear for the child's safety was marked by ambivalence and internal conflict.

> I let her go because I force myself. You have to let them be normal. (Anna, 1-year-old child died, two surviving children)

> I want her to live life and I want her to experience different relationships, or whatever, but at the same time, things have changed in the family ... I mean there's certain things of course that you have to give way on a little but, it doesn't mean you stop worrying about it the whole time they're gone. (Becky, 4-year-old child died, two surviving children)

I really try hard not to, I'll say, "have a good time at the movies" and try to leave it at that and try to hold back all the other things ... I mean, let's face it, you know, if someone said, what would you like to do with your children? Well, I want to wrap them in bubble wrap and I want to lock them in their rooms until they're 35. And maybe then let them out, perhaps. Okay, well would they be happy? Well no, so, but my instincts are telling me to do that, every second of every day. Would they be happy? Absolutely not ... That is definitely a conscious effort, to hold back. (Diane, 4-year-old child died, three surviving children)

One of the authors (SF) has encountered a relatively unique situation that represents a direct assault on a parent's survivability. Laurie was seen in psychotherapy following the death of her son (Matthew) on April 22, 2006, while serving with the Canadian Forces in Afghanistan. After her sole surviving child, Brendon, was deployed to Afghanistan approximately two years later, Laurie wrote the following:

I just can't physically or mentally bury our only surviving child. I know I couldn't survive, I just know.

Reliving the first few days and months after Matthew was killed leaves me feeling like I will never be able to breathe normally again. My world has totally shut down from the world I knew before April 22, 2006.

My fear of safety for Brendon seems to take over my every waking thought process. The pain in my chest is, at times, so overwhelming I don't think I will survive. The simplest of tasks are so daunting that I don't even allow myself to attempt them.

My sleep patterns are often interrupted with nightmares of seeing Brendon coming off the plane in a flag-draped casket. Upon waking, I feel like the walls are closing in on me, and again I find breathing difficult.

Every time we lower the flag for another fallen soldier, I get anxious. My fear is the next time the knock will be at our door ... I picture him coming home with all his body parts missing.

Brendon's six-month deployment in Afghanistan defines parental lack of control, defies controlling all you can, mocks protectiveness, and constantly threatens balance. Thankfully, he returned safely at the end of the mission.

☐ Managing a Child's Fear

As a parent's sense of safety, protection, and control was shattered so was the innocence and security of the child's world. Given the loss of these protective and soothing assumptions for *both* parents and children, the challenge became instilling surviving children with a sense of safety, while balancing it with a "healthy" awareness of the dangers that lurk in an unsafe world. This theme was salient for both fathers and mothers. The fathers expressed the following:

> My daughter was really, quite a few times she's had anxiety attacks where she feels like she can't breathe and stuff like that. So, [I said], "Let's all go get checked out." And we all got checked out [medically], everybody. (Gary, 16-year-old child died, one surviving child)

> Having seen what can happen, will [he] have faith that nature or the world is a benign place and that it won't hurt [him]? That part of it is a concern as well. I think that most people live their lives feeling protected by the law of averages. And that's gone, I don't know how much it's going to affect [him] … If your child wakes up in the morning feeling that way, is he ever going to be, never mind comfortable stepping out on his own, is he ever going to do what a young person should do which is yearn to be out on his own. You wonder about that … and it would be tragic if he didn't. (Harris, 2-year-old child died, one surviving child)

> If [she] gets in the car and she's a little slow to put her seatbelt on, and you say, "Put your seatbelt on" and she would almost say, "Well, why are you so concerned?" Well, she knows why we're concerned … I think she does know that deep down she's, maybe she's vulnerable. I think she realizes how quick life can go and I think she realizes that, which some of her friends don't. I think she struggles with that, safety issues. Hopefully she'll be okay, but, she does know it can happen, so. (Jake, 4-year-old child died, three surviving children)

Where the mothers expressed similar sensitivities over tolerating and managing their children's fears, there was evidence that they fretted over the contagious transmission of their anxiety to their apprehensive children.

> I had to work on that, trying to let her feel things were still okay, that she was going to be safe, that she could go in a car … I'm worried that that's going to be a burden on her shoulders [constant awareness of vulnerability], and I would hate to think that I was putting that on her. Really … She started sobbing and saying, "mommy, you're not going to die are you?" And that's the first thing that she thought of, and it hadn't even occurred to me that she would think [that]. So, even though you think they're all hunky dory and fine, you just scratch a little bit below the surface and it's lurking right there, just like it is with us. So, I keep that in mind all

> the time ... but, hopefully I won't make her paranoid ... You don't want to transfer that anxiety, but at the same time, I'm hoping that [she] has a healthy awareness of things. That's my goal. (Diane, 4-year-old child died, three surviving children)

> I have to guard against being overly cautious with [him]. He's starting to become more independent, and I want that, I want him to not be afraid to venture out into the world and not to worry that something will happen to him and it's, yet, you walk a fine line between being overly cautious and being frightened and also wanting to see him develop normally and you know, be naive that those kind of things can happen. It is a struggle. (Isabelle, 2-year-old child died, one surviving child)

> I guess it's a good thing [children's awareness of vulnerability], hopefully it's a good thing and I haven't made them too neurotic that they're going to be scared to move. But hopefully I've instilled some awareness. Time will tell. (Becky, 4-year-old child died, two surviving children)

Bereaved parents struggled to achieve the delicate balance of reconstructing a sense of safety for their surviving children, while also helping them maintain a "healthy" awareness of lurking dangers. This proved a difficult task and parents expressed their uncertainty as to whether they were achieving the balance. They were sensitive to the possibility that their children, too, may have experienced a rupture in their assumptive worlds and, thus, be traumatized by the death. Posttraumatic stress disorder (PTSD) is diagnosed in children and adolescents, as in adults, when the following symptoms persist for longer than one month: the unbidden intrusion of the traumatic memory into consciousness; the avoidance of stimuli associated with the traumatic incident; and hyperarousal (e.g., sleep difficulties, irritability/anger, concentration problems, and hypervigilance) (DSM-IV-TR, APA, 2000).

Establishing the existence of trauma symptoms is crucial as the presence of PTSD has the potential to significantly impede and disrupt the grieving process, e.g., if the child's fond memories of a sibling trigger trauma symptoms and, consequently, avoidance of the grieving process. It was not uncommon for parents to seek a professional consultation or assessment in order to exclude this complicating dimension of adjusting to loss. It is important to stress, however, that not all children, adolescents, or parents will inevitably be traumatized by dreadful events involving major loss—an insight not lost on the parents who participated in this research. The informed clinician, when treating bereaved children, adolescents, or adults, assesses for trauma symptoms as (even subsyndromal) PTSD will significantly complicate the grief response and impact the nature of treatment.

Although parents in this study were largely successful in striking a balance between protecting their children from danger while simultaneously encouraging their independence, this endeavor has the potential to create parental conflict and incompatibility. Consider the following case history: A family seen in psychotherapy by one of the authors (SF) had suffered the death of their 16-year-old son in a motor vehicle accident. Their remaining child, Todd (age 19), then abandoned his university studies in a neighboring city and returned home to live. In addition to their grief, within 2 years Todd's parents were witnessing his struggle to find steady employment and his abuse of alcohol. His father was adamant that Todd commit himself to either returning to university or finding reliable employment, and he had to pay rent or leave home. He was firmly of the opinion that Todd was using his brother's death to justify his maladaptive behavior and avoid facing the consequences of his actions. Todd's mother, on the other hand, strenuously objected to what she considered to be a heavy-handed policy on her husband's part. Most importantly, she was petrified that forcing Todd to leave home would inevitably result in his committing suicide, a course of action Todd had threatened in the past and from which she was most certain she could not survive. This impasse ultimately threatened the marriage and became the focus of therapeutic intervention.

☐ Reordering Priorities

In contrast to bereaved fathers, mothers now scrutinized values that defined and guided their pre-loss child-rearing and, frequently, a new set of parenting priorities emerged. They were determined to redefine relationships with their surviving children consistent with this emergent reordering of priorities.

> I no longer get angry, 'cause I can be very high strung and they [surviving children] used to see me get upset, if something broke, something stupid, like a glass that somebody gave them that was important. Well now? Couldn't care less. Who cares? And I can see them seeing that in me ... I would never let anything, anything interfere with my relationship with them. My own personal family, there's been all kinds of issues that my parents would say, "Yeah, I would disown you because of that" or whatever, I would never, ever ... They know because they've heard me say, "I

would never disown you. I won't lose you. You could never say anything to me that's bad enough that I would say don't ever come back here to this house." That will never happen. (Anna, 1-year-old child died, two surviving children)

As far as I think, when you're a young couple, you have children but you want to give them a nice home. Once you've given them a nice home you want to give them nice bedrooms. Once you've given them nice bedrooms, you want to give them nice things to put into the bedrooms. So it all comes down to providing. But nothing is to do necessarily with the nurturing, but it's to do with providing to make them happy. And now that it's happened, it does change all of our priorities. I don't care if I live in a shack at the bottom of the garden, I don't care if we have all these things. Other things can wait. As long as they have a home to come home to and a mom and a dad, they're pretty happy ... We've done a complete turnaround from doing and providing to pretty much just having our own little family. (Becky, 4-year-old child died, two surviving children)

Our son, I really had to confront him because he got very destructive in the way he was dealing with his grief. It was anger and he was doing things he shouldn't be doing. If that had been before [child] died, it would be very cut-and-dried with me. I would be very strong. And yet, I knew his pain. And it was very hard ... You don't sweat the small stuff anymore. It doesn't matter. My daughter's room doesn't matter anymore either. (Carol, 20-year-old child died, four surviving children)

The changes in parenting priorities ranged from no longer reacting to what they now perceived as the minutiae of life (e.g., tidy bedrooms, clothes put away, a broken glass) to a more fundamental shift in how they viewed parent-child relationships. This movement was propelled by the omni-present specter of loss that cast a shadow over all parental interactions with surviving children. The mothers were concerned with avoiding confrontation and fostering unconditional acceptance and understanding. Attitudes and behaviors that had the potential to rupture the relationship with their child were to be avoided at all costs.

The issue of control, and therefore protectiveness, was a central theme for bereaved parents as they continued to parent their surviving children, and it directly impacted their decisions and actions. Although there were numerous similarities in this domain, there were key differences that suggest disparate parenting priorities—productive, independent children versus children that are alive and safe. Fearing overprotectiveness would lead to intimidation in the face of life's challenges, and ultimately to deterioration in the parent-child relationship, fathers encouraged their children to challenge life. Life was still a precarious state for mothers, the world was now an unsafe and dangerous place, and they struggled on a daily basis to parent in a symmetrical manner.

Dean (2002) offered a personal glimpse into this exhausting and continuous struggle when, over 2 years following her daughter's death in a motor vehicle accident, she wrote, "... I still have this overwhelming fear and absolute conviction that everything from now on will have a tragic ending ... no sense of trust that anything could work out okay, constantly preparing myself for the next blow" (p. 111). In their interviews with bereaved mothers and fathers, Dyregrov and Dyregrov (1999) noted similar findings. Two-thirds of the 13 mothers entertained ongoing thoughts of catastrophe 12 to 15 years after the sudden death of their infants. The 12 bereaved fathers reflected that, over time, not only had they abandoned this calamitous expectation, they were somewhat surprised that it still characterized the mentation of bereaved mothers.

From the results of our study, it is clear that both mothers and fathers experienced the obliteration of their assumptive world when their child died. Although all of the mothers and fathers shared feelings of vulnerability and lack of safety, mothers devoted three times more discussion to this topic than did fathers, highlighting that this sense of vulnerability was more deeply felt and more salient in their daily experience. This is an important and intriguing difference between bereaved parents that reflects their differential ability to reconstruct shattered assumptive worlds. Possibly due to a more instrumental, cognitive, problem-solving approach to bereavement that emphasizes control and mastery (Cook, 1988; Martin & Doka, 2000), bereaved fathers were able to adequately reconstruct a revised world view that enabled a more long-term focus on goals and outcomes for their surviving children.

If bereaved mothers continue to view the world as chaotic and random, then it is no surprise that they are plagued by gnawing fears and vulnerabilities that result in heightened vigilance and protection of their surviving children. In a study of gender differences in parental grief, Rubinstein (2004) discovered that bereaved mothers had a significantly greater external locus of control and sense of hopelessness than bereaved fathers; a finding consistent with the gender discrepancy of the parents in our study. Rubinstein placed this finding within the context of the psychology of gender: "Given their social roles, women are prone to experience a decreased control over negative life events. This helplessness may stem from discrimination in workplaces, inequality in marriage, high rates of physical and sexual abuse, and the duality of being a working woman and mother" (p. 220). The results of the study by Wijngaards-de Meij, Stroebe, Schut, et al. (2008) support this hypothesis as they found that, in contrast to bereaved mothers, fathers were consistently more restoration-oriented. As previously discussed, the restoration-orientation in the DPM involves reorganizing one's life, developing a new identity, and looking to the future. This difference in the regeneration process for bereaved mothers and fathers has important clinical implications, not the least of which is a consideration of the interaction between bereavement and gender roles.

Generally, clinicians and researchers have shown a tendency to pathologize the enhanced protective stance assumed by bereaved parents; it has frequently been referred to as "overprotection," with the connotation that it is excessive, destructive, and aberrant. As is clear from our results, the death of a child obliterated a parent's assumptive world, and thereby their sense of control, and it was equally clear they could not effectively parent their surviving children from such an incapacitated position. In order to continue to parent, they had to buy back into the notion that they could implement change, that they could exert some measure of control over their environment and, subsequently, impact the safety of their surviving children. Through this lens, then, a bereaved parent's "overprotectiveness" may be considered adaptive and an indicator that they have begun the long and arduous process of reconstructing their assumptive world and reengaging their parental role.

Finally, given what we know about the assumptive world, which insulates us with baseless illusions of safety, control, and protection, and our culture that promotes and sustains pervasive death denial, Rosenblatt (2000b) suggests that bereaved parents, stripped of their illusions and denial, are actually more accurate in their assessment of danger, risk, and vulnerability than non-bereaved parents. Maybe bereaved parents are not overprotective, but rather non-bereaved parents are underprotective (Rosenblatt, 2000b)? The death of a child creates a deep psychic wound that leaves bereaved parents in the impossible and intolerable position of continuing to exist and parent feeling exposed and vulnerable. Whether more veridical or not, this position is untenable and parents work to reconstruct assumptive worlds informed by their painful experiences, and lacking the naiveté of their pre-loss perspective.

Parenting Bereaved Children
The Challenges

Parents are not the only ones profoundly impacted by a child's death as siblings are also scarred by this onerous loss. Due to the unique qualities of the sibling relationship, the death of a sister or brother has varied and long-lasting consequences (Riches & Dawson, 2000). In addition, surviving siblings suffer numerous secondary losses in the form of their parents' functional incapacity and the demise of the comforting safety, security, and predictability their family provided. For parents engulfed in grief, attempts at parenting are further complicated by the reality that, not unlike themselves, their children have been fundamentally and irrevocably changed by the confrontation with death. The data revealed parenting bereaved children to be a complex and daunting task that involved sensitively responding to the child's loss-induced personality transformations; repeatedly revisiting the loss over time; appreciating and adjusting to their children's differing grieving styles; grappling with the task of parenting a sole, bereaved child; emphasizing open communication; tolerating the helplessness of not being able to shelter their offspring from such horrific life experiences; and adequately addressing "why" the death occurred, or attempting to make sense of a senseless and incomprehensible event. In the face of seemingly insurmountable challenges to their parenting skills, and at a time when they felt diminished and least capable, it is not surprising that many sought professional help for their children and themselves. This chapter also delves into the children's perspective on their parents' changed parenting styles, as imagined by the mothers and fathers in our study. Finally, the want of another child is discussed.

☐ Changes in Surviving Children

Mothers and fathers alike noticed significant changes in their child(ren) since the death; while some of these identity transformations were considered positive and eased parenting demands, others were viewed as negative or worrisome and required more active, determined, and creative parenting. Regardless, a substantive task was to respond to their offspring in a manner that was attentive to both the grieving process and to the cognitive, behavioral, and affective developmental stages of childhood and adolescence (Fleming & Adolph, 1986). Bereaved mothers noticed:

> I think this has made them more intuitive. They understand. She'll say things at school about how kids treat other kids. She worries about those kids. That hurt, that deep hurt. I don't think that will ever go away, that's a part of her now. That's who she is. (Anna, 1-year-old child died, two surviving children)

> We never had a day's problem with him, he was one of those most placid children, he was so easy going, he was the kid who always got the first student of the month because he was such a nice kid. Very placid, easy going. Very close to [deceased] and just snapped [at death]. It was extremely hard ... He had done some things, he was getting into fights, he was just a mess. A total mess. (Carol, 20-year-old child died, four surviving children)

> It's been difficult for him. He's probably more serious than a lot of children his age would be because he's gone through the experience of losing his brother and missing him, but, he's also seen the pain that it's caused us as parents I think ... the element of trust I think is stronger because of the maturity that he's developed because of what's happened ... Because of the whole experience, I think he has a greater sensitivity for other children that are maybe being bullied or handicapped or any of those types of things. He seems very in tune with those less fortunate. People at school have said that he has great skills as sort of being the peacekeeper ... I think it's made him a much stronger, caring person. (Isabelle, 2-year-old child died, one surviving child)

The fathers also noticed changes in their children, transformations that suggested a maturity or seriousness beyond their years.

> Well, him as an individual, I find him to be very calm. He tends to be more reserved and I think that is since he lost his brother. I don't see the silliness anymore, the lack of thinking or whatever, I see a conscious effort on his part to look at what's going on ... He used to have his tantrums and stuff and he hasn't, the older he's got, those have disappeared, but, definitely since [child] died he hasn't had one. (Frank, 12-year-old child died, one surviving child)

> He has a grace about him that I think is really, really uncommon ... It might be manifesting itself in a determination to be perfect. I'm a little bit worried that he feels as if he must never fail at anything ... I do spend a little time looking at him and thinking, is he as poised as he appears to be, or is he forcing himself to be poised because he's concerned that he's not entitled to be any other way? (Harris, 2-year-old child died, one surviving child)

Personality changes in surviving children are not uncommon (Lattanzi-Licht, 1996; Lohan & Murphy, 2002), especially the noted increase in maturity (Arnold & Gemma, 1983; Fleming & Balmer, 1996). Becvar (2001) stated, "Siblings also suddenly may feel that they have aged 10 years in 10 minutes as they are forced to bear the heavy burden of their grief and acknowledge as well the fact that their family is shrinking" (p. 135). Dean (2002), in a personal account of her family's grief after the death of their daughter, concurred: "I pray to be a better parent to dear Nicholas [surviving son] in these terrible times—to give him the freedom to grow, have both 'roots and wings.' I see such old eyes in his face, eyes no sixteen-year-old should have" (p. 76).

In the face of the traumatic death of their brother or sister, Fleming and Balmer (1996) noted that resiliency was one of the most salient features of sibling adjustment—and time played a role in this. Adolescents in their first year of bereavement were often less well adjusted than their non-bereaved peers; however, by the second or third year of bereavement the adjustment scores of the bereaved and non-bereaved participants were virtually indistinguishable. In addition, the majority of bereaved adolescents presented as "wise beyond their years" and attributed this to a newfound emotional strength and maturity as a function of their sibling's death. These findings are consistent with Moos' and Shaefer's (1986) model that emphasizes the growth potential of a life transition or crisis. As previously discussed in Chapter 4, there is the distinct possibility that extremely adverse life experiences can act as a catalyst to posttraumatic growth or PTG. Although most of the research has examined adult PTG, there is a burgeoning literature exploring the phenomenon of children and adolescents growing through adversity (Cryder, Kilmer, Tedeschi, & Calhoun, 2006; Milam, Ritt-Olson, & Unger, 2004). For example, bereaved siblings have reported increased maturity, improved academic performance, higher moral values, a deeper appreciation of the value of life, and a reduction in risk-taking behavior (Balk, 1983; Fleming & Balmer, 1996; Forward & Garlie, 2003). Unquestionably, traumatic events can produce devastating consequences, but they can also promote personal growth. Cryder et al. (2006) concluded, "Suggesting that PTG is possible and identifying factors or conditions associated with PTG among children will assist clinicians in (a) attending to and assessing positive factors and (b) pursuing means to facilitate their development or enhancement and foster PTG" (p. 68).

However, one must not assume that all such life crises are met with resilience and a positive identity transformation. Research has shown that adolescents at risk for developing complications following the death of a sibling viewed themselves as outsiders and unpopular in social situations, held a worldview consistent with an externalized locus of control (i.e., the victim role), reported feeling disoriented, and stated that they were bothered by disturbing and problematic thoughts (Balmer, 1992). In contrast to their low-risk counterparts, it is suggested that these adolescents may be susceptible to self-related cognitive distortions (e.g., "No one likes me, therefore, I am worthless"), a generalized sense of being vulnerable (e.g., "I have no control over anything that happens in my life"), and bereavement-related cognitive distortions (e.g., "I sometimes see the deceased and hear them, therefore I must be going crazy"). The most appropriate treatment intervention with this group involves the use of cognitive-behavioral and psychoeducational strategies (Fleming & Robinson, 2001; Malkinson, 2007).

☐ Revisiting the Loss Over Time

Not only must parents contend with transformations in their child's identity, they are also faced with the challenge of having to explore and explain the loss at various developmental stages. Frequently, the death was reviewed as the surviving siblings matured and were able to accommodate a deeper understanding of the event and its profound impact. This can be difficult for parents as they continuously and painfully revisit the death and recognize the new levels of loss that time and maturity painfully reveal. This was poignantly demonstrated when a mother, in psychotherapy with one of the authors (SF), produced a letter recently written by her 16-year-old daughter, Tara. Some 10 years earlier, Tara's sister had died tragically in a motor vehicle accident at age 8. Tara, only 6 at the time of her sibling's death, now reflected on those painful times through the perspective of an adolescent:

> Was it hard to live with me after she died? Every time you looked at me, did you see her? Did it hurt to see me without her? Were we close ... I've seen pictures and I remember little things, but what was our relationship like? Did you and daddy change when she died? I'm crying right now, it hurts so much. Do you still think of her every day ... Do you still miss her? Does the pain ever go away?

It was the mothers in the study who most frequently referenced this component of parenting bereaved children.

> Because of the developmental stages that they go through, you have to revisit this all the time. That's what I find hard too. I get tired ... Issues are going to come up and I'm going to have to deal with those and that's what's hard. (Anna, 1-year-old child died, two surviving children)

> I found the most interesting thing to me is this grieving process regarding [surviving child]. She was 8 when he died, and she's now 15, it's changing. It's like the grief is evolving along with [her]. It's really interesting ... Because they were so close, so that's why I'm saying you know, I'm noticing her missing him in different ways [now]. It was a playmate thing before, but, it's almost like she's missing him more now I think. (Diane, 4-year-old child died, three surviving children)

> His birthday's coming, he's just aware that that's missing in his life again. (Isabelle, 2-year-old child died, one surviving child)

Revisiting the loss at various childhood and adolescent developmental stages presented unique and worrisome challenges, but it was the teenage years that were the focus of most parental concerns. The parent-child relationship during adolescence is often complex; however, with the death of a child it can become increasingly complicated and fractious. The teenage years assumed a whole new meaning for both the bereaved adolescent and parent:

> She is at that age now where she is asserting her independence ... there are times when I'm just that much more overprotective. Up to now she's

understood it. But, I think we're getting into some years where she might not. I think now she's at an age where she's coming out of that. (Carol, 20-year-old child died, four surviving children)

I know there's a part of her that is so close to us, and is so fearful of anything happening to her mom and dad. And it's her job right now as a teenager to deny those feelings and to put that distance ... It's an interesting time with her being a teenager and trying to do what nature is telling her she should be doing and that's distancing herself. And she's working really extra hard at that. You know, because I think there's a part of her that really doesn't want to ... there's a part of her that wants a relationship with mom and dad but because she's 15 she's got to fight that because she needs to be independent. (Diane, 4-year-old child died, three surviving children)

Bereaved fathers noted similar struggles and, additionally, commented on the tension and distance they perceived in their father-daughter relationships.

The teenager thing starting to click in and so, I'm just a stupid dad, what do I know? ... It's all about pushing away, you know, "I don't want you here" but, other times she's really loving and cuddly and stuff like that ... The teen years and to lose a child at that time, the parents are going to become more, or try to be more codependent on the children, keep them close by. And it's the wrong time to do it. But you can't help it as a [bereaved] parent. (Elliot, 10-year-old child died, one surviving child)

Especially at her age too. They don't want to be around having their parents pump them with a whole bunch of questions about what they're doing. So, that's hard too. "I want to go to university next year." It hurts, it hurts you to hear that, you know what I mean? It really hurts. I'd like her to maybe spend another year at home. She's too young to go. (Gary, 16-year-old child died, one surviving child)

I think it's harder for us to let go of [surviving child]. She's becoming a teenager. Independence steps [are hard], definitely. You want to keep the family close together ... Like all teenagers she sort of rebels and says, "I don't have to report in every minute of what I'm doing." There's times when I think she does let it go but she knows deep down that it's probably concerning us but I think she's being a teenager and just doing her thing ... She's at the stage now where, I'm sure most teenage girls are like this, she doesn't like to show her emotions too much to her parents. And certainly with me now, I guess most teenage girls and fathers go through the stage where they kind of pull apart. She's not, she doesn't tell me as much as she used to. That's fine, I understand that. (Jake, 4-year-old child died, three surviving children)

In many ways, parenting bereaved adolescents involved an exacerbation of contentious issues that arose for both parents and children who had not experienced a painful and debilitating loss. Hogan and DeSantis (1996) referred to the challenge of coping with the death of a sibling *and* adolescence as a form of double jeopardy, each being difficult enough to adjust to on its own, doubly so in combination. With the collision of adolescents striving for independence and autonomy and bereaved parents holding extensive and pressing concerns about safety, these transitional years were often particularly challenging and potentially disruptive. In such situations, parents and clinicians alike are confronted with the perplexing task of appreciating whether the adolescent is dealing with the "normal" conflicts inherent in each developmental phase, whether they are grappling with conflicts inherent in the grieving process, or whether there is an interaction of the two (i.e., the impact of a sibling's death affecting the course of adolescent development and maturation).

Fleming and Adolph (1986), in recognizing that "… grief responses cannot be considered in isolation; attention must be directed to the impact of loss on the conflicts and tasks of normal adolescent development" (p. 116), proposed a model of grief that combines the three tasks of adolescent development (emotional separation from parents, competency, and intimacy) with the five core issues affecting bereaved adolescents (predictability of events, self-image, belonging, fairness/justice, and mastery/control). The interaction of these two processes was evident in varying degrees in the parents' reports of their adolescents' diminishing tolerance for perceived parental overprotectiveness. But parents also commented on their teenagers' ambivalent attempts to distance and gain independence from the family. This ambivalence was noted in the many ways their children rejected age-appropriate distance and the pursuit of independence following the destruction of their assumptive world.

☐ Differing Grieving Styles

Not only do parents have to revisit the loss at various developmental stages, but those parents with more than one surviving child must deal with the differences in siblings' grieving styles and expressivity. Siblings' reactions are complex and long lasting, and they've included such varied responses as anxiety, fear, depression, anger, guilt, loneliness, peer isolation, and posttraumatic stress symptoms. No two siblings will react to the death of a brother or sister identically, and this variability requires flexibility and patience for parents who themselves are grieving—and whose flexibility and patience are severely taxed. Three of the mothers explained this challenge:

> She's not as apt to talk about it [as other sibling]. See that's the difference. She won't be as quick to tell what she's feeling. I'll have to kind of watch her. (Anna, 1-year-old child died, two surviving children)

> At the same time, you have two children that have lived through this very differently. (Becky, 4-year-old child died, two surviving children)

> He was just a mess. A total mess ... He was going through some very difficult times after his brother died and I was worried ... My second son, he's the type that acts out ... He was the one that openly grieved. He was the one that was, that I worried the most about because you could see somebody grieving, but I now know enough to know that well, you are grieving, I did it myself. That's it and that's okay. He was the one you could see it. It's [those] that grieve silently that I worry more about ... I had thought it was a little girl that wasn't dealing with her grief. But, I now know that I have rarely, I can't say I haven't seen her cry, but, she hasn't cried very much. But, my goodness she has done so much to honor his memory. (Carol, 20-year-old child died, four surviving children)

Parents with numerous surviving children face the imposing challenge of differentially responding to their children's primary and secondary losses (i.e., the loss of a friend, rival, confidant, playmate, role model, and the "loss" of their parents in a functional sense). Davies (1999) and McCown and Davies (1995) have noted that reactions to the death of a brother or sister are a function of the sibling's individual characteristics (gender, age, coping style, self-concept, previous loss history), situational variables (cause of death, duration of illness, time since death, involvement in events surrounding the death), and environmental variables (including family environment, parental grief, and parent-child communication). Although common, asynchronous or incongruous grief has the potential to be individually or collectively problematic. Marked inter-member differences in grieving may lead to estrangement, judgmental and critical responding (censorship of how grief is expressed), and contribute to further fragmentation and alienation in the family. Alternatively, incongruent grieving styles may serve to complement one another and facilitate more adaptive individual and family functioning.

☐ Now an Only Child

For a parent with surviving children there was the challenge of acknowledging and accommodating different styles of grieving and ensuring that each child was integrating the reality of their loss in their unique way. For a parent with one surviving child, a new state of affairs was introduced—that of parenting a sole, bereaved child. Parents were faced with having to adjust to a one-child family just as the child was confronted with having lost a sibling and, consequently, the role of brother or sister. Parents commented on the unique dynamics of adjusting to this situation:

> Well, it's painful to think that he's gone through the loss of a sibling and then also painful to think that as we get older, that he will be alone. He was such a fabulous brother, that I think he would have been, it was nice to see him sort of in that mentoring type of role ... There's a lot of life skills you learn by fighting with your siblings ... I worry sometimes that he has a lot more adult contact ... I sometimes worry that he feels like he's too much under a magnifying glass. You know, because he's got two parents watching him, instead of two parents having to keep an eye on two of them. (Isabelle, 2-year-old child died, one surviving child)

> It was a large impact on the sibling because now she always says, "There's me, only one now." We had to fulfill that role a lot more, like playing with the child. Yeah, and play the games and do other things, so, when you come home after a hard day at the office or whatever, and then to have to sit down and play games with her all night or to keep her, it's pretty trying at times. (Elliot, 10-year-old child died, one surviving child)

> I have friends that have only one child and I've seen their parenting styles and different things and it seems to be very different than when you have two or more children. The only thing I didn't want to do was start to swing into looking at him as the only child ... I don't think they have the flexibility. They say only children can be spoiled, well, I don't think that's always true, but, your parents' energy is constantly always on, all over them. When you get two or more, you're spread out. (Frank, 12-year-old child died, one surviving child)

> He's aware of how much of our identity hinges on him. There are times when being an only child is, I mean it *hangs* about the place. He defines the family and I'm sure there are times when he feels it's a burden ... He said, "I wish I had another brother." Nothing, nothing I know of to do about it ... The poor kid, he's been denied the family that he once had. (Harris, 2-year-old child died, one surviving child)

☐ Open Communication

A strategy implemented to address some of the challenges of parenting bereaved children was open communication. Although acknowledged as an important element of marital and family harmony before the child's death, both mothers and fathers commented on the increased importance of open communication post-loss. The mothers explained it as follows:

> We really had to talk about how we were feeling and why we were feeling that way. It wasn't to the degree [before the death] that it is now ... Importance of communication, it's so huge. (Diane, 4-year-old child died, three surviving children)

> One of us reads to him every night, we go up and snuggle with him and sort of sit in bed and read, and it's usually a time if there is something bothering him, that's usually when he'll open up and tell me what it is that's bothering him ... I think we are much more in tune with what's going on with him, I think before [the death] I wouldn't have asked him point blank, if I see him upset or something, "Do you want to talk about it, do you want to leave it awhile?" You know now just not to let those things go unnoticed. (Isabelle, 2-year-old child died, one surviving child)

Fathers shared similar thoughts on the increased importance of open communication with their surviving child(ren) since the death.

> Different ways to communicate with him. I talk to him very openly. I think it's helped that way. I think it makes it very open ... I don't know if I would have done that [be so open] before [the death]. I don't think I would have ... Communication is very important. (Frank, 12-year-old child died, one surviving child)

> It probably did become more important to us. We're pretty open. There's certain things she will communicate and things she won't, but I think if she really, she knows if she has to come to, or needs to come to us, she can. Whether she does or not it's up to her, but I think she knows she can. (Jake, 4-year-old child died, three surviving children)

As noted in Chapter 5, families with open, ongoing communication are more able to adequately adapt to a death (Jordan, Kraus, & Ware, 1993; Kissane & Lichtenthal, 2008; Rando, 1991; Vess, Moreland, & Schwebel, 1985–1986; Walsh & McGoldrick, 2004). In the aftermath of sibling death, there are also data to show that open communication within the family facilitates adjustment (Packman, Horsley, Davies, & Kramer, 2006). When bereaved siblings are allowed to frankly express their thoughts and feelings in a nonjudgmental atmosphere they feel validated, understood, and supported. But there is a caveat to this open, communicative atmosphere: If children witness the unbridled, uninhibited expression of parental grief, they may feel overwhelmed and blame themselves for causing their parents' additional distress. Consequently, they may suppress their feelings and refrain from mentioning the deceased (Horsley & Patterson, 2006). It is just such unrestrained and explosive outbursts of parental anguish and vulnerability that will guarantee the contagion effect the parents in this study feared.

Ideally, open discussion of the child's death and the individual and collective responses to it, facilitate the grief response of surviving siblings and parents. However, some individual, situational, or environmental variables may inhibit the development of such an ameliorative and therapeutic communication style. Consider the situation where 20-year-old Ben is operating a motor vehicle in which his 14-year-old sister, Julie, is a passenger. Relatively inexperienced, and driving at an excessive speed, he fails to navigate a turn in the road and the car careens out of control striking a tree. Although Ben survived the accident, Julie was fatally injured and died a few hours later in hospital. Ben was subsequently charged with dangerous driving. The parents, when seen in psychotherapy (by SF), felt open communication as a family (with Ben and their other surviving son, 8-year-old Sam) was inconceivable; they refused to express any of their hurt and anguish at Julie's death for fear of further destabilizing Ben who felt he had "killed" his sister. Ultimately, Ben was seen in individual psychotherapy to deal with his grief, anger, guilt, and his inability to speak of his sister's death. Some months later, after Sam completed a mutual-help support group for bereaved siblings, the family was seen in psychotherapy.

☐ Parental Powerlessness to Shield Children from Pain

Another problematic aspect of parenting bereaved children was the realization of parental powerlessness to shield them from the unavoidable pain of grief. The majority of mothers and one of the fathers expressed this sense of futility.

> I think that's what was the hardest thing for me to see, [surviving child] hurting. As a parent, that's probably one of the worst things. You want to take that pain away from her because you could see she was in pain and you couldn't change it. (Jake, 4-year-old child died, three surviving children)

> If I have this pain, the idea that your children have that pain is overwhelming. And this is the one time you can't, you can't as a mom take away their pain. That's awful hard. (Carol, 20-year-old child died, four surviving children)

> Because there's nothing, you can't do anything to alleviate that. There's nothing I can say, you know, I mean as a mom, you'd do anything to make your child feel better. Anything. And in this case, there's nothing. It's really hard. You really just ache for them. So, normally we like to try and work things through and I'll usually say there's not a problem we can't fix. But this is one we can't … That was a big thing, because as a mom, that's what you're supposed to do, is kiss it and make it all better. Well some things you just can't. (Diane, 4-year-old child died, three surviving children)

The profound reality of being powerless to alleviate the "hurt" and the "pain" of a sibling's grief, left parents feeling ineffectual and frustrated. Experiencing complete sadness, and the reality of a world shown to be cruel, unforgiving, and dangerous, their post-death approach to child-rearing was often characterized by feelings of powerlessness and despair.

☐ Meaning-Making

In the face of an unbearable, senseless tragedy, several mothers and one father felt it was important to provide their surviving children with wisdom, with a sense of hope, or to otherwise derive meaning from the death. This was a particularly contentious and vexing problem when the parents themselves wrestled with these very issues and, when this outcome proved to be elusive, they were left with feelings of guilt and sadness. They explained the challenge of meaning-making:

> I do worry about this, where it affects my parenting is, what am I trying to convey to him in terms of faith or morality? I think I'm pretty clear on the morality part of it, but, I've always thought that morality or moral code only works in a spiritual context. So, I've had to decouple faith and morality, which is something that still, intellectually, I don't think can be

done. But my faith is too, sometimes it's a very black thing, whatever it is it's not something that I want to convey to my son. I can't offer him that. I can never tell him things happen for a reason. I can never tell him that things work out in the end because he knows that's not true. He can never tell himself that. And I can never say it to him … One of the things I think I really owe to him is to make sense of things. And yet I'm wondering if that's going to be with us forever. The absence of an explanation, if we can't make sense of it that might linger with him. He doesn't show any signs of bitterness over it, but you know, it's one of the many things I suppose that you believe you need to do as a parent, and you can't do as a parent, and the fact that you can't do it doesn't allow you to forgive yourself for it. (Harris, 2-year-old child died, one surviving child)

So, I'm thinking it's going to get better and it doesn't. I think it's just where it [grief] is. And that's where it's going to stay. It's depressing. It's very depressing. That part of it, I don't want to give to my children. Because they have a future ahead of them and they have so much to offer with what has happened to them, but it has to be in a positive way. If they don't see that from us, they could totally turn this around and use it as a detriment. Use it as, "oh woe is me." And I don't want them to do that. So, there's that fine line. (Anna, 1-year-old child died, two surviving children)

Well, you try and create some positivity in just unbearable situations. You try and do that. I've said to her, "I'm hoping that by your example, because you've got strong feelings about some things, you can influence your friends in a positive light." I'm hoping that, for me it's really important in such a bleak landscape that you can grab onto something positive and focus on that. I do that and as parents that's what we try to do in our parenting. We try, we don't always get there … You want to impart some wisdom along the way. (Diane, 4-year-old child died, three surviving children)

An important aspect of processing loss is that of meaning-making or meaning reconstruction (Davis, 2008; Neimeyer, 2006). The ability to find meaning appears to be a critical component in the process of transforming the devastation associated with the death and reaffirming a new sense of meaning, understanding, or purpose—for individuals and for families collectively (Attig, 1996; Fleming & Robinson, 2001; Nadeau, 2008; Parkes, 1975; Rando, 1993; Worden, 2009). The search for meaning, a key component in the grieving process, is not an easy or passive endeavor; rather, it is an arduous pursuit demanding time, patience, and support. Clinicians are cautioned against attempts to rush the bereaved in this process of meaning reconstruction (Beder, 2005) as the struggle to make meaning of the death of their child is ongoing and complex. Recognizing their children also labored to make sense of a world in which a child, their sibling, could die (a reality that brings into sharp focus their own vulnerability and mortality), these parents endeavored to impart meaning and wisdom regarding the death, but they frequently failed to do so.

☐ Seeking Professional Help

As these bereaved parents have documented, there were myriad challenges inherent in parenting bereaved children and, given their profound devastation and reduced capacity to perform even the most basic parental tasks, they felt woefully inadequate. Aware of their precarious situation, both mothers and fathers discussed the professional help they sought and their reasons for seeking it.

> I made sure that she saw [psychologist] because I needed to make sure that there was nothing that I was missing with her. Like certain signals that she was giving out that I wasn't getting … It was just very good, because as a parent you like to be the one to provide all the answers and put the ointment on the wound. But, when you're bereaved, quite honestly, you know you don't have all the answers. And there comes a point when you just need to have the external help and let somebody else, in a professional manner, can maybe give your child something that you're just not capable of doing. Physically or mentally. That's the one thing I'm so glad I did. I needed to hear from [psychologist], "She's okay, she's fine." I needed to hear that because I didn't feel I was capable … So I highly recommend for bereaved moms and dads if they feel overwhelmed with parenting, are they doing the right thing for their child, are their own personal feelings getting in the way of maybe the bigger picture, to seek outside professional help. Very good idea. (Diane, 4-year-old child died, three surviving children)

> I mean who knows what she's thinking? She doesn't talk to us a whole lot. I mean, she comes and sees [psychologist]. So, she comes and talks to her when she needs some help or try to get straightened around a bit. (Gary, 16-year-old child died, one surviving child)

> We wanted to make sure, it was only a year after [child] died, that we were doing the right things as her parents, so we wanted to make sure that a professional, when she looks at her, says we're not doing anything wrong or that, in her opinion seems to be okay. But, [psychologist] did say to us, when she becomes a teenager, she may want to come back and start to talk as she gets older. She hasn't done that at this stage, she may not need

to. But we're always aware of the fact that if she wants to she can do that. (Jake, 4-year-old child died, three surviving children)

Many of the parents chose professional help for their surviving children or adolescents, either for long-term intervention or an assessment to ascertain if they were "okay." Although this may be the prudent option in the case of a sudden, violent death, or when parents suspect their child's grief may be complicated by anxiety, depression, or trauma, we are not suggesting that *all* bereaved siblings need a referral to a mental health practitioner. As previously noted, children and adolescents often exhibit a resiliency in the face of loss that is truly admirable. In addition, bereaved siblings may derive significant benefits from socializing with their friends, maintaining a "normal" routine, or participating in a mutual-help bereavement program.

In contrast to professional intervention, mutual-help groups offer a number of distinct benefits for bereaved siblings, including alleviating feelings of loneliness and uniqueness; providing an environment that normalizes and validates their grief; illustrating both mastery and coping models; demanding behaviors that more closely resemble those occurring in a natural social setting; and offering a distinctive social function for the participants. One such program, Bereaved Families of Ontario–Toronto (see Appendix A), is designed to provide a safe environment in which children and adolescents can explore and express the emotional vicissitudes of their grief. The unique evolution of each group is a function of the age and developmental level of participants, the mode(s) of expression found most effective by the participants (e.g., verbal, written, drawings, clay), and the leadership styles of the coleaders (Fleming & Balmer, 1995). This model, using a professional with expertise in child development and a bereaved adolescent as cofacilitators, allows for the monitoring of the children's behavior and affect, and enables feedback to the parents at the conclusion of each group.

☐ Taking the Child's Perspective

We were curious to know what bereaved parents would say about their children's perceptions of changes in parenting style. It was here that the circular questioning technique was employed. All parents were asked, "If you could speak from the perspective of _____ (name[s] of surviving child[ren]), what are the changes in your parenting that s/he would have noticed since _____'s (child's name) death?" Since this was a directly asked question to each participant, all of the mothers and fathers responded.

In reflecting on their children's perceptions, parents included predictable comments that reflected themes that had been discussed throughout the interviews; however, unexpected findings also emerged. Consider the following comment from a bereaved mother:

> Well, they would say that I cared more about [deceased child]. I've heard them say it in different ways and in different conversations. So, they would say that mommy cared more about him. And that he was the one that was special to me ... It's not true, it's the circumstances that did it, but to a little child, they don't understand that ... They know I was not there for them. (Anna, 1-year-old child died, two surviving children)

Other mothers touched on themes that they had previously discussed but now focussed on how their children would perceive these changes.

> She would say that I don't trust anybody. And that I don't let her do anything ... He would probably feel that I'm a little too protective, invading his territory or something. (Becky, 4-year-old child died, two surviving children)

> Oh, what a question! That's a great question and I'm having trouble with it ... They would say I'm more in touch, that I make a bigger effort to stay in contact with them. I'm more concerned and show it. He would probably say I was a pain in the neck as well. My daughter as well, in regards to my protectiveness. She would definitely say that I wasn't as free as the other moms. (Carol, 20-year-old child died, four surviving children)

> I think she just really has a really deep-seated knowledge that, as a mom, I'm just there no matter what. I'm just totally there for her on every level. She can absolutely count on me. (Diane, 4-year-old child died, three surviving children)

> I think he would have said, just we're more, the protectiveness. Probably asking him more often if he's okay. You know, just being more attentive to him. Just wanting to share more things with him, because, I haven't got, you know, another child to share that with anymore ... I think he knows we don't like to see him upset. And as a result, he could use it to his advantage, you know, he could play with it. I don't think he would. (Isabelle, 2-year-old child died, one surviving child)

Fathers also reflected on how their children might regard their post-loss parenting style:

> Good question. Well, she might say, "He's at home more now." Maybe, "He spends more time with me." I try to. "Dad is more protective." (Elliot, 10-year-old child died, one surviving child)

> I think he might say I'm probably more quiet than I used to be ... I used to yell at them once in a while, still do that though. But now it's only him. But, not that often, now most of the time I let it slide. (Frank, 12-year-old child died, one surviving child)

> Well, "He's chilled out a lot." I used to rant and rave. (Gary, 16-year-old child died, two surviving children)

> He might say that I'm gentler. (Harris, 2-year-old child died, one surviving child)

> Well, where she's at right now, she'd probably say we're overprotective. Maybe if she was honest, she'd probably say we're more in tune with her. (Jake, 4-year-old child died, three surviving children)

When considering their children's perceptions, the majority of mothers spoke of protectiveness and a deepening in the relationship between parent and child; in contrast, the fathers more frequently commented on the mellowing or reduction in disciplinary expressiveness. Of course, this is not true of every mother and every father interviewed, there was some variation in their reports, but in terms of general themes, this was a salient difference when assuming the child's perspective on parental changes. Again we see the heightened focus on protection and vulnerability expressed by mothers.

There is scant research into the perceptions of parenting style following the death of sibling. In one of the few studies, Pantke and Slade (2006) found that, compared to university students who did not report the prenatal or infant death of a child in their family when they were 5 years or younger, bereaved respondents recalled their mothers exhibiting a more protective, controlling parenting style. These qualities were not ascribed to the parenting style of bereaved fathers. In other words, there was no significant difference between the bereaved group and the non-bereaved group on perceptions of control and protectiveness demonstrated by their fathers. Pantke and Slade interpreted this gender difference as evidence that the grief response was more devastating and enduring for bereaved mothers than bereaved fathers. This is possible; however, it is also possible that bereaved fathers are not necessarily less distressed than mothers. Rather, they may have been more effective at implementing cognitive strategies designed to rebuild their assumptive world to a degree that allows a reduction in fear and vulnerability, and this translated into a reduced need for parental protection and control.

☐ The Want of Another Child

Despite the challenges of parenting bereaved children and the difficulty of parenting while grieving, every parent with the sole exception of one mother who considered herself past childbearing and child-rearing age, discussed the want of another child. Even in her interview, however, she reflected on the joy of having a grandchild in the family and her desire to be a foster parent to a child in a developing country. One possible interpretation could be that she is extending her parenting role through her grandchild and through participation in a foster parent's plan. All other parents, however, directly discussed the desire for another child and the complexity inherent in it. The mothers expressed the emotion and difficulties surrounding this issue:

> I would've loved to have more children and I didn't have that opportunity. I would have given the world to have another child. I would have done anything ... Once they [surviving children] have children, and wanting to be around them, and I say this to people, I want them to have lots of kids. Because they're going to have the children I wasn't able to have. (Anna, 1-year-old child died, two surviving children)

> Just before the accident, I had had a partial hysterectomy so my womb was removed. And then I had the accident. I still had fallopian tubes and I still had ovaries and I was still producing eggs. Therefore, we could still have our own baby, but somebody else would have to carry it ... Went through the attempt [surrogacy] four times and it didn't work ... So we kept trying and trying [to find another surrogate] ... Tried again [with another woman] and the pregnancy tests were all coming back negative ... So now there are four embryos left and I have to make the decision what we were going to do with them ... Yeah babies, so, I'm waiting for one to be put on my doorstep now ... But, I would love to have another baby ... Yeah, I'm keeping my eyes open. (Becky, 4-year-old child died, two surviving children)

> Unfortunately, time ran out. Time ran out on us. We didn't, you don't anticipate that kind of thing. It seemed like a cruel blow on top of everything else. After [child] died, my hormone levels were checked and they said basically I had gone into menopause, either from shock or just would have happened anyway ... With us wanting to have more children, we explored in vitro. And I did become pregnant but lost the first time that we did it. We tried four more times after that with no success. We kind of just this past fall, we put that, that was the last time and we just said that we can't continue on, just emotionally it was too hard to walk that line ... And we talked about adoption, and maybe if, I think if we had pursued that route at the time, now I'm nervous about it. (Isabelle, 2-year-old child died, one surviving child)

Although not faced with the cruel disappointment and emotional roller coaster that these women experienced, the one mother who was able to have more children experienced concerns of her own. She explained her thoughts and feelings on being pregnant after the death of her child:

> I truly feel she is a gift and this is meant to be ... But, this is a lifetime commitment, forever. You know, let's face it. At that point I didn't know if I was going to make it into next week, let alone be around to look after the safety and welfare and well-being of another baby for the next sixty, fifty years or whatever. Even if they're fifty, they're still your kids. I don't think anybody in their right mind, at that point would have said, sure, we'll have another one of those. And it's like, I don't know, I mean, because it's taking on more risks if something did happen, could I live through this again? I don't know. I don't feel I could go through this again. And having more children opens you up to that possibility. And that's the other thing. You don't have children with that lovely thought of, my life is perfect, I have my children. It's more that thought of, oh my God, more chances that something's going to happen. Isn't that awful? But that's how you change. (Diane, 4-year-old child died, three surviving children)

The want of another child was no less complex for the fathers. Relatively soon after the death of their child, all of the fathers, save one, expressed the wish to conceive a child, and the one exception revisited his initial decision with the passage of time. He stated:

> Well, I guess it was within the first two weeks that [child] died, [wife] came to me and said that she wanted to have another baby. And I said, "There's no way." I was no and she wanted to do it. And it was not a good situation. I told her, "Another baby is not going to replace [deceased child]." And I told her, "The way I feel right now, I don't have enough energy to

put into anybody else. I don't have enough energy for myself." I was asked about it several times and just said, "No." But what's kind of unique is that actually, just very recently I've been thinking about and wondering if we should have some more children ... I don't think we had any closure on [child's] death at that point [when topic of another child was first raised]. We've spent a lot of time in the past two years in getting results or answers, you know, we've learned an awful lot about it. The genetic component, it's stuff you need to know. (Frank, 12-year-old child died, one surviving child)

The remaining fathers had tried to have other children, but only one succeeded. Here are their experiences:

We talked about having another child. If it happened, it would happen, which it didn't. And we talked about adopting but didn't pursue it. (Elliot, 10-year-old child died, one surviving child)

I would but we couldn't. We're past the point of being able to conceive anymore. It was hard when [wife] had to go in to have her operation, that was really, really emotional. I was a wreck. It was like the final thing, nothing else could be done as far as having another child. I even thought some crazy thing like you know, even my daughter, if she got pregnant. I wouldn't even get mad at her for maybe even if she wanted to keep the baby, I'd be willing to bring it up, you know? And I never told my wife that, but I said to myself, if she ever came home, "Dad, I made a mistake, I'm pregnant" you know, I would have maybe just said, if she'd have wanted to go through with it, it would have been okay with me, I don't think I would have got mad at her. So, that's the way I thought, but I never told her or my wife about that ... But we had no choice. We felt kind of cheated I guess. (Gary, 16-year-old child died, two surviving children)

We talked about it very shortly after [child's] death. What happens though, is [wife] at the age of 37 entered menopause. So another child was not an option. Tried to climb up on the cliff again and got kicked off again. But that one, that particular one I don't feel personally tortured about because I think that the feeling is much more acute with [wife]. I think it was absolutely brutal for her ... We tried in vitro fertilization, about four or five attempts that all failed ... We've talked about adoption or fostering ... I've sort of asked [wife] and she hasn't taken the bait so I don't think that she had an easy time with it. (Harris, 2-year-old child died, one surviving child)

For the one father who was able to have more children, a host of other concerns arose. He explained:

> Now when we found out she was pregnant that was really emotional because that was, that was hard. Because then, is he going to be a little boy? And I think we struggled and initially that's why I think we felt we needed to know. So, we decided we needed to know, just for our own mental, to prepare ourselves. Because if it was going to be a boy, we had to really psych ourselves up for that. Because she was a girl, obviously all the comparisons were taken away. Because it wasn't another boy, that helped. But it was still hard. (Jake, 4-year-old child died, three surviving children)

The desire to have another child, although a salient reflection for bereaved parents, is emotionally charged and complex. And, whether successful or not, they are caught in a catch-22 situation. More specifically, for those who were able to conceive, their ebullience was tempered by the pervasive fear for the safety of the new arrival (and that of their older children). Parents who were unable to have another child were left with a longing that could not be satisfied, another level of sorrow they had to endure. This finding, that both mothers and fathers expressed a desire for another child, highlighted once again the lived duality of the devastation of the death and the movement toward regeneration.

The bereavement literature has a long history of viewing a child conceived after the death of a child as a "replacement" and at risk of a compromised identity (Cain & Cain, 1964; Poznanski, 1972). Krell and Rabkin (1979) maintained, "a decision may be taken to produce a replacement ... the new offspring is intended to fill the family void ... the newcomer is perceived as a replacement, dealt with as a reincarnation, and hemmed in by diffuse conscious and unconscious expectations" (p. 474). Increasingly, this interpretation is being called into question; in fact, if our data are indicative, many parents do not desire to "replace" the deceased child, they do not necessarily wish to have a child of the same sex, nor do they hope there is a physical resemblance between the new arrival and the deceased. Rather, their consistent and foremost desire was that the baby be healthy and, secondarily, they valued the uniqueness of the new arrival—not his/her similarity to the deceased child. Hagemeister and Rosenblatt (1997) and Rosenblatt (2000a) found that many bereaved parents had wanted another child but hoped that the child would ideally be different in obvious ways from the child who died; an individual in his or her own right. The child may not be a replacement, but instead an attempt to restore the parental role (Hagemeister & Rosenblatt, 1997; Rosenblatt, 2000a). As such, we do not see the desire for another child to be a pathological phenomenon but rather an opportunity to regenerate the family and the diminished parental role.

Grout and Romanoff (2000) also cautioned against conceptualizing subsequent children as "replacements." Instead, they posit that there is a difference between "replacing a loss and replacing a person," adding that clinical terms such as "replacement child" do not represent the full complexity of parental representations of the child and the family (Grout & Romanoff, 2000, p. 109). Finally, Grout and Romanoff stated that the concept of the replacement child derives from the belief that there is a prescribed pathway through grief to resolution, and any deviation from this path is considered unhealthy. As new formulations of grief theory are explored and embraced, and with a lack of empirical support, the replacement model is increasingly in disfavor.

The desire of bereaved parents to have another child can also be viewed through the lens of evolutionary psychology (Archer, 1999). Considering children to hold the greatest potential to transmit their parents' genes to future generations, then the more children a set of parents produces, the greater the reproductive potential, and the greater the possibility of genetic information enduring across generations. This motivation, although likely not conscious, may fuel a bereaved parent's yearning for more children. Wijngaards-de Meij et al. (2005), in a study of parental adjustment after the death of a child, found that the number of surviving children was inversely related to self-reported grief symptoms in bereaved parents. Furthermore, the authors found that grief and depression decreased more rapidly for parents who conceived after the death than for parents who did not conceive. The evolutionary approach can account for these findings (Archer, 1999; Wijngaards-de Meij et al., 2005); however, one must guard against inferring causality. Furthermore, although the evolutionary perspective offers the potential to shed light on this very common reaction in bereaved parents, it does not account for the psychological factors that influence both grief and the desire to procreate. Moreover, it does not account for bereaved parents' desire to adopt or foster a child after the death; a child with whom there is no shared genetic code.

Finally, it is the clinical experience of one of the authors (SF) that the desire to conceive may represent a bereaved parent's attempt to re-establish or exert control. Although death ruptured the relationship with their beloved child and left them powerless to reverse this cataclysm, bereaved parents may reclaim a sense of power and control through the creation of new life. Shortly after the drowning death of Kelly's 22-month-old daughter, Delaney, she defiantly declared, "I may have not had a say in my daughter's dying, but *I* will determine if I have another child or not. That cannot be taken from me!" In a cruel twist of fate, Kelly suffered yet another devastating loss when the onset of premature menopause at age 35 prevented her from conceiving another child and poignantly illustrated her abject helplessness. The presentation of this hypothesis is not to say that this is the sole motivation for wanting to conceive, but it may be a component of a more complex understanding of the multifaceted nature of control after the death of a child.

CHAPTER 9

Afterword

Throughout this book, parenting surviving children after the death of a child has been explored from the standpoint of research and clinical practice. The intersection of these two perspectives results in a rich and comprehensive understanding of bereaved parenting. In this final chapter, the overarching themes of directions for future research, the impact of qualitative research on the participant and the researcher, and general implications for practice are presented.

☐ Future Research

The participants in this study were a relatively homogeneous group of bereaved mothers and fathers, and it is important to recognize limits to the generalizability of these data, e.g., inappropriately applying these results to culturally diverse groups. Bereaved parents from other cultural backgrounds may have very different worldviews and grief experiences (Reif, Patton, & Gold, 1995; Rosenblatt, 2008). Furthermore, the participants in this study were highly psychologically minded. Each bereaved parent was able to communicate his or her thoughts, emotions, and experiences in a deep and introspective manner, and within the context of a largely nondirective interview. Likewise, the clients in the case examples were engaged in psychotherapy with similar psychological demands. Finally, all of the parents were either involved with the mutual help organization,

Bereaved Families of Ontario, or in psychotherapy. There may be important differences in the experiences of bereaved parents who seek support through mutual help groups or through psychological services than those who do not. Awareness of these possible differences is important when considering these results and offers directions for future research on bereaved parenting.

Future research exploring the experience of parenting surviving children after the death of a child could encompass many perspectives. First, interviewing bereaved parents from various cultural backgrounds would prove useful in determining the degree to which the results presented here represent their experiences, noting and exploring areas of discrepancy. Second, a focus on single parents' experiences would be a useful endeavor given the increasing number of single parents and the overwhelming nature of parental bereavement. Third, it may prove useful to interview couples together to assess their experiences of bereaved parenting. This exploration might unearth both the common and discrepant components of joint bereaved parenting in the dynamic, interactive, co-constructive atmosphere of a shared interview, which could be taken a step further to include surviving children and their unique perspective on the parenting they received post-loss. Finally, as grandparents often take an active role in the lives of their grandchildren, their perspectives on parenting and grief would be important to investigate.

☐ The Impact of Qualitative Research

In contrast to the quantitative approach to research, qualitative data collection involves a dynamic, interpersonal interaction between those conducting the research and those participating in it. As a qualitative researcher, you are not separate from the phenomenon under study—contact with participants is not limited to the completion of questionnaires and number crunching; rather, you are firmly part of the process and essential to it. In this instance, the face-to-face encounter with bereaved parents as they explored the painful nuances of their losses insured that their voices echoed throughout the analysis of the interviews. The stories are real and the images generated are vivid and enduring. It is not an option to retreat into the role of a detached researcher. You have met each participant individually. You sat with them as they entrusted you with their story. In this research, each parent shared their private, personal, and most painful experience of all—the death of their child. Receiving that information came with a heavy responsibility—a responsibility to apply the method diligently and consistently, a responsibility to represent each parent's story accurately and sensitively, and a responsibility to the legacy of the beloved children whose absence is forever grieved.

What is the impact of participating in qualitative research? Despite the concerns of others (notably members of research ethics boards), participants in qualitative bereavement research frequently note the benefits they realize as a result of their participation (Buckle, Corbin Dwyer, & Jackson, 2010). The research interview, often the cornerstone of the qualitative approach, is commonly perceived as therapeutic and meaningful by participants (e.g., Jordan, 2000; Rosenblatt, 1995). Indeed, the parents who participated in the research for this book unanimously expressed the benefits of their participation. In the analysis of the impact of participation in qualitative bereavement research, both the risks *and* benefits must be fully considered.

The second question regarding the impact of qualitative research addresses the other participant in the interview—the researcher. What is the impact of conducting qualitative research? In qualitative research, and the grounded theory method in particular, the meaning is always present in the words of the participants. The distance provided by assigning numbers to participants' experiences is absent. Furthermore, from interview to analysis, the subjectivity of the researcher is explicitly recognized and accounted for throughout the process. The influence of the researcher on the research is duly noted, as is the influence of the research on the researcher (e.g., Corbin Dwyer & Buckle, 2009). Being a qualitative researcher studying bereavement makes it difficult to compartmentalize the devastation of others when relating to a core fear of every person—the death of a loved one. The images of maimed and dying children do not leave you with the completion of the analysis. The knowledge of accidents and medical conditions and the dire consequences resulting from everyday decisions does not lie sterile and contained in the "analysis." Instead, the images, the knowledge, and the stories penetrate the boundaries of the researcher role and permeate other, personal aspects of one's life, e.g., parenting style, spousal relationships, and interactions with siblings and friends.

Conducting bereavement research impacts the assumptive world of the researcher. Exposure to parents' stories of the deaths of their children and their palpable pain demands accommodation in the assumptive world of the researcher. When you do not distance yourself from the pain with reasons why this could not happen to you, you open yourself to the realization that your assumptive world is an illusion. This realization frequently brings fear, anxiety, insecurity—and more conscious living.

While there are costs for the researcher in conducting qualitative bereavement research, there are also rich and varied benefits. It was a rare honor to share in the lives of the parents who participated in this research, and to honestly and deliberately explore life in the face of death and loss. There was a sacredness or reverence present as a result of bearing witness to such pain and devastation. These parents provided poignant examples of immeasurable strength, commitment to survival, and astounding courage, although they would not necessarily agree that they were particularly courageous. Their unending, all-encompassing love for their deceased children stood in fierce defiance of death, strong and true amid the destruction and ruin of their lives. And that was the fundamental life force from which all else was constructed as they painstakingly began to regenerate their lives. One cannot witness their powerful pain, enduring love, and dedication to the legacy of their children without being changed in important and life-altering ways. With exposure to the trauma comes exposure to the resilience, growth, and profound love.

☐ Implications for Practice

The research results presented in this book have important clinical implications. Specific therapeutic techniques and approaches have been explored throughout the book; as such, the implications for practice outlined in this section are more general in nature. First, the detailed descriptions of parenting offer insight into the daily struggles of bereaved parents and the coping mechanisms they employ. For practitioners working with bereaved parents, it is important to address the daily difficulty of negotiating grieving and parenting. Based on the results of this study, all bereaved parents functioned at a lower level in their parenting role after the death. While this reduced functioning is to be expected, it is important to assess the level of functioning as well as the degree to which bereaved parents feel overwhelmed and depleted.

Astute practitioners working with bereaved parents will be aware of the broader family context and the impact of a child's death on this system. Role changes and shifting boundaries are expected after the loss of a significant member. While it is important to attend to the individual in his or her grief, it is of equal importance to avoid partitioning the person from the rest of the family. Consideration must be given to how each member is adjusting to the death and to the cataclysmic changes in the family. Within this focus on roles and family structure is the on-going relationship with the deceased. The facilitation of an ongoing relationship with the deceased child through the concept of legacy and relocating or redefining the relationship is an important clinical consideration when working with bereaved parents.

The presence of trauma increases the likelihood of grief complications for the bereaved must not only contend with the loss of their loved one but also with the impact of trauma. The most salient features of trauma, including arousal, numbness/avoidance, and reliving, have the potential to impede, complicate, or magnify the process of grieving (Nader, 1997). Awareness and knowledge of the impact of trauma in bereavement, therefore, has significant clinical implications. The importance of assessing the degree to which trauma is present for a bereaved individual, especially a bereaved parent, is not to be understated. The results of this assessment will determine the direction of intervention. Where the signs and symptoms of trauma are present, trauma work should be the focus of early intervention before grief is fully attended to.

When considering the impact of trauma, one must also consider the degree to which bereaved parents were able to reconstruct their assumptive worlds—a process essential to continuing in the parenting role. Based on the responses of the parents in this study, there were clear differences in the degree to which mothers and fathers were able to engage in this reconstruction. The destruction of the assumptive world was clear for both as they shared how they felt exposed, unprotected, and deeply vulnerable in a world now considered unsafe and unpredictable. It appears that the fathers in this study had been able to adequately reconstruct their assumptive world to a sufficient degree that allowed a longer-term focus on goals and outcomes for their surviving children, possibly due to a more instrumental, cognitive problem-solving approach to grieving. Conversely, the mothers had greater difficulty reconstructing an assumptive world that allowed them to once again feel a measure of safety and trust. This has important clinical implications for not only does it affect the grief process but also the ongoing parenting role. It is essential to explore the degree to which bereaved mothers and fathers have been able to adequately reconstruct their assumptive worlds, bearing in mind that gender differences may be at play in the process, and respond with therapeutic interventions tailored to the individual process and potential impediments to reconstruction.

Just as exposure to the devastation and trauma of bereavement has the potential to significantly and personally impact the qualitative researcher, it also has the potential to impact the practitioner as well. There are risks associated with exposure to intense suffering and trauma inherent in clinical work with this population, and the very qualities of a good therapist increase the potential for risk—empathy, authenticity, and genuine engagement. The importance of assessment has been iterated throughout this book and is also relevant to this discussion. However, in this case it is self-assessment and self-monitoring that is the focus of attention. Practitioners are encouraged to make self-care a priority and engage in ongoing monitoring of their responses and reactions resulting from their work with bereaved parents, which will not only enhance the care they provide to their clients but will also preserve and potentially enhance their own psychological health. Tedeschi and Calhoun (2004a) offer specific suggestions to minimize the risks of this work: (a) control overall caseloads and the number of clients experiencing great loss and trauma within a caseload; (b) set realistic goals for therapy with bereaved parents, recognizing the life-long process of adjusting to the death of a child; (c) commit to regular consultation with a trusted colleague to debrief and decompress; (d) incorporate journaling about your experiences into an overall self-care plan; (e) take time away from work and protect that time with the same commitment that you would apply to your client's time; (f) attend to the regular maintenance of physical health; (g) engage fully in life-affirming and life-enhancing relationships and experiences.

It is crucial to recognize that the significant impact of this work is not always negative or disconcerting. In fact, the practitioner working with bereaved parents has a unique and privileged opportunity to realize benefits or personally positive aspects of engaging in this work. The lessons born of loss that bereaved parents share in therapy have the potential to enhance the therapist's own life and relationships. Bearing witness to the devastation of parental bereavement breaks the habituation inherent in routine and perceived stability. You are reminded to cherish your life and your loved ones when you are open to the pain of your clients in response to all they have lost. This realization can bring anxiety, but it can also bring a sense of deeper presence and gratitude in your own relationships and experiences. Finally, working with bereaved parents is a very hopeful endeavor. By their example, you realize it is possible to survive even the most devastating loss. By their example, you witness resilience, courage, and the power of a parent's love for a child. It is transformative and life-affirming.

Once you become acquainted with death in an open and honest manner, either vicariously or directly, you can never forget this acquaintance, you cannot claim you have not met. Like many relationships, your relationship with death will have benefits and costs, and it requires work to negotiate and constantly renegotiate a comfortable interaction. When you recognize the ever-presence of death in your life, as a researcher, a practitioner, and a human being, it changes you irrevocably.

☐ In Summary

With the death of a child, parents are irrevocably changed. Their lives are damaged beyond repair and must be painfully reconstructed anew. This reconstruction is often shrouded in ambivalence. To rebuild is to look to the future, which is almost impossible when the pull is so strong to stay in the past with their beloved child, and the reality of death makes the future seem tenuous. To rebuild demands energy and engagement when the overriding experience is depletion and distraction. To rebuild means to move forward, without their child, a thought almost too abhorrent to imagine. But rebuild they must. Bereaved parents must rebuild from the wreckage of their lives—their surviving children require it.

Grief is a normal experience. It is not to be pathologized or medicalized. It is to be understood, compassionately and empathetically. This is not to deny the potential for complications or the need for intervention. Skilled assessment is essential to determine a parent's strengths and areas requiring clinical attention. However, when the utter devastation of parental bereavement is fully considered, even the most seasoned researcher or practitioner cannot help but be moved by the poignant example of survival and resilience evident in each bereaved mother and father. Many bereaved parents attribute their survival and growth to the legacy of their children—what a profound legacy.

APPENDIX A

Bereaved Families of Ontario
Toronto, Canada*

Bereaved Families of Ontario-Toronto (BFO-T) was established in 1978 by four bereaved mothers who recognized the benefit of mutual support. From its inception, the core values of understanding, compassion, integrity, diversity, building relationships, and mutual support have informed and transformed the development of the organization. At the heart of the BFO is the belief that, with access to an emotionally safe place to grieve, everyone carries within themselves the capacity to heal.

Bereavement support programs developed from the philosophy that, while the experience of grief is unique to each individual, spending time and sharing space with others who are similarly bereaved allows people to explore, talk, and learn about grief in a manner and pace that makes sense for them. Bereaved people often feel that they are unable to openly discuss or express their grief for fear of being judged or causing discomfort to others. The chance to talk about how loss affects their lives with someone who has *been there* can be vitally important in learning to live with a "new normal" after the death of a loved one. The connection and validation offered through confidential meetings in like-loss groups can be an essential antidote against the isolation and estrangement people often face after a significant loss. The programs and services offered through BFO-T serve as a reminder that "you don't have to go through this alone."

---

* The following information relates specifically to the programs offered through Bereaved Families of Ontario-Toronto. Each affiliate across the Province of Ontario offers different programming and should be contacted directly for information regarding specific services, outreach projects, and volunteer opportunities. See www.bereavedfamilies.net for affiliate contact information.

☐ Peer and Mutual Support

BFO-T programs are based on a peer/mutual support model. Peer support refers to the concept that the facilitators of the programs are not mental health professionals delivering formal counseling or psychotherapy; rather, they are similarly bereaved people (peers) who are able to offer support to others because of their personal lived experience with loss and the training they have received at BFO-T. At the foundation of the peer support model is the belief that the grief an individual experiences following the death of a loved one is a normal and natural response to loss and, as such, does not necessarily require professional intervention. BFO-T also believes that peer facilitators, who are further along in their journey of learning to live with grief, represent beacons of hope and reflections of possibility that reassure and offer solace to those facing the difficult road ahead.

Mutual support refers to the process of sharing common experiences within a safe, encouraging environment. It is the mutually beneficial exchange of support and information that can reduce isolation and increase self-efficacy by allowing the individual who requires support to also be a supporter. This reciprocal exchange provides people with an opportunity to give what they also need, while learning to help themselves in the process.

The BFO-T mutual support model sustains the bereaved as they receive and provide support inside a confidential and nurturing environment. Participation in a bereavement group involves sharing personal experiences and stories about the deceased while bearing witness to the experiences and stories of others. Trust and respect are established as connections develop among the members; this, in turn, creates an atmosphere where authentic expressions of grief are permitted and encouraged. The group experience validates and normalizes individual experiences, and the opportunity to help others while being helped facilitates the restoration of a sense of purpose that has often been ruptured by the experience of loss.

☐ Group Facilitators

Each group facilitator is a volunteer who has completed the BFO-T Volunteer Training Program. This training is offered free of charge and involves more than 45 hours of comprehensive didactic and experiential exposure to issues such as grief, mutual support, group facilitation, and BFO-T's mission and values. Peer facilitators have experienced a similar loss to those they support in both one-to-one interactions and within the group program. They have often received support from being a previous participant in a BFO group and are now far enough along in their own journey to be able to provide assistance to others who are grieving.

☐ Group Advisors

A unique feature of BFO-T's structure is its close working relationship with the professional community. Professional advisors are volunteers who have been assigned to each mutual support group. Before each session, a professional advisor meets with peer facilitators for supervision and support. Professional advisors are social workers, psychologists, therapists, counselors, teachers, and other healthcare and social service professionals who have expertise in topics related to group development and process, adjustment to loss, trauma, and the mutual support model.

☐ Programs and Services

The original mission of BFO-T was to provide support to parents who had experienced the death of a child, however, this mandate was soon expanded to meet the diverse needs of bereaved *families*. Currently, in addition to bereaved parents, programs are now offered for children (4–12 yrs); youth (13–17 yrs.); young adults (18–30 yrs.) who have lost a parent, caregiver, or close friend; parents who have experienced the perinatal or neonatal death of an infant up to one year; and groups for adults over the age of 30 who have lost a sibling, spouse, partner, or parent.

BFO-T's values include a commitment to principles of access, equity, and inclusion. The goal is to ensure that the programs are accessible, facilitate connections, and reduce the isolation often experienced by bereaved people. How an individual responds to loss is determined by a number of factors. Some of these include the cause of death, loss history, as well as gender, culture, race, faith, sexual orientation, and other aspects of social identity. In addition to influencing responses to loss, the experience of oppression or discrimination impacts an individual's access to services, their sense of safety in a group setting, and/or their grief experience.

BFO-T recognizes that for some individuals the term "peer" can be described both by shared loss and/or shared cultural/social experiences that, in turn, can inform the way individuals define belonging, comfort, and safety. Therefore, groups have been established for people to connect in "like" community groups, i.e., groups for bereaved mothers, drop-in groups for bereaved mothers in the Black community, partner/spousal loss groups, and groups for members of the Lesbian Gay Bisexual Transgendered and Queer Communities (LGBTQ) who have experienced the loss of a sibling, spouse, partner, or parent.

☐ Intake Process

BFO-T does not offer individual or group counseling or psychotherapy. When a person initially contacts the organization, they are informed of the various programs and invited to complete a brief intake (by phone or mail) to gather client contact and loss information. The intake process also includes questions asking who the caller might be most comfortable meeting during the initial one-to-one session, e.g., someone of the same culture/race/faith/gender/age, someone who has experienced the same type of loss, and any other considerations that the client or interviewer feels should be considered. This might mean that if a newly bereaved parent is also a single mother, she may be most comfortable meeting with a volunteer who has managed a similar family situation; or a young father who has experienced the loss of his spouse to cancer may be more comfortable meeting with another male volunteer who has experienced losing a spouse to a similar disease; or a woman whose brother has been the victim of gun violence may want to meet with someone who understands the import of having a family member murdered.

Once the intake process is completed, BFO-T arranges a one-to-one match with a volunteer who has experienced a similar loss; prospective participants are encouraged to attend with a partner, supportive friend, or family member.

One-to-One Meeting

The confidential one-to-one session offers the unique opportunity to meet with someone who has experienced a similar loss. This initial meeting provides the opportunity for a bereaved person to share their story with someone who has "been there"; they can receive immediate understanding and solace, and explore the possibility of joining a mutual support group. For the newly bereaved, this might be the first time they have been invited to speak about the deceased, to utter their name, to talk openly about the intensity and extent of their grief and, because they are sitting with someone who has survived a similar loss, to actually contemplate surviving this unspeakable horror.

The one-to-one session is also the occasion for the facilitator to discuss the realities of joining a group, to provide information about the group format and structure, and to explore whether the timing is right to join a group. Just as BFO-T endorses the belief that everyone grieves uniquely and that there is no right or wrong way to grieve, we also believe that people need to access support when *they* are ready. For some people, this may mean contacting the organization days after their loss and, for others, this could mean many years later. The first meeting with a similarly bereaved volunteer is also the time to explore the implications of sharing personal stories of loss with group members as well as hearing and holding the stories of other bereaved individuals.

At the end of the one-to-one meeting, it may be determined by the client and peer facilitator that it is not an appropriate time to enter a group. This may happen because they do not have the time to commit to every session considering the changes they are facing, they would prefer individual counseling as opposed to group support, or perhaps they would prefer to wait until the next series of groups. Regardless of the reason, they are invited to use BFO-T's lending library, borrow articles and information related to grief and grief support, access information and other resources (including our websites: http://www.bfotoronto.ca and www.soul2soul.ca for youth), or become a new member and receive support through our newsletter. Whatever the client decides, information and assistance are available in many forms.

☐ Mutual Support Bereavement Groups

BFO-T offers closed groups of 8–12 people with membership usually based on like-loss experiences. Groups generally meet once a week, in 2-hour sessions, for 10 weeks to facilitate learning to live with the "new normal" of life following the death of a loved one. Each group is cofacilitated by two trained peer facilitators who are there to establish and maintain a safe atmosphere for members to explore their grief. Group participation helps to reduce feelings of isolation, normalize the grief experience, and nurture the resiliency of people so they are better able to identify their own inner resources and coping strategies.

The topics explored within the group sessions vary depending on many factors including age of participants, type of loss, and the needs that emerge within each group. Members also participate in their own unique way and at their own pace, which influences the topics that are discussed and the guidelines that are established in the first session. Members and peer facilitators are responsible for creating the group's guidelines that will shape the structure of their experience; relevant issues include confidentiality, the sharing of time equally, respect for individual differences, and the importance of empathetic listening.

The initial session is focused on building trust and safety so that each member has the opportunity to share their individual story of loss without having to worry about interruptions, questions, or judgments. The first session is also the time that group members receive affirmation for the courage, openness, and energy it takes to begin the process of seeking and accepting support. Often, the first session can feel grueling, and participants are reminded that having taken the first step and, with deliberate engagement in the grief process, the intensity of their grief will continue to change over time. The middle group sessions tend to focus on topics related to memorials/rituals/funerals, the sharing of mementos related to their loved one, grief reactions, the impact of loss on family and relationships, coping strategies, how to survive holidays and other significant anniversaries, and strategies associated with surviving such a painful and poignant experience.

The final or closing session can be emotionally difficult for the participants. After spending nine weeks building connections with similarly bereaved people in a place that has become safe, the ending of a mutual support group can feel like another loss. Part of the final session is about encouraging members to discuss the pain of endings, what they have learned in the group, and how their grief has changed in the process. New skills and transformations are acknowledged and affirmed by group members and peer facilitators, while remaining challenges are addressed. If they are comfortable, the group exchanges contact information so that members have continued informal access to their new network of support.

☐ BFO-T Groups

Children's Program (4–6 Years, 7–9 Years, 10–12 Years)

These groups are for children who have experienced the death of a parent/caregiver or sibling. They are expressive-arts based, composed of five to eight children, and delineated by age. Each evening group meets once a week for an hour and a half. There are nine sessions in total: the first session is an orientation for parents/caregivers only; sessions two to eight are for the children with their facilitators; and the ninth session is for individual feedback between the parent/caregiver, child, and facilitators.

Children's groups are cofacilitated by two trained, peer facilitators who experienced similar losses as children and/or have direct experience working with children. A professional advisor (someone who works with children in a professional capacity, e.g. a teacher, therapist, social worker, psychologist, or child and youth worker) meets with the facilitators before each session to offer consultation or guidance around issues specific to the unique needs of bereaved children.

Concurrent Parenting Group

This group provides peer support and psycho-education to the parents/caregivers of the children participating in the Children's Program. The group, which runs concurrent to the children's sessions, provides parents/caregivers with information and resources on how to respond to the diverse needs of grieving children. This group is cofacilitated by two trained peer facilitators who have experience working directly with children and have either experienced the death of a parent/caregiver or sibling as a child or the loss of a spouse or child as a parent.

Youth Program (13–17 Years)

Each group meets once a week in the evening for an hour and a half. There are nine sessions in total, with a follow-up session planned for six to eight weeks after termination. Group discussion, art, media, and music are used to explore the far-reaching impact of grief on young people; topics are determined by the unique needs of the individual members and the group as a whole. The group is cofacilitated by two trained peer facilitators who have experienced loss during adolescence. As with all groups, these facilitators are supported by a professional advisor.

Community-Based Programming for Youth (13–24 Years)

BFO-T also offers bereavement support groups for youth in schools, detention centers, shelters, and agency settings. The length, duration, and content of these sessions, which draw on the expressive arts, media, music, and group discussion, varies depending on the needs of the group members. More recently, peer support skills training has been offered so that members can also learn how to support bereaved peers in addition to accessing support for themselves. The groups are often cofacilitated in collaboration with school or agency-involved staff.

Soul 2 Soul Summer Program (13–24 Years)

This program is for Black and racialized youth who are living in under-resourced communities in Toronto, and who have experienced the death of a close friend or family member. The program provides bereavement support through culturally relevant activities and experiences, as well as training in the development of peer support skills which can be used to support other youth who have experienced loss. Leadership opportunities are available to the older youth in the program who, supported by staff, provide mentorship to younger participants. These groups use media arts, film, music, and theatre to explore the impact of grief, loss, and violence on youth. Several theatrical pieces have been developed to raise public awareness and create a forum for open dialogue about youth-identified support needs. The Soul 2 Soul summer program is facilitated by BFO-T staff, volunteers, and community artists.

Young Adults (18–30 Years)

For young adults who have experienced the death of a parent/caregiver or sibling, these evening groups meet weekly for two-hour sessions over 10 weeks. Group discussion is used to explore the impact of grief and topics are determined by the unique needs and experience of the group members. The group is cofacilitated by two trained peer facilitators and supported by a professional advisor.

Adult (30 + Years)

These groups, for adults who have experienced the death of a parent/sibling/spouse or partner, follow the same structure, schedule, and format as the Young Adults' group. Within the adult program, BFO-T also offers groups for men and women who are members of the LGBTQ communities who have lost a partner/spouse, parent, or sibling, and who are more comfortable meeting with other members of their identified community.

Infant Loss (Any Age)

For parents who have experienced the perinatal or neonatal death of an infant up to one year; this includes miscarriage, babies who are born still, and newborn/infant deaths.

Parental Loss (Any Age)

For parents who have experienced the death of a child older than one year. Groups are offered in the daytime and evening as the demand arises.

☐ Conclusion

All BFO-T services are provided free of charge. The organization is volunteer-based and depends on the generous donations of individuals, foundations, and corporations to maintain the accessibility and impact of our core programs and outreach.

BFO-T acknowledges the courage it takes to reach out for support, especially when surrounded by so many people who would rather deny the reality of grief, who are uncomfortable with its manifestations, and who communicate messages to "move on" and "get over it." BFO-T offers the opportunity to share one's story, to have it witnessed and understood by someone who has survived a similar experience and learned how to live with loss—this is how the healing begins.

As a community, BFO-T believes the intense grief following the death of a loved one is a normal and natural response to loss. In providing a confidential and open environment for bereaved people to come together, connect, and share their personal stories of loss, it becomes possible to nurture hope and see the possibility of life after loss. Mutual support, and the people who provide it, are the starting place where isolation is met with relationships, and fear of judgment is met with understanding. One bereaved mother, initially a group participant and currently a BFO-T volunteer, explained, "We hold our pain, afraid to imagine any other intimacy, urged forward in our healing until one day you find yourself present in your body. Perhaps the eyes look a little older after having cried the oceans of the world. The heart is bandaged, yet somehow still beating."

Sarah Henderson, M.A.
Coordinator of Children and Youth Programs
Bereaved Families of Ontario – Toronto
28 Madison Avenue
Toronto, ON M5R 2S1
Canada
Internet: www.bfotoronto.ca
www.soul2soul.ca

APPENDIX B

Appendix B

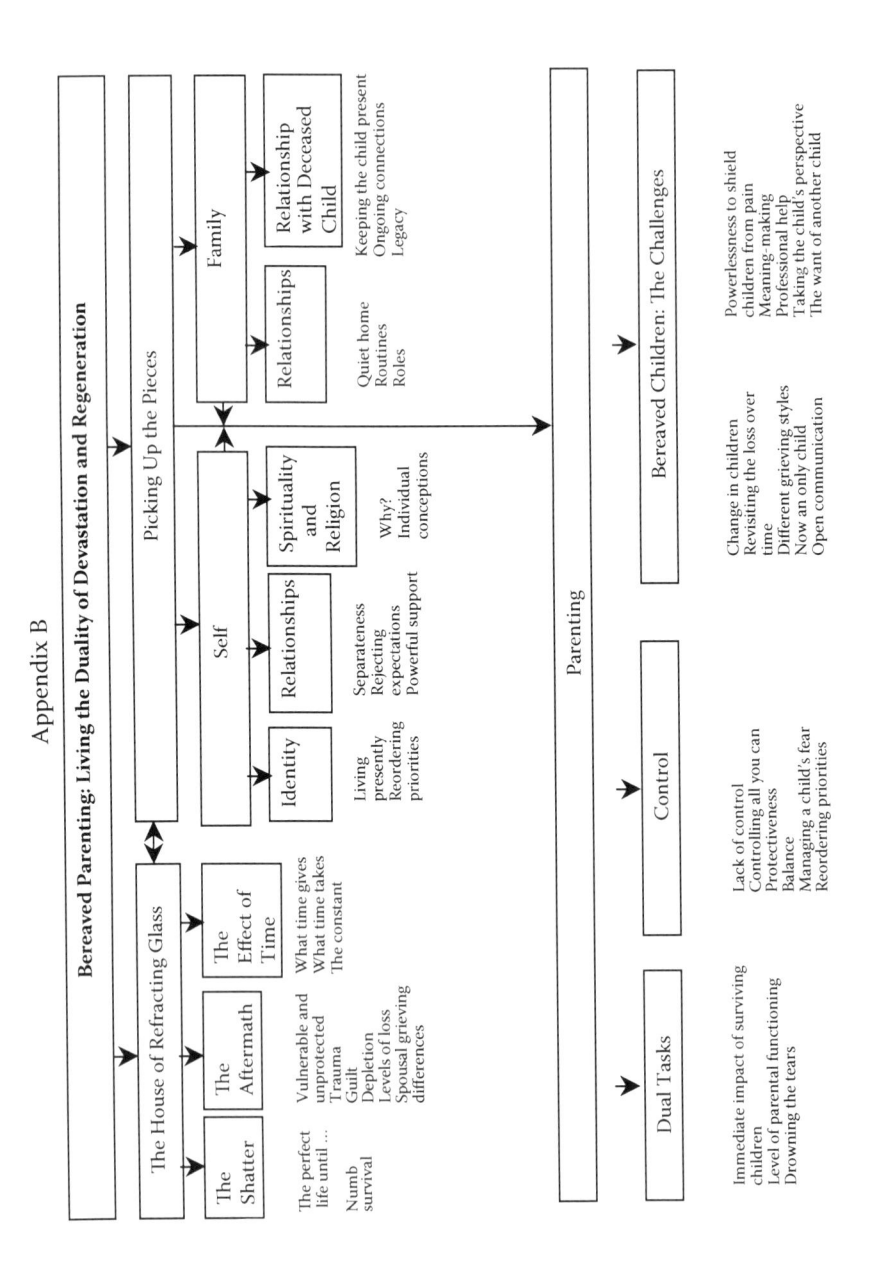

Bereaved Parenting: Living the Duality of Devastation and Regeneration

The House of Refracting Glass

- The Shatter
  - The perfect life until …
  - Numb survival
- The Aftermath
  - Vulnerable and unprotected
  - Trauma
  - Guilt
  - Depletion
  - Levels of loss
  - Spousal grieving differences
- The Effect of Time
  - What time gives
  - What time takes
  - The constant

Picking Up the Pieces

- Self
  - Identity
    - Living presently
    - Reordering priorities
  - Relationships
    - Separateness
    - Rejecting expectations
    - Powerful support
  - Spirituality and Religion
    - Why?
    - Individual conceptions
- Family
  - Relationships
    - Quiet home
    - Routines
    - Roles
  - Relationship with Deceased Child
    - Keeping the child present
    - Ongoing connections
    - Legacy

Parenting

- Dual Tasks
  - Immediate impact of surviving children
  - Level of parental functioning
  - Drowning the tears
- Control
  - Lack of control
  - Controlling all you can
  - Protectiveness
  - Balance
  - Managing a child's fear
  - Reordering priorities
- Bereaved Children: The Challenges
  - Change in children
  - Revisiting the loss over time
  - Different grieving styles
  - Now an only child
  - Open communication
  - Powerlessness to shield children from pain
  - Meaning-making
  - Professional help
  - Taking the child's perspective
  - The want of another child

REFERENCES

Ainsworth, M. D. S., Blehar, M. C., Waters, E., & Wall, S. (1978). *Patterns of attachment: A psychological study of the strange situation*. Hillsdale, NJ: Lawrence Erlbaum.

American Psychiatric Association (APA) (2000). *Diagnostic and statistical manual of mental disorders, fourth edition, text revision (DSM-IV-TR)*. Washington, DC: American Psychiatric Association.

Anderson, M. J., Marwitt, S. J., Vandenberg, B., & Chibnall, J. T. (2005). Psychological and religious coping strategies of mothers bereaved by the sudden death of a child. *Death Studies, 29*, 811–826.

Annells, M. (1996). Grounded theory method: Philosophical perspectives, paradigm of inquiry, and postmodernism. *Qualitative Health Research, 6*, 379–393.

Archer, J. (1999). *The nature of grief: The evolution and psychology of reactions to loss*. London: Routledge.

Arnold, J. H., & Gemma, P. B. (2008). The continuing process of parental grief. *Death Studies, 32*, 658–673.

Attig, T. (1996). *How we grieve: Relearning the world*. New York: Oxford University.

Baker, J. E. (1997). Minimizing the impact of parental grief on children: Parent and family interventions. In C. R. Figley, B. E. Bride, & N. Mazza (Eds.), *Death and trauma: The traumatology of grieving* (pp. 139–157). Washington, DC: Taylor & Francis.

Balk, D. E. (1983). Adolescents' grief reactions and self-concept perceptions following sibling death: A study of 33 teenagers. *Journal of Youth and Adolescence, 12*, 137–161.

Balmer, L. E. (1992). *Adolescent sibling bereavement: Mediating effects of family environment and personality*. Unpublished doctoral dissertation, York University, Toronto, Ontario, Canada.

Barrera, M., D'Agostino, N. M., Schneiderman, G., Tallett, S., Spencer, L., & Jovcevska, V. (2007). Patterns of parental bereavement following the loss of a child and related factors. *Omega, 55*, 145–167.

Barrera, M., O'Connor, K., D'Agostino, N. M, Spencer, L., Nicholas, D., Jovcevska, V., Tallet, S., & Schneiderman, G. (2009). Early parental adjustment and bereavement after childhood cancer death. *Death Studies, 33*, 497–520.

Beck, A. T. (1967). *Depression: Clinical, experimental and theoretical aspects*. New York: Harper and Row.

Beck, A. T. (1976). *Cognitive therapy and the emotional disorders*. New York: International Universities Press.

Becvar, D. S. (2001). *In the presence of grief: Helping family members resolve death, dying, and bereavement issues*. New York: Guilford Press.

Beder, J. (2005). Loss of the assumptive world—How do we deal with death and loss? *Omega, 50*, 255–265.

Bennett, S. M., Litz, B. T., Lee, B. S., & Maguen, S. (2005). The scope and impact of perinatal loss: Current status and future directions. *Professional Psychology: Research and Practice, 36(2)*, 180–187.

Boelen, P. A., Stroebe, M., Schut, H., & Zijerveld, A. M. (2006). Continuing bonds and grief: A prospective analysis. *Death Studies, 30*, 767–776.

Boelen, P. A., van den Bout, J., & de Keijser, J. (2003). Traumatic grief as a disorder distinct from bereavement-related depression and anxiety: A replication study with bereaved mental health care patients. *American Journal of Psychiatry, 160*, 1339–1341.

Bohannon, J. R. (1990). Grief responses of spouses following the death of a child: A longitudinal study. *Omega, 22*, 109–121.

Bohannon, J. R. (1991). Religiosity related to grief levels of bereaved mothers and fathers. *Omega, 23*, 153–159.

Bonanno, G. A., & Kaltman, S. (1999). Toward an integrative perspective on bereavement. *Psychological Bulletin, 125*, 760–776.

Borg, S., & Lasker, J. (1982). *When pregnancy fails: Coping with miscarriage, stillbirth, and infant death*. London: Routledge & Kegan Paul.

Bowen, E. J. (1990). *Families facing death*. Lexington, MA: Lexington Books.

Bowlby, J. (1969). *Attachment and loss: Vol. 1. Attachment*. London: Hogarth Press.

Bowlby, J. (1973). *Attachment and loss: Vol. 2. Separation: Anxiety and anger*. London: Hogarth Press.

Bowlby, J. (1980). *Attachment and loss. Vol. 3. Loss: Sadness and depression*. London: Hogarth Press.

Brabant, S., Forsyth, C., & McFarlain, G. (1995). Life after the death of a child: Initial and long term support from others. *Omega, 31*, 67–85.

Breslau, N., Lucia, V. C., & Davis, G. C. (2004). Partial PTSD versus full PTSD: An empirical examination of associated impairment. *Psychological Medicine, 34*, 1205–1214.

Broderick, C. B. (1993). *Understanding family process: Basics of family systems theory*. Newbury Park: Sage.

Broderick, C., & Smith, J. (1979). General systems approach to the family. In W. Burr, R. Hill, F. I. Nye, & I. L. Reiss (Eds.), *Contemporary theories about the family* (Vol. 2, pp. 112–128). New York: Free Press.

Buckle, J. L. (1998). *Intervention in maternal bereavement: The efficacy of mutual-help groups*. Unpublished master's thesis, York University, Toronto, Ontario, Canada.

Buckle, J. L., Corbin Dwyer, S., & Jackson, M. (2010). Qualitative bereavement research: Incongruity between the perspectives of participants and research ethics boards. *International Journal of Social Research Methodology, 13*, 111–125.

Cain, A. C., & Cain, B. S. (1964). On replacing a child. *Journal of the American Academy of Child Psychiatry, 3*, 443–456.

Clayton, P. J., & Darvish, H. S. (1979). Course of depressive symptoms following the stress of bereavement. In J. E. Barrett, R. M. Rose, & G. Klerman (Eds.), *Stress and mental disorder* (pp. 121–136). New York: Raven Press.

Cleiren, M. P., Diekstra, R. F., Kerkhof, A. J., & van der Wal, J. (1994). Mode of death and kinship in bereavement: Focusing on "who" rather than "how." *Crisis, 15*, 22–36.

Conway, V., & Feeney, J. (1997). Attachments and grief: A study of parental bereavement. *Journal of Family Studies, 3*, 36–42.
Cook, J. A. (1988). Dad's double binds: Rethinking fathers' bereavement from a man's studies perspective. *Journal of Contemporary Ethnography, 17*, 285–308.
Corbin Dwyer, S., & Buckle, J. L. (2009). The space between: On being an insider-outsider in qualitative research. *International Journal of Qualitative Methods, 8*, 54–63.
Cordell, A., & Thomas, N. (1990). Fathers and grieving: Coping with infant death. *Journal of Perinatology, 10*, 75–80.
Corden, A., Sainsbury, R., & Sloper, P. (2002). When a child dies: Money matters. *Illness, Crisis & Loss, 10*, 125–137.
Cryder, C. H., Kilmer, R. P., Tedeschi, R. G., & Calhoun, L. G. (2006). An exploratory study of posttraumatic growth in children following a natural disaster. *American Journal of Orthopsychiatry, 76*, 65–69.
Das, V. (1993). Moral orientations to suffering. In L. C. Chen, A. Kleinman, & N. C. Ware (Eds.), *Health and social change in international perspective* (pp. 139–167). Boston: Harvard University Press.
Davies, B. (1999). *Shadows in the sun: The experiences of sibling bereavement in childhood*. Philadelphia: Brunner/Mazel.
Davies, R. (2004). New understandings of parental grief: literature review. *Journal of Advanced Nursing, 46*, 506–513.
Davis, C. G. (2008). Redefining goals and redefining self: A closer look at posttraumatic growth following loss. In M. S. Stroebe, R. O. Hansson, H. Schut, & W. Stroebe (Eds.), *Handbook of bereavement research and practice: Advances in theory and intervention* (pp. 309–325). Washington, DC: American Psychological Association.
Davis, C. G., Lehman, D. R., Wortman, C. B., Silver, R. C., & Thompson, S. C. (1995). The undoing of traumatic life events. *Personality and Social Psychology Bulletin, 21*, 109–124.
Dean, W. (2002). *Journaling a pathway through grief: One family's journey after the death of a child*. Toronto: Key Porter Books.
Detmer, C. M., & Lamberti, J. W. (1991). Family grief. *Death Studies, 15*, 363–374.
DeVries, B., Dalla Lana, R., & Falek, V. (1994). Parental bereavement over the life course: A theoretical intersection and empirical review. *Omega, 29*, 47–70.
Dijkstra, I. C., & Stroebe, M. S. (1998). The impact of a child's death on parents: A myth (not yet) disproved? *Journal of Family Studies, 4*, 159–185.
Dobson, K. S., & Shaw, B. F. (1987). Specificity and stability of self-referent encoding in clinical depression. *Journal of Abnormal Psychology, 96*, 34–40.
Doka, K. (2002). How could God? In J. Kauffman (Ed.), *Loss of the assumptive world: A theory of traumatic loss* (pp. 49–54). New York: Brunner-Routledge.
Dyregrov, A., & Dyregrov, K. (1999). Long-term impact of sudden infant death: A 12- to 15-year follow-up. *Death Studies, 23*, 635–661.
Edelstein, L. (1984). *Maternal bereavement: Coping with the unexpected death of a child*. Toronto: Praeger.
Elliott, R., Fischer, C. T., & Rennie, D. L. (1999). Evolving guidelines for publication of qualitative research studies in psychology and related fields. *British Journal of Clinical Psychology, 38*, 215–229.
Fanos, J. H. (1996). *Sibling loss*. New Jersey: Lawerence Erlbaum Associates.

Field, N. P. (2008). Whether to relinquish or maintain a bond with the deceased. In M. Stroebe, R. Hansson, H. Schut, & W. Stroebe (Eds.). *Handbook of bereavement research and practice: Advances in theory and intervention* (pp. 113–132). Washington, DC: American Psychological Association.

Field, N. P., Nichols, C., Holen, A., & Horowitz, M. J. (1999). The relation of continuing attachment to adjustment in conjugal bereavement. *Journal of Consulting and Clinical Psychology, 67,* 212–218.

Figley, C. R. (1999). Introduction. In C. R. Figley (Ed.), *Traumatology of grieving: Conceptual, theoretical, and treatment foundations* (pp. xv–xxi). Philadelphia: Brunner/Mazel.

Fish, W. C. (1986). Differences of grief intensity in bereaved parents. In T. A. Rando (Ed.), *Parental loss of a child* (pp. 415–428). Illinois: Research Press Company.

Fleming, S. J., & Adolph, R. (1986). Helping bereaved adolescents: Needs and responses. In C. A. Corr & J. N. McNeil (Eds.), *Adolescence and death* (pp. 97–118). New York: Springer Publishing.

Fleming, S. J., & Balmer, L. E. (1995). Bereaved Families of Ontario: A mutual-help model for families experiencing death. In L. A. DeSpelder & A. L. Strickland (Eds.), *The path ahead: Readings in death and dying* (pp. 281–294). Mountain View, CA: Mayfield.

Fleming, S. J., & Balmer, L. E. (1996). Bereavement in adolescence. In C. A. Corr & D. E. Balk (Eds.), *Handbook of adolescent death and bereavement* (pp. 139–154). New York: Springer.

Fleming, S. J., & Bélanger, S. K. (2001). Trauma, grief, and surviving childhood sexual abuse. In R. A. Neimeyer (Ed.), *Meaning reconstruction & the experience of loss* (pp. 311–329). Washington, DC: American Psychological Association.

Fleming, S. J., & Robinson, P. J. (1991). The application of cognitive therapy to the bereaved. In T. M. Vallis, J. L. Howes, & P. C. Miller (Eds.), *The challenge of cognitive therapy: Applications to nontraditional populations* (pp. 135–158). New York: Plenum.

Fleming, S. J., & Robinson, P. J. (2001). Grief and cognitive-behavioural therapy: The reconstruction of meaning. In M. Stroebe, R. O. Hansson, W. Stroebe, & H. Schut (Eds.), *Handbook of bereavement research: Consequences, coping, and care* (pp. 647–669). Washington, DC: American Psychological Association.

Fletcher, P. N. (2002). Experiences in family bereavement. *Family & Community Health, 25,* 57–70.

Ford, J. D., & Saltzman, W. (2009). Family systems therapy. In C. A. Courtois & J. D. Ford (Eds.), *Treating complex traumatic stress disorders: An evidence-based guide* (pp. 391–414). New York: Guilford.

Forward, D. R., & Garlie, N. (2003). Search for new meaning: Adolescent bereavement after the sudden death of a sibling. *Canadian Journal of School Psychology, 18,* 23–53.

Fraley, R. C. (2002). Attachment stability from infancy to adulthood: Meta-analysis and dynamic modeling of developmental mechanisms. *Personality and Social Psychology Review, 6,* 123–151.

Freud, S. (1957). Mourning and melancholia. In J. Strachey (Ed. & Trans.), *Standard edition of the complete psychological works of Sigmund Freud* (Vol. 14: pp. 237–260). London: Hogarth Press. (Original work published 1917).

Gamino, L. A., Sewell, K. W., & Easterling, L. W. (2000). Scott and White grief study—Phase 2: Toward an adaptive model of grief. *Death Studies, 24*, 633–660.

Gilbert, K. (2001, December). Traumatic loss and the family. *National Council on Family Relations Newsletter, 46*, 18–19.

Glaser, B. G. (1992). *Emerging vs. forcing: The basics of grounded theory analysis*. Mill Valley, CA: The Sociology Press.

Glaser, B. G., & Strauss, A. L. (1967). *The discovery of grounded theory: Strategies for qualitative research*. New York: Aldine Publishing.

Grout, L. A., & Romanoff, B. D. (2000). The myth of the replacement child: Parents' stories and practices after perinatal death. *Death Studies, 24*, 93–113.

Gudmundsdottir, M., & Chesla, C. A. (2006). Building a new world: Habits and practices of healing following the death of a child. *Journal of Family Nursing, 12*, 143–164.

Hagemeister, A. K., & Rosenblatt, P. C. (1997). Grief and the sexual relationship of couples who have experienced a child's death. *Death Studies, 21*, 231–252.

Hagman, G. (1995). Mourning: A review and reconsideration. *International Journal of Psychoanalysis, 76*, 909–925.

Helmrath, T. A., & Steinitz, E. (1978). Death of an infant: Parental grieving and the failure of social support. *The Journal of Family Practice, 6*, 785–790.

Higgins, M. (2002). Parental bereavement and religious factors. *Omega, 45*, 187–207.

Hogan, N. S., & DeSantis, L. (1996). Adolescent sibling bereavement: toward a new theory. In C. A. Corr & D. E. Balk (Eds.), *Handbook of adolescent death and bereavement* (pp. 173–195). New York: Springer.

Horowitz, M. J., Siegel, B., Holen, A., Bonnano, G., Milbrath, C., & Stinson, C. H. (1997). Diagnostic criteria for complicated grief disorder. *American Journal of Psychiatry, 154*, 904–910.

Horsley, H., & Patterson, T. (2006). The effects of a parent guidance intervention on communication among adolescents who have experienced the sudden death of a sibling. *American Journal of Family Therapy, 34*, 119–137.

Horwitz, A. V., & Wakefield, J. C. (2007). *The loss of sadness: How psychiatry transformed normal sorrow into depressive disorder*. New York: Oxford University Press.

Horwitz, S. H. (1997). Treating families with traumatic loss: Transitional family therapy. In C. R. Figley, B. E. Bride, & N. Mazza (Eds.), *Death and trauma: The traumatology of grieving* (pp. 211–230). Washington, DC: Taylor & Francis.

Imber-Black, E. (2004). Rituals and the healing process. In F. Walsh & M. McGoldrick (Eds.), *Living beyond loss: Death in the family* (2nd ed., pp. 340–357). New York: W. W. Norton.

Janoff-Bulman, R. (1992). *Shattered assumptions: Towards a new psychology of trauma*. New York: The Free Press.

Janoff-Bulman, R. (2004). Posttraumatic growth: Three explanatory models. *Psychological Inquiry, 15*, 30–34.

Janoff-Bulman, R. & Berg, M. (1998). Disillusionment and the creation of values: From traumatic losses to existential gains. In J. H. Harvey (Ed.), *Perspectives on loss: A sourcebook* (pp. 35–47). Philadelphia: Brunner-Mazel.

Jordan, J. R. (2000). Research that matters: Bridging the gap between research and practice in thanatology. *Death Studies, 24*, 457–467.

Jordan, J. R., Kraus, D. R., & Ware, E. S. (1993). Observations on loss and family development. *Family Process, 32,* 425–440.
Kagan, H. (1998). *Gili's book: A journey into bereavement for parents and counselors.* New York: Teachers College Press.
Kamm, S., & Vandenberg, B. (2001). Grief communication, grief reactions, and marital satisfaction in bereaved parents. *Death Studies, 25,* 569–582.
Kastenbaum, R. J. (2007). *Death, society, and human experience.* (9th ed.). Boston: Pearson.
Kauffman, J. (2002). Introduction. In J. Kauffman (Ed.), *Loss of the assumptive world: A theory of traumatic loss* (pp. 1–9). New York: Brunner-Routledge.
Kelley, L. P., Weathers, F. W., McDevitt-Murphy, M. E., Eakin, D. E., & Flood, A. M. (2009). A comparison of PTSD symptom patterns in three types of civilian trauma. *Journal of Traumatic Stress, 22,* 227–235.
Kim, K., & Jacobs, S. (1991). Pathologic grief and its relationship to other psychiatric disorders. *Journal of Affective Disorders, 21,* 257–263.
Kissane, D. W., & Lichtenthal, W. G. (2008). Family focused grief therapy: From palliative care into bereavement. In M. Stroebe, R. O. Hansson, H. Schut, & W. Stroebe (Eds.), *Handbook of bereavement research and practice: Advances in theory and intervention* (pp. 485–510). Washington, DC: American Psychological Association.
Klass, D. (1988). *Parental grief: Solace and resolution.* New York: Springer.
Klass, D. (1995). Solace and immortality: Bereaved parents' continuing bond with their children. In L. A. DeSpelder & A. L. Strickland (Eds.), *The path ahead* (pp. 246–259). London: Mayfield.
Klass, D. (1997). The deceased child in the psychic and social worlds of bereaved parents during the resolution of grief. *Death Studies, 21,* 147–175.
Klass, D., Silverman, P., & Nickman, S. L. (Eds.). (1996). *Continuing bonds: New understandings of grief.* Washington, DC: Taylor & Francis.
Klass, D., & Walter, T. (2001). Processes of grieving: How bonds are continued. In M. Stroebe, R. Hansson, W. Stroebe, & H. Schut (Eds.), *Handbook of bereavement research: Consequences, coping, and care* (pp. 431–448). Washington, DC: American Psychological Association.
Knapp, R. J. (1986). *Beyond endurance: When a child dies.* New York: Schocken.
Krell, R., & Rabkin, L. (1979). The effects of sibling death on the surviving child: A family perspective. *Family Process, 18,* 471–477.
Kübler-Ross, E. (1969). *On death and dying.* New York: Macmillan.
Lamberti, J. W., & Detmer, C. M. (1993). Model of family grief assessment and treatment. *Death Studies, 17,* 55–67.
Lang, A., & Gottlieb, L. (1991). Parental grief reactions and martial intimacy in bereaved and nonbereaved couples: A comparative study. In D. Papadatou & C. Papadatos (Eds.), *Children and death* (pp. 267–275). Washington, DC: Hemisphere.
Lang, A., & Gottlieb, L. (1993). Marital intimacy after infant death. *Death Studies, 17,* 233–256.
Lattanzi-Licht, M. (1996). Helping families with adolescents cope with loss. In C. A. Corr & Balk, D. E. (Eds.), *Handbook of adolescent death and bereavement* (pp. 219–234). New York: Springer.

Leahy, J. M. (1992–1993). A comparison of depression in women bereaved of a spouse, child, or parent. *Omega, 26,* 207–217.

Li, J., Hansen, D., Mortensen, P. B., & Olsen, J. (2002). Myocardial infarction in parents who lost a child: A nationwide prospective cohort study in Denmark. *Circulation, 106,* 1634–1639.

Li, J., Johansen, C., Bronnum-Hansen, H., Stenager, E., Koch-Henriksen, N., & Olsen, J. (2004). The risk of multiple sclerosis in bereaved parents: A nationwide study in Denmark. *Neurology, 62,* 726–728.

Li, J., Johansen, C., Hansen, D., & Olsen, J. (2002). Cancer incidence in parents who lost a child. *Cancer, 95,* 2237–2242.

Li, J., Laursen, T. M., Precht, D., Olsen, J., & Mortensen, P. (2005). Hospitalization for mental illness among parents after the death of a child. *New England Journal of Medicine, 352,* 1190–1196.

Li, J., Precht, D. H., Mortensen, P. B., & Olsen, J. (2003). Mortality in parents after the death of a child in Denmark: A nationwide follow-up study. *The Lancet, 361,* 363–367.

Lohan, J. A., & Murphy, S. A. (2002). Parents' perceptions of adolescent sibling grief responses after an adolescent or young adult child's sudden, violent death. *Omega, 44,* 77–95.

Main, M. (1995). Discourse, prediction and recent studies in attachment: Implications for psychoanalysis. In T. Shapiro & R. M. Emde (Eds.), *Research in psychoanalysis: Process, development, outcome* (pp. 209–245). Madison, CT: International Universities Press.

Main, M., & Solomon, J. (1986). Discovery of a new, insecure-disorganized/disoriented attachment pattern. In T. B. Brazelton & M. Yogman (Eds.), *Affective development in infancy* (pp. 24–124). Norwood, NJ: Ablex.

Main, M., & Solomon, J. (1990). Procedures for identifying infants as disorganized/disoriented during the Ainsworth Strange Situation. In M. T. Greenberg, D. Cicchetti, & E. M. Cummings (Eds.), *Attachment in the preschool years* (pp. 121–160). Chicago, IL: University of Chicago Press.

Malkinson, R. (2007). *Cognitive grief therapy: Constructing a rational meaning to life following loss.* New York: W. W. Norton & Company.

Martin, T. L., & Doka, K. J. (2000). *Men don't cry ... women do: Transcending gender stereotypes of grief.* Philadelphia: Brunner/Mazel.

Matthews, L. T., & Marwit, S. J. (2006). Meaning reconstruction in the context of religious coping: Rebuilding the shattered asssumptive world. *Omega, 53,* 87–104.

McClowry, S. G., Davies, E. B., May, K. A., Kulenkamp, E. J., & Martinson, I. M. (1987). The empty space phenomenon: The process of grief in the bereaved family. *Death Studies, 11,* 361–374.

McCown, D., & Davies, B. (1995). Patterns of grief in young children following the death of a sibling. *Death Studies, 19,* 41–53.

Middleton, W. R., Raphael, B., Burnett, P., & Martinek, N. (1998). A longitudinal study comparing bereavement phenomena in recently bereaved spouses, adult children, and parents. *Australian and New Zealand Journal of Psychiatry, 32,* 235–241.

Milam, J. E., Ritt-Olson, A., & Unger, J. (2004). Posttraumatic growth among adolescents. *Journal of Adolescent Research, 19,* 192–204.

Miles, A. S., & Demi, M. S. (1984). Toward the development of a theory of bereavement guilt: Sources of guilt in bereaved parents. *Omega, 14*, 299–314.

Miles, A. S., & Demi, M. S. (1994). Bereavement guilt: A conceptual model with applications. In I. Corless, B. Germino, & M. Pittman (Eds.), *Dying, death, and bereavement: Theoretical perspectives and other ways of knowing* (pp. 171–188). Boston: Jones and Bartlett.

Moos, R. H., & Shaefer, J. A. (1986). Life transitions and crises: A conceptual overview. In R. H. Moos (Ed.), *Coping with life crises: An integrated approach* (pp. 3–28). New York: Plenum Press.

Moriarty, H. J., Carroll, R., & Cotroneo, M. (1996). Differences in bereavement reactions within couples following the death of a child. *Research in Nursing and Health, 19*, 461–469.

Murphy, S. A. (1996). Parent bereavement stress and preventive intervention following the violent deaths of adolescent or young adult children. *Death Studies, 20*, 441–452.

Murphy, S. A. (2008). The loss of a child: Sudden death and extended illness perspectives. In M. S. Stroebe, R. O. Hansson, H. Schut, & W. Stroebe (Eds.), *Handbook of bereavement research and practice: Advances in theory and intervention* (pp. 375–395). Washington, DC: American Psychological Association.

Nadeau, J. W. (1998). *Families making sense of death*. Thousand Oaks, CA: Sage.

Nadeau, J. W. (2008). Meaning-making in bereaved families: Assessment, intervention, and future research. In M. S. Stroebe, R. O. Hansson, H. Schut, & W. Stroebe (Eds.), *Handbook of bereavement research and practice: Advances in theory and intervention* (pp. 511–530). Washington, DC: American Psychological Association.

Nader, K. O. (1997). Childhood traumatic loss: The interaction of trauma and grief. In C. R. Figley, B. E. Bride, & N. Mazza (Eds.), *Death and trauma: The traumatology of grieving* (pp. 17–41). Washington, DC: Taylor & Francis.

Neimeyer, R. A. (1998). *Lessons of loss: A guide to coping*. Florida: PsychoEducational Resources.

Neimeyer, R. A. (2006). Re-storying loss: Fostering growth in the posttraumatic narrative. In L. Calhoun & R. Tedeschi (Eds.), *Handbook of posttraumatic growth: Research and practice* (pp. 68–80). Mahwah, NJ: Lawrence Erlbaum.

Neimeyer, R. A. & Hogan, N. S. (2001). Quantitative or qualitative? Measurement issues in the study of grief. In M. Stroebe, R. O. Hansson, W. Stroebe, & H. Schut (Eds.), *Handbook of bereavement research: Consequences, coping, and care* (pp. 89–118). Washington, DC: American Psychological Association.

Oglethorpe, R. J. L. (1989). Parenting after perinatal bereavement—A review of the literature. *Journal of Reproductive and Infant Psychology, 7*, 227–244.

Ogrodniczuk, J. S., & Piper, W. E. (2003). Recognizing complicated grief in clinical practice. *Canadian Journal of Psychiatry, 48*, 713.

Oliver, L. E. (1999). Effects of a child's death on the marital relationship: A review. *Omega, 39*, 197–227.

Ott, C. H. (2003). The impact of complicated grief on mental and physical health at various points in the bereavement process. *Death Studies, 27*, 249–272.

Oxford English Reference Dictionary (2nd ed.). (1996). Oxford: Oxford University Press.

Packman, W., Horsley, H., Davies, B., & Kramer, R. (2006). Sibling bereavement and continuing bonds. *Death Studies, 30*, 817–841.

Pantke, R., & Slade, P. (2006). Remembered parenting style and psychological well-being in young adults whose parents had experienced early child loss. *Psychology and Psychotherapy: Theory, Research and Practice, 79*, 69–81.

Parkes, C. M. (1971). Psycho-social transitions: A field of study. *Social Science and Medicine, 5*, 101–115.

Parkes, C. M. (1975). What becomes of redundant world models? A contribution to the study of adaptation to change. *British Journal of Medical Psychology, 48*, 131–137.

Parkes, C. M. (1988). Bereavement as a psychosocial transition: Processes of adaptation to change. *Journal of Social Issues, 44*, 53–65.

Parkes, C. M. (2002). Grief: Lessons from the past, visions of the future. *Death Studies, 26*, 267–385.

Parkes, C. M. (2006). *Love and loss: The roots of grief and its complications.* London: Routledge.

Peppers, L. G., & Knapp, R. J. (1980). *Motherhood and mourning: Perinatal death.* New York: Praeger

Poznanski, E. O. (1972). The replacement child: A saga of unresolved parental grief. *Behavioral Pediatrics, 81*, 1190–1193.

Prigerson, H. G., Bierhals, A. J., Kasl, S. V., Reynolds, C. F., Shear, M. K., Day, N., Beery, L. C., Newsom, J. T., & Jacobs, S. (1997). Traumatic grief as a risk factor for mental and physical morbidity. *American Journal of Psychiatry, 154*, 616–623.

Prigerson, H. G., Bridge, J., Maciejewski, P. K., Beery, L. C., Rosenheck, R. A., Jacobs, S. C., Bierhals, A. J., Kupfer, D. J., & Brent, D. A. (1999). Influence of traumatic grief on suicidal ideation among young adults. *American Journal of Psychiatry, 156*, 1994–1995.

Prigerson, H. G, Frank, E., Kasl, S. V., Reynolds, C. F., Anderson, B., Zubenko, G. S., Houck, P. R., George, C. J., & Kupfer, D. J. (1995). Complicated grief and bereavement-related depression as distinct disorders: Preliminary empirical validation in elderly bereaved spouses. *American Journal of Psychiatry, 152*, 22–30.

Prigerson, H. G., Maciejewski, P. K., Reynolds, C. F., Bierhals, A. J., Newsom, J. T., Fasiczka, A., Frank, E., Doman, J., & Miller, M. (1995). The inventory of complicated grief: A scale to measure maladaptive symptoms of loss. *Psychiatry Research, 59*, 65–79.

Prigerson, H. G., Shear, M. K., Frank, E., Beery, L. C., Silberman, R., Prigerson, J., & Reynolds, C. F. (1997). Traumatic grief: A case of loss-induced trauma. *American Journal of Psychiatry, 154*, 1003–1009.

Prigerson, H. G., Vanderwerker, L. C., & Maciejewski, P. K. (2008). A case for inclusion of prolonged grief disorder in DSM-V. In M. S. Stroebe, R. O. Hansson, H. Schut, & W. Stroebe (Eds.), *Handbook of bereavement research and practice: Advances in theory and intervention* (pp. 165–186). Washington, DC: American Psychological Association.

Rando, T. A. (1986a). The unique issues and impact of the death of a child. In T. A. Rando (Ed.), *Parental loss of a child* (pp. 5–43). Champaign, IL: Research Press.

Rando, T. A. (1986b). Individual and couples treatment following the death of a child. In T. A. Rando (Ed.), *Parental loss of a child* (pp. 341–413). Champaign, IL: Research Press.

Rando, T. A. (1988). *Grieving: How to go on living when someone you love dies.* Lexington, MA: Lexington Books.

Rando, T. A. (1991). Parental adjustment to the loss of a child. In D. Papadatou & C. Papadatos (Eds.), *Children and death* (pp. 233–253). Washington, DC: Hemisphere.

Rando, T. A. (1993). *Treatment of complicated mourning.* Champaign, IL: Research Press.

Rando, T. A. (1994). Complications in mourning traumatic death. In I. Corless, B. Germino, & M. Pittman (Eds.), *Death, dying, and bereavement: Theoretical perspectives and other ways of knowing* (pp. 253–271). Boston: Jones and Bartlett.

Rando, T. A. (2003). Public tragedy and complicated mourning. In M. Lattanzi-Licht & K. Doka (Eds.), *Living with grief: Coping with public tragedy* (pp. 263–274). New York: Brunner-Routledge.

Reif, L. V., Patton, M. J., & Gold, P. B. (1995). Bereavement, stress, and social support in members of a self-help group. *Journal of Community Psychology, 23,* 292–306.

Rennie, D. L. (1994). Human science and counseling psychology: Closing the gap between research and practice. *Counselling Psychology Quarterly, 7,* 235–250.

Rennie, D. L. (1995a). On the rhetorics of social science: Let's not conflate natural science and human science. *The Humanistic Psychologist, 23,* 321–332.

Rennie, D. L. (1995b). Plausible constructionism as the rigor of qualitative research. *Methods: A Journal for Human Science,* Annual Edition, 42–58.

Rennie, D. L. (1995c). Strategic choices in a qualitative approach to psychotherapy process research. In L. T. Hoshmand & J. Martin (Eds.), *Research as praxis: Lessons from programmatic research in therapeutic psychology* (pp. 198–220). New York: Teachers College Press.

Rennie, D. L. (1996). Fifteen years of doing qualitative research on psychotherapy. *British Journal of Guidance and Counselling, 24,* 317–327.

Rennie, D. L. (1998). Grounded theory methodology: The pressing need for a coherent logic of justification. *Theory and Psychology, 8,* 101–119.

Rennie, D. L. (2000). Grounded theory methodology as methodical hermeneutics: Reconciling realism and relativism. *Theory and Psychology, 10,* 481–502.

Rennie, D. L., & Fergus, K. D. (2006). Embodied categorizing in the grounded theory method: Methodical hermeneutics in action. *Theory and Psychology, 16,* 483–503.

Rennie, D. L., Phillips, J. R., & Quartaro, G. K. (1988). Grounded theory: A promising approach to conceptualization in psychology? *Canadian Psychology, 29,* 139–150.

Rennie, D. L., Watson, K. D., & Monterio, A. M. (2002). The rise of qualitative research in psychology. *Canadian Psychology, 43,* 179–189.

Riches, G., & Dawson, P. (1996). Making stories and taking stories: Methodological reflections on researching grief and marital tension following the death of a child. *British Journal of Guidance and Counselling, 24,* 357–365.

Riches, G., & Dawson, P. (2000). *An intimate loneliness: Supporting bereaved parents and siblings.* Buckingham: Open University Press.

Riley, L. P., LaMontagne, L. L., Hepworth, J. T., & Murphy, B. A. (2007). Parental grief responses and personal growth following the death of a child. *Death Studies, 31,* 277–299.

Roach, S. S., & Nieto, B. C. (1997). *Healing and the grief process.* Toronto: Delmar.

Robinson, P. J., & Fleming, S. J. (1992). Depressotypic cognitive patterns in major depression and conjugal bereavement. *Omega, 25*, 291–305.

Rosenblatt, P. C. (1995). Ethics of qualitative interviewing with grieving families. *Death Studies, 19*, 139–155.

Rosenblatt, P. C. (1996). Grief that does not end. In D. Klass, P. R. Silverman, & S. L. Nickman (Eds.), *Continuing bonds: New understandings of grief* (pp. 45–58). Washington, DC: Taylor & Francis.

Rosenblatt, P. C. (2000a). *Parent grief: Narratives of loss and relationship.* Philadelphia: Brunner/Mazel.

Rosenblatt, P. C. (2000b). Protective parenting after the death of a child. *Journal of Personal & Interpersonal Loss, 5*, 343–360.

Rosenblatt, P. C. (2004). Grieving while driving. *Death Studies, 28*, 679–686.

Rosenblatt, P. C. (2008). Grief across cultures: A review and research agenda. In M. S. Stroebe, R. O. Hansson, H. Schut, & W. Stroebe (Eds.), *Handbook of bereavement research and practice: Advances in theory and intervention* (pp. 207–222). Washington, DC: American Psychological Association.

Rosof, B. D. (1994). *The worst loss: How families heal from the death of a child.* New York: Henry Holt and Company.

Rothman, J. C. (1997). *The bereaved parents' survival guide.* New York: Continuum.

Roy, D. J. (1988). After a death ... interpreting the silence. *Journal of Palliative Care, 4*, 5–6.

Rubin, S. S. (1993). The death of a child is forever: The life course impact of child loss. In M. S. Stroebe, W. Stroebe, & R. O. Hansson (Eds.), *Handbook of bereavement: Theory, research, intervention* (pp. 285–299). Cambridge, England: Cambridge University.

Rubin, S. S. (1996). The wounded family: Bereaved parents and the impact of adult child loss. In D. Klass, P. R. Silverman, & S. L. Nickman (Eds.), *Continuing bonds: New understandings of grief* (pp. 217–232). Washington, DC: Taylor & Francis.

Rubin, S. S. (1999). The two-track model of bereavement: Overview, retrospect, and prospect. *Death Studies, 23*, 681–714.

Rubin, S. S., & Malkinson, R. (2001). Parental response to child loss across the life cycle: Clinical and research perspectives. In M. S. Stroebe, R. O. Hansson, W. Stroebe, & H. Schut (Eds.), *Handbook of bereavement research: Consequences, coping, and care* (pp. 219–240). Washington, DC: American Psychological Association.

Rubin, S. S., Malkinson, R., & Witztum, E. (2003). Trauma and bereavement: Conceptual and clinical issues revolving around relationships. *Death Studies, 27*, 667–690.

Rubin, S. S., Nadav, O. B., Malkinson, R., Koren, D., Goffer-Shnarch, M., & Michaeli, E. (2009). The Two-Track Model of Bereavement Questionnaire (TTBQ): Development and validation of a relational measure. *Death Studies, 33*, 305–333.

Rubinstein, G. (2004). Locus of control and helplessness: Gender differences among bereaved parents. *Death Studies, 28*, 211–223.

Sanders, C. M. (1980). A comparison of adult bereavement in the death of a spouse, child, and parent. *Omega, 10*, 303–322.

Schiff, H. S. (1977). *The Bereaved Parent.* New York: Crown Publishing.

Schut, H., de Keijser, J., van den Bout, J., & Dijkhuis, J. (1991). Post-traumatic stress symptoms in the first year of conjugal bereavement. *Anxiety Research, 4*, 225–234.

Schwab, R. (1990). Paternal and maternal coping with the death of a child. *Death Studies, 14*, 407–422.

Schwab, R. (1992). Effects of a child's death on the marital relationship: A preliminary study. *Death Studies, 16*, 141–154.

Schwab, R. (1996). Gender differences in parental grief. *Death Studies, 20*, 103–114.

Schwab, R. (1997). Parental mourning and children's behavior. *Journal of Counseling and Development, 75*, 258–265.

Shapiro, E. R. (1994). *Grief as a family process: A developmental approach to clinical practice.* New York: Guilford Press.

Sherkat, D., & Reed, M. (1992). The effects of religion and social support on self-esteem and depression among the suddenly bereaved. *Social Indicators Research, 26*, 259–275.

Silverman, G. K., Jacobs, S. C., Kasl, S. V., Shear, M. K., Maciejewski, P. K., Noaghiul, F. S., & Prigerson, H. G. (2000). Quality of life impairments associated with diagnostic criteria for traumatic grief. *Psychological Medicine, 30*, 857–862.

Silverman, G. K., Johnson, J. G., & Prigerson, H. G. (2001). Preliminary explorations of the effects of prior trauma and loss on risk for psychiatric disorders in recently widowed people. *Israel Journal of Psychiatry and Related Sciences, 38*, 202–215.

Silverman, P. R., & Klass, D. (1996). Introduction: What's the problem? In D. Klass, P. R. Silverman, & S. L. Nickman (Eds.), *Continuing bonds: New understandings of grief* (pp. 3–27). Washington, DC: Taylor & Francis.

Simpson, M. A. (1997). Traumatic bereavements and death-related PTSD. In C. R. Figley, B. E. Bride, & N. Mazza (Eds.), *Death and trauma: The traumatology of grieving* (pp. 3–16). Washington, DC: Taylor & Francis.

Sprang, G., & McNeil, J. (1995). *The many faces of bereavement: The nature and treatment of natural, traumatic, and stigmatized grief.* New York: Brunner/Mazel.

Stern, P. N. (1994). Eroding grounded theory. In J. M. Morse (Ed.), *Critical issues in qualitative research methods.* Thousand Oaks, CA: Sage.

Strauss, A., & Corbin, J. (1990). *Basics of qualitative research: Grounded theory, procedures and techniques.* Newbury Park, CA: Sage.

Strauss, A., & Corbin, J. (1994). Grounded theory methodology: An overview. In N. K. Denzin, & Y. S. Lincoln (Eds.), *Handbook of qualitative research* (pp. 273–285). Thousand Oaks, CA: Sage.

Stroebe, M. S. (2002). Paving the way: From early attachment theory to contemporary bereavement research. *Mortality, 7*, 127–138.

Stroebe, M. S. (2004). Religion in coping with bereavement: Confidence of convictions or scientific scrutiny? *The International Journal for the Psychology of Religion, 14*, 23–36.

Stroebe, M. S., Hansson, R. O., Schut, H., & Stroebe, W. (2008). Bereavement research: Contemporary perspectives. In M. S. Stroebe, R. O. Hansson, H. Schut, & W. Stroebe (Eds.), *Handbook of bereavement research and practice: Advances in theory and intervention* (pp. 3–25). Washington, DC: American Psychological Association.

Stroebe, M. S., & Schut, H. (1999). The dual process model of coping with bereavement: Rationale and description. *Death Studies, 23,* 197–224.

Stroebe, M. S., & Schut, H. (2001). Meaning making in the dual process model of coping with bereavement. In R. A. Neimeyer (Ed.), *Meaning reconstruction and the experience of loss* (pp. 55–73). Washington, DC: American Psychological Association.

Stroebe, M. S., & Schut, H. (2005–2006). Complicated grief: A conceptual analysis of the field. *Omega, 52,* 53–70.

Stroebe, M. S., Schut, H., & Stroebe, W. (1998). Trauma and grief: A comparative analysis. In J. H. Harvey (Ed.), *Perspectives on loss: A sourcebook* (pp. 81–96). Philadelphia: Brunner/Mazel.

Stroebe, W., & Schut, H. (2001). Risk factors in bereavement outcome: A methodological and empirical review. In M. S. Stroebe, R. O. Hansson, W. Stroebe, & H. Schut (Eds.), *Handbook of bereavement research: Consequences, coping, and care* (pp. 349–371). Washington, DC: American Psychological Association.

Talbot, K. (2002). *What forever means after the death of a child.* New York: Routledge.

Tedeschi, R. G., & Calhoun, L. G. (2004a). *Helping bereaved parents: A clinician's guide.* New York: Routledge.

Tedeschi, R. G., & Calhoun, L. G. (2004b). Posttraumatic growth: Conceptual foundations and empirical evidence. *Psychological Inquiry, 15,* 1–18.

Tursman, R. (1987). *Pierce's theory of scientific discovery: A system of logic as conceived as semiotic.* Bloomington: Indiana University Press.

Uren, T. H., & Wastell, C. A. (2002). Attachment and meaning-making in perinatal bereavement. *Death Studies, 26,* 279–308.

Vance, J. C., Boyle, F. M., Najman, J. M., & Thearle, M. J. (1995). Gender differences in parental psychological distress following perinatal death or sudden infant death syndrome. *British Journal of Psychiatry, 167,* 806–811.

Varney Sidmore, K. (1999–2000). Parental bereavement: Levels of grief as affected by gender issues. *Omega, 40,* 351–374.

Vess, J., Moreland, J., & Schwebel, A. I. (1985–1986). Understanding family role reallocation following a death: A theoretical framework. *Omega, 16,* 115–128.

Vickio, C. J. (1999). Together in spirit: Keeping our relationships alive when loved ones die. *Death Studies, 23,* 161–175.

Walsh, F., & McGoldrick, M. (2004). Loss and the family: A systemic perspective. In F. Walsh & M. McGoldrick (Eds.), *Living beyond loss: Death in the family* (2nd ed., pp. 3–26). New York: W. W. Norton.

Walsh, K., King, M., Jones, L., Tookman, A., & Blizard, R. (2002). Spiritual beliefs may affect outcome of bereavement: Prospective study. *British Medical Journal, 324,* 1–5.

Wijngaards-de Meij, L., Stroebe, M., Schut, H., Stroebe, W., van den Bout, J., van der Heijden, P. G. M., & Dijkstra, I. (2005). Couples at risk following the death of their child: Predictors of grief versus depression. *Journal of Consulting and Clinical Psychology, 73,* 617–623.

Wijngaards-de Meij, L., Stroebe, M., Schut, H., Stroebe, W., van den Bout, J., van der Heijden, P. G. M., & Dijkstra, I. (2007). Patterns of attachment and parent's adjustment to the death of their child. *Personality and Social Psychology Bulletin, 33,* 537–548.

Wijngaards-de Meij, L., Stroebe, M., Stroebe, W., Schut, H., van den Bout, J., van der Heijden, P. G. M., & Dijkstra, I. (2008). The impact of circumstances surrounding the death of a child on parents' grief. *Death Studies, 32,* 237–252.

Wing, D. G., Clance, P. R., Burge-Callaway, K., & Armistead, L. (2001). Understanding gender differences in bereavement following the death of an infant: Implications for treatment. *Psychotherapy, 38,* 60–73.

Woodgate, R. L. (2006). Living in a world without closure: Reality for parents who have experienced the death of a child. *Journal of Palliative Care, 22,* 75–82.

Worden, J. W. (1982). *Grief counseling and grief therapy: A handbook for the mental health practitioner.* New York: Springer.

Worden, J. W. (2002). *Grief counseling and grief therapy: A handbook for the mental health practitioner* (3rd ed.). New York: Springer.

Worden, J. W. (2009). *Grief counseling and grief therapy: A handbook for the mental health practitioner* (4th ed.). New York: Springer.

Wortman, C. B., & Silver, R. C. (2001). The myths of coping with loss revisited. In M. S. Stroebe, R. O. Hansson, H. Schut, & W. Stroebe (Eds.), *Handbook of bereavement research* (pp. 405–430). Washington, DC: American Psychological Association.

Zisook, S., Paulus, M., Shuchter, S. R., & Judd, L. L. (1997). The many faces of depression following spousal bereavement. *Journal of Affective Disorders 45,* 85–95.

Zisook, S., & Shuchter, S. R. (1991). Depression through the first year after the death of a spouse. *American Journal of Psychiatry, 148,* 1346–1352.

Zuroff, D. C., Blatt, S. J., Sanislow, C. A., Bondi, C. M., & Pilkonis, P. A. (1999). Vulnerability to depression: Reexamining state dependence and relative stability. *Journal of Abnormal Psychology, 108,* 76–89.

INDEX

A

Aftermath
  immediate, 117
  overview, 45-46
Anxieties, post-death, 138-141
Attachment styles, 14-15, 15-16
Attachment theory
  centrality of attachments to children, 61
  grief, role of attachment in, 12-13
  importance of, 14
  styles of attachments, 14-15, 15-16
Attachments. *See* Attachment styles; Attachment theory

B

Beck's Depression Inventory, 6
Bereaved parenting. *See also* Bereavement; Parents, bereaved
  active process of, 41
  Aftermath, overview of, 45-46
  assumptive world, destruction of, 48-49, 50-51
  circumstances of death, impact of, 54
  complexity of, 38, 117
  depletion, emotional and physical, 58-60, 122
  dread, feelings of, 48
  duality of, 37, 113, 115-116
  future research areas, 169-170
  guilt (*See* Guilt)
  helplessness, feelings of, 48, 49
  House of Refracting Glass, 38, 42-44, 45
  immediate aftermath of death, in, 117
  integrated grief reaction, 122-123
  mother's role, 114-115
  parental functioning, level of, 119-122
  Picking Up Pieces (*See* Picking Up Pieces)
  Shatter, The, 38, 44-45
  social networks of parents, reactions of, 63
  spousal differences in (*See* Spousal differences in grief)
  surviving children, needs of, 116, 117-118
  time, influence of, 68, 69-71
  trauma of (*See* Trauma)
  vulnerability, feelings of, 45-51
Bereavement. *See also* Bereaved parenting; Grief; Parents, bereaved
  definition, 3-4
  DSM-IV-TR category, 5
  Dual Process Model of Coping with Bereavement (DPM) (*See* Dual Process Model of Coping with Bereavement (DPM))
  interplay of social, cultural, and religion and, 4-5
  qualitative methodology (*See* Qualitative methodology to bereavement)
  spousal, 5
  Two-Track Model of Bereavement (TTMoB) (*See* Two-Track Model of Bereavement (TTMoB))

C

Child, deceased
  legacy of, 105-110
  need for parents to talk about, 81-82
  ongoing bond/connection to, desire for, 102-104, 108
  presence or connection to, 104-105
Cultural influences on bereavement, 4-5

D

Depression
  cognitive theory of, 6
  melancholia, 7
  neurovegetative symptoms, 7
  symptoms of, 5
Dual Process Model of Coping with Bereavement (DPM), 15-16, 41

203

orientation types, 125–126, 127
oscillation process, 126–127
predictions, 126

E

Evolutionary psychology, 166

F

Family
  boundaries, blurring of, 99–100
  changes after child's death, 1–2
  communication styles, impact of, 110
  connectedness, impact of, 110–111
  definition of, 17
  flexibility of, 18
  grief response of, 17–18
  increased closeness following death, 92–93
  redistribution of roles, 101–102
  roles, changes in, 96–102
  routines, changes in, 94
  stability, 95
  surviving siblings (*See* Siblings, surviving)
  variables impacting reaction to death of child, 17–18
Fathers. *See* Bereaved parenting; Spousal differences in grief

G

Grief. *See also* Bereavement
  attachment theory (*See* Attachment theory)
  complicated type, 9–11
  definition of, 4
  depression, co-morbidity with, 5–8
  differences in unexpected deaths versus expected/illness deaths, 3
  family response (*See* Family)
  integrated grief reaction, 122–123
  intensity of, 68
  phase theory, 13
  post-traumatic stress disorder, co-morbidity with, 8–9
  prolonged grief disorder, 10–11
  psychoanalytic perspective, 12
  raw, 124
  siblings, of (*See* Siblings, surviving)
  spousal differences in (*See* Spousal differences in grief)
  stage theory, 13
  stuck, being, 18
  symptoms of, 3
  task theory, 14
Grief Experience Inventory, 2–3
Grounded theory method
  abductions, 26–27
  comparative analysis, constant, 24–25
  methodical hemeneutics, relationship between, 26
  overview, 22–23
  protocols, 32
  relativism and realism, tension between, 26
  theoretical memoing, 25, 33–34
  theoretical sampling, 23–24
Guilt
  counterfactual thinking, 57–58
  parental feelings of failing, 56
  typology of, 57

H

House of Refracting Glass, 38, 42–44, 45

K

Kübler-Ross, Elisabeth, 13

L

Losses
  benevolence, belief in, 2
  complexity of, 61
  future hopes and expectations, 2
  intensity of, 1
  levels of, 60–61
  physical, 1
  types of, 3–4

M

Melancholia, 7
Methodical hermeneutics, 25–27
Minnesota Multiphasic Personality Inventory, 2–3
Mothers. *See* Bereaved parenting; Spousal differences in grief
Mourning. *See also* Bereavement; Grief
  definition of, 4
  variations in, 4

O

Organ donation, 105

Index **205**

Oscillation, 126–127

P

Parents, bereaved. *See also* Bereaved parenting
 affective disorders of, 3
 balance, desire for, 137–138
 comforting others, 83–84
 control, feeling of lack of, 130–131
 desire for another child, 162–167
 future expectations changes after child's death, 2
 need to discuss deceased child, 81–82
 powerlessness, feelings of, 155–156
 priorities of, 141–143
 protectiveness of other children, 132–136
 rejection by others, 80–81
 self-identity changes after child's death, 1, 2, 74–75, 78–79
 spousal differences (*See* Spousal differences in grief)
 superficiality, rejection of, 83
 support for, from others, 85–87
Picking Up Pieces
 active process of, 73
 normal, new, 73
 overview, 38–39, 73–74
 priorities, reordering of, 77, 78
 reconstruction of identity, 75–76
 relationships with others, impact on, 80–87
 self-identity, impact on, 73–74
 spirituality and religion (*See* Spirituality and religion)
 time, changes in perceptions of, 76–77
Posttraumatic stress disorder
 grief, co-morbidity with, 8–9, 125
 grief, similarity to, 8, 53
 grief, *versus*, 8, 10
 persistence of reliving of trauma, 53
 symptoms, 8, 53, 55–56, 140
Professional help
 advisors, support groups, 179
 bereaved family programs, 179–180
 children's programs, 182–183
 clinical implications of bereaved parenting research, 172–174
 facilitators, 178–179
 intake process, 180–181
 mutual support models, 178, 181–182
 psychotherapy for bereaved parents, 54
 siblings, for, 158–159
 support groups, 169–170, 177–186
Prolonged grief disorder, 10–11

Q

Qualitative methodology to bereavement
 categorizing, 35, 36, 37
 circular questioning, 29–30
 clinical implications, 172–174
 credibility checks, 36
 criteria for inclusion, 28–29
 data analysis, 34–36
 deceased children, profiles of, 27–28
 ethical considerations, 32
 grounded theory method (*See* Grounded theory method)
 impact of research, 170–172
 interviews, 29–31
 memoing, 33–34
 overview, 22–23
 participants, 27–29
 transcription of interviews, 33

R

Religion. *See* Spirituality and religion
Resiliency, 67

S

Self-help groups, 15
Shatter, The, 38, 44–45
Siblings, surviving. *See also* Family
 adolescents, 148, 151
 changes in, 146–148
 cognitive distortions, 148
 communication, importance of, 154–155
 developmental stages, 148–151
 experiences of, 22
 fears of, 138–141
 grief styles, 151–152
 long-lasting consequences of death of sibling, 145
 meaning/wisdom, imbuing with, 156–158
 needs of, 116, 117
 only child, creation of, 153
 perspectives of, 159–162
 protectiveness of, 132–136
Spirituality and religion
 betrayal, feelings of, 87–88
 influence on bereavement, 4–5

mothers *versus* fathers, differences in, 88–90
reexamination of, 89–90
shattering of, 88
why, question of, 87
Spousal differences in grief
commonalities, 66–67
coping strategies, 64
fathers' perspectives on differences, 62–63
fathers, unique relationship lost through child's death, 2
intensity, differences in, 64
intuitive *versus* instrumental grieving styles, 66
mother, unique relationship lost through child's death, 2
mothers' perspectives on differences, 62
mothers', support for from friends, 85–87
overview, 62
religion and spirituality differences, 88–90
roles, changes in, 97–99
routines in families, changes in, 94–95
severity and diversity of reactions, 64
social networks of parents, reactions of, 63
social roles, relationship to, 64–65
time, influence of, 68, 69

T

Trauma
circumstances of death, impact of, 54
descriptions of, 51, 52
grief, as element of, 52–53
growth following, 79–80
mental images associated with, 51, 52, 54
posttraumatic stress disorder, relationship between, 53–56
qualitative differences in, 55–56
rape/murder of child, case study of, 50–51
subsiding, 52
symptoms of, 140
Two-Track Model of Bereavement (TTMoB), 16–17, 41–42
description of, 124
Track I, 124–125
Track II, 124, 125